THE LETTER

to

THE HEBREWS

THE LETTER

to

THE HEBREWS

Translated
with an Introduction and Interpretation
by

WILLIAM BARCLAY

THE WESTMINSTER PRESS
PHILADELPHIA

First published by The Saint Andrew Press
Edinburgh, Scotland
First Edition, March, 1955
Second Edition, April, 1957

Library of Congress Catalog Card No. 58–5149

Typeset in Great Britain
Printed in the United States of America

GENERAL INTRODUCTION

It may truly be said that this series of Daily Bible Studies began almost accidentally. A series which the Church of Scotland was using came to an end, and another series was immediately required. I was asked to write a volume on *Acts*, and, at the moment, had no intention beyond that. But one volume followed another, until the demand for one volume became a plan to write on the whole New Testament.

The translation which is given in each volume claims no special merit. It was included in order that the reader might be able to carry both the text of the New Testament and the comments on it wherever he went, and that he might be able to read it anywhere. While I was making the translation, the translations of Moffatt, Weymouth, and Knox were ever beside me. *The American Revised Standard Version*, *The Twentieth Century New Testament*, and *The New Testament in Plain English*, by Charles Kingsley Williams, have been in constant use. Since its publication, I have consistently consulted *The Authentic New Testament*, translated by Hugh J. Schonfield.

I cannot see another edition of these books going out to the public without expressing my very deep and sincere gratitude to the Church of Scotland Publications Committee for allowing me the privilege of first beginning, and then continuing, this series. And in particular I wish to express my very great gratitude to the convener, Rev. R. G. Macdonald, O.B.E., M.A., D.D., and to the committee's secretary and manager, Rev. Andrew McCosh, M.A., S.T.M., for constant encouragement and never-failing sympathy and help.

As these volumes went on, the idea of the whole series developed. The aim is to make the results of modern scholarship available to the non-technical reader in a form that it does not require a theological education to understand; and then to seek to make the teaching of the New Testament books relevant to life and work to-day. The whole aim of these books is summed up in Richard of Chichester's famous prayer; they are meant to enable men and women to know Jesus Christ more clearly, to love Him more dearly, and to follow Him more nearly. It is my prayer that they may do something to make that possible.

FOREWORD

WHEN we come to read the *Letter to the Hebrews* we come to read what is, for the person of to-day, the most difficult book in the whole New Testament. *Hebrews* was never at any time an easy book to read. Even when it was first written it was written by a scholar for a little group of scholars. The knowledge which it demands of the Old Testament and of the Hebrew sacrificial system was never the possession of every man; and, if it was difficult for the people to whom it was first written, it will be still more difficult for us to-day. But I believe that there is no book in the New Testament which is more worth the effort to understand. I believe that no New Testament book gives us such a glorious picture of Jesus Christ, in all the splendour of His manhood and in all the majesty of His deity. I know that those who read *Hebrews* will find it difficult, but it is my earnest prayer that many will persevere until for them this great book has unlocked its treasures.

As I wrote this exposition I have made constant use of certain books, for the literature on *Hebrews* is very extensive. For those who read Greek the commentary in the Macmillan series by B. F. Westcott is still unsurpassed although it was written as long ago as 1889. The volume by Moffatt in the International Critical Commentary is a monument of scholarship to which I am much indebted. Of commentaries on the English text that by F. D. V. Narborough in the Clarendon Bible is small, but very suggestive and illuminating. The commentary by T. H. Robinson in the Moffatt Commentary is not one of the outstanding volumes in that series, although it is useful. The commentary by E. C. Wickham in the Westminster Commentaries series is in every way first-class. There have been many first-class studies on *Hebrews*. That by E. F. Scott is specially good, as is also that by A. Nairne. *Let us go on, the Secret of Christian Progress in the Epistle to the Hebrews,* by W. H.

Griffith Thomas is outstandingly helpful. But to this day by far the best work on the thought of *Hebrews* is *The Epistle to the Hebrews, the first Apology for Christianity,* by A. B. Bruce. Of all interpreters A. B. Bruce stands supreme. I have one debt that I cannot but acknowledge. The first man whom I ever heard lecture on *Hebrews* was the late W. M. Macgregor, my teacher when I was a student in Trinity College. These lectures I will never forget. To me they were the high-water mark of the work of him who was the greatest interpreter of the New Testament I ever met. If this present book has anything of good in it, it remains due to the inspiration of W. M. Macgregor. I am bound to say that there may be debts in this book which I have not acknowledged. That is because it has been my duty and privilege for seven years now to lecture to students on *Hebrews*, and, over the years, I have collected material, and have sometimes failed to note from where it came. If I have quoted the work of others without acknowledgment, I ask their pardon.

I hope that there are many who will undertake the adventure of reading this great letter of the New Testament. It is my prayer that the reading of it will bring to many that access to the presence of God in which the nameless writer of the *Letter to the Hebrews* saw the very essence of all religion.

CONTENTS

THE LETTER TO THE HEBREWS

CONTENTS

INTRODUCTION

God fulfils Himself in many Ways

Religion has never been and can never be the same thing to all men. " God," as Tennyson said, " fulfils Himself in many ways." George Russell said: " There are as many ways of climbing to the stars as there are people to climb." There is a well-known saying which tells us very truly and very beautifully that " God has His own secret stairway into every heart." Broadly speaking, there have been four great conceptions of religion. (i) To some men religion is *inward fellowship with God*. It is a union with Christ so close and so intimate that the Christian can be said to live in Christ, and Christ can be said to live in him. That was Paul's conception of religion. Religion to him was something which mystically and mysteriously united him with God. (ii) To some, religion is that which gives a man *a standard for life and a power to reach that standard*. Religion is the law for a good life, and the power to keep that law. On the whole, that is what religion was to James and to Peter. It was something which showed them what life ought to be, and which enabled them to make life what it ought to be. (iii) To some men religion is *the highest satisfaction of their minds*. Their minds seek and seek, until they find that they can rest in God. It was Plato who said that " the unexamined life is the life not worth living." There are some men who must understand or perish. Their minds must be satisfied. On the whole, that is what religion was to John. The first chapter of John's gospel is one of the greatest attempts in the world to state religion in a way that really satisfies the mind. (iv) To some men religion is *access to God*. It is that which brings them into the very presence of God. It is that which removes the barriers, which takes away the estrangements, and opens the door to the living presence of the living God. That is what religion was to the writer of the *Letter to the Hebrews*. With that idea his mind is haunted and dominated. He found in Christ the one person who could take him into the very presence of God. The door that had been shut was opened because of what Jesus was and did. His whole idea of religion is summed up in the great passage in *Hebrews* 10: 19-23.

> " Having therefore boldness to enter into the holiest by the blood of Jesus, by a new and living way, which He has consecrated for us through the veil that is His flesh, let us draw near with a true heart in full assurance of faith."

If the writer to the Hebrews had one text and one summons, it was: " *Let us draw near.*"

The double Background

The writer to the Hebrews had a double background, and into both these backgrounds this idea came. He had a *Greek background.* Ever since the time of Plato, five hundred years before, the Greeks had been haunted by the contrast between the real and the unreal, the seen and the unseen, the temporal and the eternal. It was the Greek idea that somewhere there is a real world, of which this world is only a poor and shadowy and imperfect copy. Plato had the idea that somewhere there is a world of perfect *forms* or *ideas* or *patterns*, of which everything in this world is an imperfect copy. To take a simple instance, somewhere there is laid up the pattern, the idea, the form of a perfect chair of which all the chairs in this world are inadequate copies. Plato said: " The Creator of the world had designed and carried out His work according to an unchangeable and eternal pattern of which the world is but a copy." Philo, who took his ideas from Plato, said: " God knew from the beginning that a fair copy could never come into being apart from a fair pattern; and that none of the objects perceivable by sense could be flawless which was not modelled after an archtype and spiritual idea, and thus, when He prepared to create this visible world, He shaped beforehand the ideal world in order to constitute

the corporeal after the incorporeal and godlike pattern."
When Cicero was talking of the laws men know and use
on earth, he said: " We have no real and life-like likeness
of real law and genuine justice; all we enjoy is a shadow
and a sketch." The thinkers of the ancient world all
had this idea, that somewhere there is a real world, of
which this world is only a kind of pale shadow, an imperfect
copy. Here we can only guess and grope; here we can
only work with shadows and copies and imperfect things.
But in the unseen world there are the real things, the
perfect things, the world as God conceived it. When
Newman died they erected a statue to him, and on the
pedestal of it there are the Latin words: *Ab umbris et
imaginibus ad veritatem,* " Away from the shadows and the
semblances to the truth." If that be so, clearly the great
task of this life is to get away from the shadows and the
imperfections and to reach *reality.* It is exactly that that
the writer to the Hebrews claims that Jesus Christ can
enable us to do. To the Greek the writer to the Hebrews
would have said, did in fact say: " All your lives you
have been searching for reality; all your lives you have
been trying to get from the shadows to the truth. That
is just what this Jesus Christ can enable you to do."

The Hebrew Background

But the writer to the Hebrews also had a *Jewish background.* To the Jew it was always a dangerous thing to
come too near to God. " No man," said God to Moses,
" shall see my face and live " (*Deuteronomy* 33: 20).
It was Jacob's astonished exclamation at Peniel: " I
have seen God face to face and my life is preserved "
(*Genesis* 32: 30). When Manoah realised who his visitor
had been, he said in terror to his wife: " We shall surely
die because we have seen God." The great day of Jewish
worship was the Day of Atonement. That was the one
day of all the year when the High Priest entered the

Holy of Holies where the very presence of God was held to dwell. No man ever entered in except the High Priest, and he entered in only on that day. When he did so enter in, the law laid it down that he must not linger in the Holy Place for long " lest he put Israel in terror." It was dangerous to enter the presence of God, and if a man waited too long he might be struck dead.

In view of this there entered into Jewish thought the idea of a *covenant*. A covenant meant that God, in His grace and of His own initiative, in a way that was quite unmerited and quite undeserved, approached the nation of Israel, and offered them a special relationship with Himself. In a unique way they would be His people and He would be their God. He was offering them a special access to Himself. But that access was conditional on one thing—it was conditional on the observance by the people of the law that He gave to them. We can see this relationship being entered into and this law being accepted in the dramatic scene in *Exodus* 24: 3-8. So then Israel had access to God, *but only if she kept the law*. To break the law was sin, and sin interrupted the access to God, put up a barrier which stopped the way to God. It was to take away that barrier that the whole system of the Levitical priesthood and sacrifices was constructed. The law was given; man sinned; the barrier was up; the sacrifice was made; and the sacrifice was designed to restore the lost relationship, to give back the forfeited access, to open the closed way to God. But the whole experience of life was that that was precisely what sacrifice could not do. Over and over again sacrifice had to be made; the priests themselves were sinning men and had to offer sacrifices for their own sins first of all; no animal sacrifice can ever really remove the guilt of sin. It was the proof of the ineffectiveness of the whole system that for ever and for ever sacrifice had to go on and on and on. Sacrifice was a losing and ineffective battle to remove the barrier that sin had erected between man and God.

THE LETTER TO THE HEBREWS

The Perfect Priest and the Perfect Sacrifice

What men needed was a *perfect priest* and **a perfect** *sacrifice*, someone who was such that he could bring to God a sacrifice which once and for all opened the way of access to God. That, said the writer to the Hebrews, is exactly what Christ did. He is the perfect priest, because He is at once perfectly man and perfectly God. In His manhood He can take man to God, and in His Godhead He can take God to man. He has no sin. The perfect sacrifice He brings is the sacrifice of Himself, a sacrifice so perfect that it never needs to be made again. To the Jew the writer to the Hebrews said: " All your lives you have been looking for the perfect priest who can bring the perfect sacrifice and give you access to God and take away the barriers and put you for ever into a right relationship with God. That is what you have in Jesus Christ, and in Him alone."

So to the Greek the writer to the Hebrews said: " You are looking for the way from the shadows to reality; you will find it in Jesus Christ." So to the Jew the writer to the Hebrews said: " You are looking for that perfect sacrifice which will open the way to God which your sins have closed; you will find it in Jesus Christ." To the writer to the Hebrews Jesus was the one person on earth who gave access to reality and access to God. That is the key-thought of the whole letter.

The Riddle of the New Testament

So much is clear, but when we turn to the other questions of introduction the *Letter to the Hebrews* is wrapped in mystery. E. F. Scott wrote: " The *Epistle to the Hebrews* is in many respects the riddle of the New Testament." When we ask when it was written, to whom it was written, and who wrote it, we can only guess and grope. The very history of the letter shows how its mystery made it to be treated with a certain reserve and suspicion. It was a long time before the *Letter to the Hebrews* became an unquestioned New Testament book. The first list of New Testament books, The Muratorian Canon, compiled about A.D. 170, does not mention it at all. The great Alexandrian scholars, Clement and Origen, knew it and loved it but agreed that its place as scripture was disputed. Of the great African fathers, Cyprian never mentions it, and Tertullian knows that its place was disputed. Eusebius, the great Church historian, says that it ranked among the disputed books. It was not until the time of Athanasius, in the middle of the fourth century, that *Hebrews* was definitely accepted as a New Testament book, and even Luther was not too sure about it. It is a strange thing to think how long this great book had to wait for full authority and full recognition. Of any New Testament book we have to ask, when was it written, to whom was it written, and who wrote it? Let us try to answer these questions as far as we can.

When was it written?

The only information we have must come from the letter itself. Clearly it is written for what we might call second generation Christians (2: 3). The story was transmitted to its recipients by those who had heard the Lord. The community to whom it was written were not new to the Christian faith; they ought to have been mature (5: 12). They must have had a long history for they are summoned to look back on the former days (10: 32). They had a great history behind them, and heroic martyr figures on which they ought to look back for inspiration (13: 7). The thing that will help us most in dating the letter is the references to persecution. It is clear that at one time their leaders had died for their faith, for they are urged to remember the exit from life of these great figures (13: 7). It is clear that they themselves had not yet suffered persecution, for they had not yet resisted unto blood (12: 4). It is also clear that they have had ill-treatment to suffer for they have had to undergo the pillaging of their goods (10: 32-34). And it is clear from the whole outlook of the letter that there is a risk of persecution about to come. From all that it is safe to say that this letter must have been written in days between two persecutions, in days when Christians were not actually persecuted, but were nonetheless unpopular with their fellow men. Now the first persecution was in the time of Nero in the year A.D. 64; and the next persecution was in the time of Domitian about A.D. 85. Somewhere between these dates this letter was written. There was the memory of persecution behind them to inspire them with the story of its heroes; there was the prospect of persecution in front of them, for which they must nerve themselves; there was daily hatred and hostility which sometimes issued in ill-treatment. We can place this letter between the days of Nero and Domitian, more likely nearer to Domitian. If we take the date as A.D. 80 we shall not be far wrong.

To whom was it written?

Next, we ask the question, " To whom was the *Letter to the Hebrews* written? " Once again we will have to be dependent on such hints as we get from the letter itself. One thing is certain—it cannot have been written to any of the great Churches or the name of the place to which it was written could not have so completely vanished. Let us set down what we do know. The letter was written to a long-established Church (5: 12). It was written to a Church which had at some time in the past suffered persecution (10: 32-34). It was written to a Church which had had great days and which had had great teachers and leaders (13: 7). It was written to a Church which had not been directly founded by the apostles (2: 3). It was written to a Church which had been marked by generosity and liberality (6: 10). Now we do have one direct hint. Amongst the closing greetings we find the sentence, as the Authorised Version translates it: "They of Italy salute you" (13: 24). To translate it more accurately, it ought to be: "Those who are from Italy salute you" (*hoi apo tēs Italias*). Now taken by itself that phrase could mean either that the letter was written *from* Italy or that it was written *to* Italy. But much more likely it means that it was written *to* Italy. Suppose I am in Glasgow and I am writing to some place abroad, I would not likely say, "All the people from Glasgow salute you": I would much more likely say, "All the people in Glasgow salute you." But suppose I am somewhere abroad where there is a little colony of Scots, I might well say, "All the people here from Glasgow send you their greetings." This little phrase much more naturally means that the letter was sent to Italy from abroad by someone whose home was in Italy, and who, for some reason, was away from home. So then we may say that the letter was written *to Italy*; and if it was written to Italy it was almost certainly written to Rome. But quite certainly it was not written to the Church at Rome as a whole. If it had been it would never have lost its title. And furthermore, as we read it we cannot help getting the impression that it was written to a small body of like-minded persons. Still further, it was obviously written to a scholarly group. From 5: 12 we can see that these people had long been under instruction and that they were preparing themselves to become teachers of the Christian faith. Still further, *Hebrews* demands such a knowledge of the Old Testament and such a knowledge of the tabernacle and of the priests and of the system of sacrifice that it must always have been a book written by a scholar for scholars. When we sum it all up, we can say that *Hebrews* is a letter written by a great teacher, written by a man whom we would call a professor, to a little group or college of Christians in Rome. He was their teacher; at the moment he was separated from them; he was afraid that they were drifting away from the faith;

and so he wrote this letter to them. It is not so much a letter as it is a talk. It does not begin like a letter, as Paul's letters do, although it ends with greetings as a letter does. The writer himself calls it " a word of exhortation." We will not be wrong if we think of *Hebrews* as a letter written to a little group of people who were training to be teachers in the Christian Church. It was written to them by their own teacher at a time when he could not come to them in person.

By whom was it written?

Perhaps the most insoluble problem of all is the problem, Who wrote the *Letter to the Hebrews?* It was precisely that uncertainty which kept this letter so long on the fringes of the New Testament. The title in the earliest days is simply, *To the Hebrews*. No author's name is given. In the earliest days no one connected it directly with the name of Paul. Clement of Alexandria used to think that Paul might have written it and that perhaps he wrote it in Hebrew and Luke translated it, for the style is quite different from the style of Paul. Origen made the famous remark that " who wrote the *Letter to the Hebrews* only God knows for certain." Tertullian thought that Barnabas wrote it. Jerome says the Latin Church did not receive it as Paul's and when he is speaking of the author says, " the writer to the Hebrews whoever he was." Augustine felt the same way about it. Luther declared that Paul could never have written it because the thought is not his. And Calvin said that " he could not bring himself to think that this letter was a letter of Paul." At no time in the history of the Church did men ever really think that Paul wrote *Hebrews*. How then did it get attached to his name? It all happened very simply. When the New Testament came into its final form there was of course argument about which books were to be included and which were not. To settle it one test was used. Was a book the work of an apostle, or was it at least the work of one who had been in direct contact with the apostles? Now by this time the *Letter to the Hebrews* was known and loved throughout the Church. Most people felt like Origen that God only knew who wrote it; but they read it and loved it and wanted it. So there was only one thing to do with it. It *must* go into the New Testament and there was only one way to ensure that it would, and that was to include it with the thirteen letters of Paul, the great letter writer. So *Hebrews* won its way into the New Testament on the grounds of its own supreme greatness, but to get in it had to be included with the letters of Paul and had to come under his name. People knew quite well that the style was not Paul's and the thought was not Paul's, but they included it among his letters because no man knew who wrote it, and it must go in.

The Author of Hebrews.

Can we guess who the author was? Many candidates for the authorship have been put forward. We can only glance at three of the many suggestions. (i) Tertullian thought that Barnabas wrote *Hebrews*. Barnabas was a native of Cyprus; the people of Cyprus were famous for the excellence of the Greek they spoke; and *Hebrews* is written in the best Greek in the New Testament. Barnabas was a Levite (Acts 4: 36) and of all men in the New Testament he would have had the closest knowledge of the priestly and the sacrificial system on which the whole thought of the letter is based. Barnabas is called a son of *consolation*; the Greek word is *paraklēsis*; and the *Letter to the Hebrews* calls itself a word of *paraklēsis* (13: 22), a word of *exhortation* or *consolation*. Barnabas was one of the few men who were acceptable to both Jews and Greeks and who were at home in both worlds of thought. It might be that Barnabas wrote this letter, but if he did it is strange that his name should vanish in connection with it. (ii) Luther was sure that Apollos wrote *Hebrews*. Apollos, according to the New Testament mention of him, was a

Jew, born at Alexandria, an eloquent man and mighty in the scriptures (Acts 18: 24ff; I Corinthians 1: 12; 3: 4). The man who wrote this letter certainly knew the scriptures; he was certainly eloquent; and he certainly thought and argued in the way that a cultured Alexandrian would. It is certainly true that the man who wrote *Hebrews* was a man like Apollos in thought and in background. (iii) The most romantic of all conjectures is that of Harnack, the great German scholar. He thought that maybe Aquila and Priscilla wrote it between them. Aquila was a teacher (Acts 18: 26). Their house in Rome was a Church in itself (Romans 16: 5). Harnack thought that that is why the letter begins with no greetings and why the writer's name has vanished—because the main author of *Hebrews* was a woman and a woman was not allowed to teach.

But when we come to the end of conjecture, we can only say as Origen said seventeen hundred years ago, that only God knows who wrote the *Letter to the Hebrews*. To us this man must remain for ever a voice and nothing more; but we can be thankful to God for the work of this great nameless one who wrote with incomparable skill and beauty about this Jesus who to him—and to us—is the way to reality and the way to God.

HEBREWS

THE END OF FRAGMENTS

Hebrews I: 1-3

> It was in many parts and in many ways that God
> spoke to our fathers in the prophets in time gone past;
> but in the end of these days He has spoken to us in
> One who is a Son, a Son whom He destined to enter
> into possession of all things, a Son by whose agency He
> made the universe. He was the very effulgence of God's
> glory; He was the exact expression of God's very
> essence. He bore everything onwards by the word
> of His power; and after He had made purification
> for the sins of men, He took His royal seat at the right
> hand of the glory in the heights.

THIS is the most sonorous piece of Greek in the whole
New Testament. It is a passage that any classical Greek
orator would have been proud to write. The writer of the
Letter to the Hebrews has brought to it every artifice of
word and rhythm that the beautiful and flexible Greek
language could provide. In Greek the two adverbs which
we have translated *in many parts* and *in many ways* are
single words. They are the words *polumerōs* and *polutropōs*.
The Greek word *polu-* in such a combination means *many*.
And it was a habit of the great Greek orators, like Demosthenes, the greatest of them all, to weave such sonorous
adjectives into the first paragraph of a speech. The writer
to the Hebrews felt that, since he was going to speak of the
supreme revelation of God to men, he must clothe his
thought in the noblest language that it was possible to
find. A great thought demanded a great dress. There is
something of interest even here. The man who wrote this
letter must have been trained in Greek oratory. When
he became a Christian he did not throw his training away.
He used the talent he had in the service of Jesus Christ.
Everyone knows the lovely legend of the acrobatic tumbler
who became a monk. He felt that he had so little to offer.
One day someone saw him go into the chapel and stand

I

before the statue of the Virgin Mary. He hesitated for a moment; and then he began to offer all that he had to offer; he began to go through his acrobatic routine, doing all the gymnastic tricks he had learned. When he had completed his tumbling he knelt in adoration; and then, says the legend, the statue of the Virgin Mary came to life, stepped down from her pedestal and gently wiped the sweat from the brow of the acrobat who had offered all he had to give. When a man becomes a Christian he is not asked to abandon all the gifts and the talents he once had; he is asked to use them in the service of Jesus Christ and of His Church.

The basic idea of this whole letter is that Jesus Christ alone brings to men the full revelation of God, and that He alone enables men to enter into the very presence of God. So the writer begins by contrasting Jesus with the prophets who had gone before. He talks about Jesus coming *in the end of these days*. The Jews divided all time into two ages—the present age and the age to come. In between they set The Day of the Lord. The present age was wholly human and wholly bad; the age to come was to be the golden age of God. The Day of the Lord, in between, was to be like the birth-pangs of a new age. So this writer says, " The old time is passing away; the age of incompleteness is gone; the time of human guessing and groping is at an end; the new age, the age of God, has dawned in Christ." He saw the world and the thought of men enter, as it were, into a new beginning with Jesus Christ. In Jesus, God had entered humanity, eternity had invaded time, and things could never be the same again.

He chooses to begin to contrast Jesus with the prophets, for the prophets were always believed to be in the secret counsels of God. Long ago Amos had said: " The Lord God will do nothing but He revealeth His secrets to His servants the prophets " (Amos 3: 7). Philo had said: " The prophet is the interpreter of the God who speaks within." He had said: " The prophets are interpreters of the God who uses them as instruments to reveal to men that which He wills." In later days this doctrine had been completely mechanised. Athenagoras spoke of God moving the mouths of the prophets as a man might play upon a musical instrument, and of the Spirit breathing into them as a flute-player breathes into a flute. Justin Martyr spoke of the divine coming down from heaven and sweeping across the prophets as a plectrum sweeps across a harp or a lute. In the end men came to put it in such a way that the prophets had really no more to do with their message than a musical instrument has to do with the music it plays, or a pen with the message which it writes. That was over-mechanising the matter; for it remains true that even the finest musician is to some extent at the mercy of his instrument and could not produce great music out of a piano in which certain notes were missing or out of tune, and even the finest penman is to some extent at the mercy of his pen. God could not reveal more than men could understand. God's revelation comes through the minds and the hearts of men. And that is exactly what the writer to the Hebrews saw.

He says that the revelation of God, the truth, which came through the prophets, was *in many parts* (*polumerōs*) and *in many ways* (*polutropōs*). There are two ideas there. (i) The revelation of the prophets had a variegated grandeur which made it a tremendous thing. From age to age the prophets had spoken, always fitting their message to their age, always seizing that facet of the truth which was relevant to the men to whom they spoke. It was never a static and outworn thing. It was never out-of-date and irrelevant and imcomprehensible. It was adapted to the need of every age. (ii) But, at the same time, that revelation was fragmentary, and had to be presented in such a way that the limitations of the time would understand. It was *fragmentary*. One of the most interesting things is to see how time and again the prophets are characterised by one idea. For instance, *Amos* is " *a cry for social justice.*"

Isaiah had grasped the *holiness of God*. *Hosea*, because of his own bitter home experience, had realised the wonder of *the forgiving love of God*. Each prophet, out of his own experience of life, and out of the experience of Israel, had grasped and expressed a *fragment*, a *part* of the truth of God. No prophet had grasped the whole round orb of truth; but with Jesus it was different. Jesus was not a part of the truth; He was the whole truth. He was not a fragmentary revelation of God; He was the full revelation of God. In Him God displayed not some facet of His truth; God displayed *Himself* full revealed to men. Further, the prophets had used many methods. They had used the method of *speech*. When speech had failed they had used the method of *dramatic action*. (Cp. I Kings II: 29-32; Jeremiah 13: 1-9; 27: 1-7; Ezekiel 4: 1-3; 5: 1-4). The prophet had had to use human methods to transmit his part of the truth of God. Again, it was different with Jesus. Jesus revealed God *by being Himself*. It was not so much what He said and did that shows us what God is like; it is what He *is*. The revelation of the prophets was great and manifold, but it was fragmentary and presented by such methods as they could find to make it effective; but the revelation of God in Jesus was complete, and was presented in Jesus Himself. In a word, the prophets were the *friends* of God; but Jesus was the *Son*. The prophets grasped *part* of the mind of God; but Jesus *was* the mind of God. It is to be noted that it is no part of the purpose of the writer to the Hebrews to belittle the prophets; it is his aim to establish the supremacy of Jesus Christ. He is not saying that there is a *break* between the Old Testament revelation and that of the New Testament; he is stressing the fact that there is *continuity*, but continuity that ends in *consummation*.

The writer to the Hebrews uses two great pictures to describe what Jesus was. He says that He was the *apaugasma* of God's glory. *Apaugasma* can mean one of two things in Greek. It can mean *effulgence*, the light which shines forth, or it can mean *reflection*, the light which is reflected. Here it means, more likely, *effulgence*. Jesus is the shining of God's glory among men. He says that He was the *charactēr* of God's very essence and substance and being. Now, in Greek, *charactēr* means two things. It means, first, a *seal*; and it means, second, the *mark*, the *impression*, that the seal leaves on the wax. Now, the impression has the exact form of the seal; it reproduces exactly, and in every detail, the shape of the seal. So, when the writer to the Hebrews said that Jesus was the *charactēr* of the very being of God, he meant that Jesus is the exact image and expression of God, that just as if you look at the impression, you see exactly what the seal which made it is like, so if you look at Jesus you see exactly what God is like. Jesus is not fragmentary and incomplete; He is the full and exact expression of God.

C. J. Vaughan has pointed out that this passage tells us six great things about Jesus.

(i) The original glory of God belongs to Him. He is the effulgence of God's glory. Now here is a wonderful thought. Jesus is God's glory; therefore, we see with amazing clarity that the glory of God consists not in crushing men and in tyrannising over them and in reducing them to abject servitude, but in serving men and loving men and in the end dying for men. The glory of God is not the glory of shattering power, but the glory of suffering love.

(ii) The destined empire belongs to Jesus. The New Testament writers never doubted the ultimate triumph of Jesus. Think of it. They are thinking of a Galilaean carpenter who was crucified as a criminal on a Cross on a hill outside the city of Jerusalem. They themselves faced savage persecution and they were the humblest of people. As Sir William Watson said of them,

> " So to the wild wolf Hate were sacrificed
> The panting, huddled flock, whose crime was Christ."

And yet they never doubted the ultimate triumph. They

were quite certain that God's love was backed by God's power, and that in the end the kingdoms of the world would be the kingdoms of the Lord and of His Christ. We would do well to grasp again the fact-defying optimism of the early Church.

(iii) The creative action belongs to Jesus. The early Church had one great thought. They held that the Son had been God's agent and instrument in creation; that in some way God had originally created the world through His Son. They were filled with the thought that the One who had created the world would be the One who re-created that same world; that the One who made the world must be the One who would also redeem the world.

(iv) The sustaining power belongs to Jesus. He carries all things onward by His power. That is to say, these early Christians had a tremendous grip of the doctrine of *providence*. They did not think of God as creating the world, and then, as it were, leaving the world to itself. Somehow and somewhere they saw in life and in the world a power that was carrying the world and carrying each life on to a destined end. They believed,

> " That nothing walks with aimless feet,
>   That not one life shall be destroy'd,
>   Or cast as rubbish to the void,
> When God hath made the pile complete."

(v) To Jesus belonged the redemptive work. He made purification for the sins of men. By His sacrifice He paid the price of sin; by His continual presence He liberates from sin.

(vi) To Jesus belongs the mediatorial exaltation. He has taken His place on the right hand of glory; but the tremendous thought of the writer to the Hebrews is that He is there, not as our judge, but as the one who makes intercession for us, so that, when we enter into the presence of God, we go, not to hear God's justice prosecute us, but to hear God's love plead for us.

THE LETTER TO THE HEBREWS

ABOVE THE ANGELS

Hebrews I: 4-14

He was the superior to the angels, in proportion as He had received a more excellent rank than they. For to which of the angels did God ever say: " It is my *Son* that you are; it is I who this day have begotten you "? And again: " I will be to Him a Father, and He will be to Me a Son." And again, when He brings His honoured one into the world of men, He says: " And let all the angels of God bow down before Him." As for the angels, He says: " He who makes His angels winds, and His servants a flame of fire." But, as for the Son, He says: " God is your throne for ever and for ever, and the sceptre of righteousness is the sceptre of your kingdom. You have loved justice and hated lawlessness; therefore God has anointed you, even your God, with the oil of exultation above your fellows." And, " You in the beginning, O Lord, laid the foundations of the earth, and the heavens are the work of your hands. They shall perish but you remain unalterable. All of them will grow old like a garment, and like a mantle you will fold them up, and they will be changed. But you are ever yourself, and your years will not fail." To which of the angels did He ever say: " Sit at my right hand till I make your enemies your footstool "? Are they not all ministering spirits, continually being despatched on service, for the sake of those who are destined to enter into possession of salvation?

IN the previous passage the writer had been concerned to prove the superiority of Jesus over all the prophets who had gone before. Now he is concerned to prove His superiority over the angels. That he thinks it worth while to do this proves the place that belief in angels had in the thought of the Jews of His day. At this time belief in angels was on the increase. The reason was that men were more and more impressed with what is called the transcendence of God. Men felt more and more the distance and the difference between God and man. They felt that God was ever farther and farther away and more and more

7

unknowable and unreachable. The result was that they came to think of the angels as intermediaries between God and man. They had begun to feel that God was so far away from man that He could not speak direct to man, nor could man directly speak to Him; and so they began to believe that the angels bridged the gulf and that God spoke to man through the angels, and that part of the duty of the angels was to carry the prayers of man into the presence of God. We see this process happening very particularly in one special instance. In the Old Testament the law was given direct by God to Moses. There was no need of any intermediary between God and man. The communication was not through any third party but direct. But in New Testament times the Jews believed that God gave the law first to angels and that the angels passed it on to Moses because direct communication between man and God was unthinkable (cp. Acts 7: 53; Galatians 3: 19).

Let us look at some of the basic Jewish beliefs about the angels, and as we look at them we will see them reappearing in this passage. God lived surrounded by His angelic hosts (Isaiah 6; I Kings 22: 19). Sometimes the angels are thought of as God's army (Joshua 5: 14f). In Greek the word for *angels* is *aggeloi* and in Hebrew it is *mal'akim*. In both languages the word means *messenger* as well as *angel*. In fact, *messenger* is its ordinary and commoner meaning. The angels are really the beings who are the instruments in the bringing of God's word and the working of God's will in the universe of men. They are, as it were, the go-betweens, the liaison officers, between God and man. They were said to be spirits who were made of an ethereal fiery substance like blazing light. They were created either on the second or the fifth day of creation. They do not eat or drink and they do not beget children. Sometimes they were believed to be immortal, although they could be annihilated by God, but there was another belief about their existence as we shall see. Some of them, the seraphim, the cherubim and the ofanim (-*im* is the Hebrew plural ending of nouns) were always around the throne of God. They were thought of as having more knowledge than men, especially more knowledge of the future, but they did not possess that knowledge as it were by right, but rather because of " what they had heard behind the curtain." It is almost as if the angels eavesdropped on the purposes and plans of God. They were thought of as the kind of entourage, the *familia*, of God. They were thought of as God's senate or counsel. God did nothing without consulting His angels. For instance, when God said: " Let *us* make man " (Genesis 1: 26) it was to the angel senate that He was speaking. Often the angels remonstrated with God and laid objections to His purposes. In particular, they objected to the creation of man, and at that time troops of them were annihilated; and they objected to the giving of the law and attacked Moses on his way up Mount Sinai. This was because they were jealous and did not wish to share any of their place or prerogatives with any other creature.

There were millions and millions of angels. It was not till quite late that the Jews assigned names to the angels. At first the angels were nameless and anonymous; but later they came to give them names. There were, in particular, the seven angels of the presence, who were the archangels. Of these the principal ones were Raphael, Uriel, Phanuel, Gabriel, who was the angel who brought God's messages to men, and Michael, who was the angel who presided over the destinies of Israel. The angels had many duties. They brought God's messages to men. In that case they took their message and delivered it and vanished (Judges 13: 26). They intervened for God in the events of history (2 Kings 19: 35, 36). There were two hundred angels who controlled the movements of the stars and kept them in their courses. There was an angel who controlled the never-ending succession of the years and months and days. There was an angel, a mighty prince, who was over the sea. There were angels of the frost, the dew, the rain, the snow, the hail, the thunder and the lightning. There were angels who were wardens of hell and torturers of the damned. There were recording angels who wrote down in books every single word which every man spoke. There were destroying angels, and angels of punishment. There was Satan, the prosecuting angel, who for 364 days of the year, on every day except the Day of Atonement, assiduously and continuously brought charges against men before God. There was the angel of death who went out only at God's bidding and who impartially delivered His summons to good and evil alike. Every nation had its guardian angel who had the *prostasia*, the presidency over the nation. Every individual had his guardian angel. Even little children had their angels (Matthew 18: 10). So many were the angels that the Rabbis could even say: " Every blade of grass has its angel."

There was one special belief, held only by some, which is indirectly referred to in this passage which we are studying. The common belief was that the angels were immortal; but there were some who held a very different belief. Some believed that the angels lived only one day. There was a rabbinic belief in some schools that " every day God creates a new company of angels who utter a song before Him and are gone." " The angels are renewed every morning and after they have praised God they return to the stream of fire from whence they came." 4 Esdras 8: 21 speaks of the God " before whom the heavenly host stand in terror and at Thy word change to wind and fire." A rabbinic homily makes one of the angels say: " God changes us every hour. . . . Sometimes He makes us fire, at other times wind." That is what the writer to the Hebrews means when He talks of God making His angels wind and fire.

With this vast angelology there was a very real danger that the angels would come, in men's belief, to intervene between God and men. It was necessary to show that the Son was greater far than they, that he who knew the Son needed no angel to be his intermediary between himself and God. The writer to the Hebrews does it by choosing what were for him a series of proof texts in which the Son was given a higher place than was ever given to any angel. The texts he quotes are as follows: Psalm 2: 7; 2 Samuel 7: 14; Psalm 97: 7 or Deuteronomy 32: 43; Psalm 104: 4; Psalm 45: 7, 8; Psalm 102: 26, 27; Psalm 110: 1. Some of these texts differ from the version which appears in our Bibles, because the writer to the Hebrews was quoting from the Septuagint, the Greek version of the Old Testament, which is not always the same as the original Hebrew from which our Bible is translated. To us some of the proof texts he chooses seem very strange. For instance, 2 Samuel 7: 14 is in the original a simple and direct reference to Solomon and has nothing to do with the Son or the Messiah. Psalm 102: 26, 27 is a reference to God and not to the Son. But whenever the early Christians found a text with the word *son* or the word *Lord* they considered themselves quite entitled to take it right out of its context and to apply it to Jesus. Whatever that method may seem like to us, it was entirely convincing to them.

There was one danger which the writer to the Hebrews wished at all costs to avoid. The doctrine of angels is a very lovely thing; but it has one danger. It puts a series of beings between man and God. It introduces a series of beings, other than Jesus, through whom man makes approach to God. That is clearly seen in the Jewish belief that the angels brought God's messages to men and that the angels brought men's prayers to God. In Christianity there is no need for anyone else in between. Because of Jesus and what Jesus did we have direct access to God. As Tennyson had it:

" Speak to Him thou for He hears, and Spirit with
  spirit can meet—
Closer is He than breathing, and nearer than
  hands and feet."

The writer to the Hebrews has caught and lays down the
great truth that we must ever remember—that we need
no man, that we need no supernatural being to bring us
into the presence of God. Jesus Christ broke every barrier
down and opened the way direct for us to God.

THE SALVATION WE DARE NOT NEGLECT

Hebrews 2: 1-4

We must, therefore, with very special intensity pay
attention to the things that we have heard. For,
if the word which was spoken through the medium
of the angels proved itself to be certified as valid,
and if every transgression and disobedience of it
received its just recompense, how shall we escape
if we neglect so great a salvation, a salvation of such
a kind that it had its origin in the words of the Lord,
and was then guaranteed to us by those who had heard
it from His lips, while God Himself added His own
witness to it by signs and wonders and manifold
deeds of power, and by giving us each a share of the
Holy Spirit, according as He willed it ?

HERE the writer is arguing from the less to the greater.
He has in his mind two revelations. The one was the
revelation of the law which came *by the medium of the
angels*, that is to say, the Ten Commandments. Now
any breach of that law, or any disobedience to it, was
followed by strict and just punishment. The other was
the revelation which came *through the medium of Jesus
Christ, the Son*. Because it came in and through the Son
it was infinitely greater than the revelation of God's
truth brought by the angels; and therefore any transgression of it, any refusal to listen to it, must of necessity
be followed by a far greater and a far more terrible punish-

ment. If men cannot neglect the revelation which came *through the angels*, how much less can they neglect the revelation which came *through the Son*?

In the first verse there may quite possibly be an even more vivid picture than there is in the translation which we have used. The two key words are *prosechein* and *pararrein*. In the way we have taken it *prosechein* is taken to mean *to pay attention to*, which is one of its commonest meanings. *Pararrein* is a word of many meanings. It is used of something flowing or slipping past; it can be used for a ring that has slipped off the finger; for a particle of food that has slipped down the wrong way; of a topic that has slipped into the conversation; of a point which has escaped someone in the course of an argument; of some fact that has slipped out of the mind; of something that has ebbed or leaked away. It is regularly used of something which has carelessly or thoughtlessly been allowed to slip away and become lost. These are the senses in which we have taken these two words. But both have another sense; both have a nautical sense. *Prosechein* can mean *to moor a ship*; and *pararrein* can be used of a ship which has been carelessly allowed to drift past a harbour or a haven because the mariner has forgotten to allow for the wind or the current or the tide. So, then, this first verse could be very vividly translated: " Therefore, we must the more eagerly anchor our lives to the things that we have been taught, lest the ship of life drift past the harbour and be wrecked." There is a vivid picture there—the picture of a ship drifting to destruction because the pilot sleeps while the insidious current sweeps the ship past the harbour until it is wrecked. For most of us the threat of life is not so much that we should plunge into disaster, but that we should drift into sin. There are few people who deliberately and in a moment turn their backs on God; there are many who day by day drift farther and farther away from Him. There are not many who in one moment of time commit some disastrous sin; there are many who, bit by bit and almost imperceptibly, involve themselves in some situation, and suddenly awake to find that they have ruined life for themselves and broken someone else's heart. We would do well to be continually on the alert against the peril of the drifting life.

The writer to the Hebrews characterises the sins for which the law brings its punishment under two headings: he calls them *transgression* and *disobedience*. The first of these words is *parabasis*, which literally means *the stepping across a line*. There is a line drawn both by knowledge and by conscience, and to step across that line is sin. The second of these words is *parakoē*. *Parakoē* is an interesting word. It begins by meaning *imperfect hearing*, as, for instance, the hearing of a deaf man. Then it goes on to mean *careless hearing*, the kind of hearing which through carelessness and inattention either misunderstands or fails to catch that which has been said. It ends by meaning *unwillingness to hear*, and therefore *disobedience to the voice of God*. It is the deliberate shutting of the ears to the commands and the warnings and the advice and the invitations of God.

The writer to the Hebrews ends this paragraph by stating three ways in which the Christian revelation is unique.

(i) It is unique in its *origin*. It came direct from the words of Jesus Himself. It was first spoken by the Lord. That is to say, it does not consist of guessings and gropings after God; it is the very voice of God Himself which comes to us in Jesus Christ.

(ii) It is unique in its *transmission*. It came to the people to whom the writer to the Hebrews was writing, from men who had themselves heard it direct from the lips of Jesus. It will always remain true that the one man who can pass on the Christian truth to others is the man who knows Christ " other than at second hand." We can never teach what we do not know; and we can only teach others of Christ when we know Him ourselves.

(iii) It is unique in its *effectiveness*. It issued in signs and wonders and manifold deeds of power. Someone once congratulated Thomas Chalmers after one of his great speeches. " Yes," he said, " but *what did it do?* " As Denney used to say, the ultimate object of Christianity is to make bad men good; and the proof of real Christianity is still the fact that it can change the lives of men. The moral miracles of Christianity are still plain for all to see.

THE RECOVERY OF MAN'S LOST DESTINY

Hebrews 2: 5-9

> It was not to angels that He subjected the order of things to come of which we are speaking. Somewhere in scripture someone bears this witness to that fact: " What is man that you remember him? Or the son of man that you visit him? For a little time you made him lower than the angels; you crowned him with glory and honour; you set him over the work of your hands; you subjected all things beneath his feet." The fact that all things have been subjected to him means that nothing has been left unsubjected to him. But as things are, we see that all things are not in a state of subjection to him. But we do see Him who was for a little while made lower than the angels, Jesus Himself, crowned with glory and honour because of the suffering of His death, a suffering which came to Him in order that, by the grace of God, He might drain the cup of death for every man.

THIS is by no means an easy passage of which to grasp the meaning; but when we do grasp it, the meaning is a tremendous thing. The writer begins with a quotation from Psalm 8: 4-6. Now if we are ever to understand this passage correctly we must understand one thing— *the whole reference of Psalm 8 is to man*. It is the Psalm which sings of the glory that God gave to *man*. There is in it no reference to the Messiah and no reference to Jesus at all. Its reference is altogether to man. There is one phrase in this psalm which makes it difficult for us to grasp that. That is the phrase *the son of man*. We are so used to hearing that phrase applied to Jesus that we tend always to take it to refer to Him. But in Hebrew *a son of man* always means simply *a man*. We have only to turn to the book of the prophet Ezekiel to see that that is true. Again and again, more than eighty times, God addresses Ezekiel as *son of man*. " Son of man, set thy face toward Jerusalem " (Ezekiel 21: 2). " Son of man, prophesy and say. . . . " (Ezekiel 30: 2). The normal meaning of *son of man* in Hebrew is nothing other than *man*, as indeed it is in English also. In the psalm quoted here the two parallel phrases: " What is man that you remember him? " and " Or the son of man that you visit him? " are different ways of saying exactly the same thing. The psalm is a great lyric cry of the glory of man as God meant it to be. It is in fact an expansion of the great promise of God at creation in Genesis 1: 28, when God said to man: " Have dominion over the fish of the sea, and over the fowl of the air, and over every living thing that moveth upon the earth." In fact the glory of man is even greater than the Authorised Version would have us to understand. The Authorised Version has it: " Thou hast made him a little lower than the angels " (Psalm 8: 5). Now that is a correct translation of the *Greek* of the Psalm but it is not a correct translation of the *original Hebrew*. In the original Hebrew it is said that man is made a little lower than the *Elohim*; and *Elohim* is the regular Hebrew word for *God*. What the psalmist wrote about man really was: " Thou hast made him little less than God," which, in fact, is the translation of the American Revised Standard Version of the Psalms. So then this psalm sings of the glory of man, who was made little less than divine, and whom God meant to have dominion over everything in the world.

But, the writer to the Hebrews goes on, in point of fact the situation with which we are confronted is very different. Man was meant to have dominion over everything *but he has not.* He is a creature who is frustrated by his circumstances, defeated by his temptations, girt about with his own weakness. He who should be free is bound; he who should be a king is a slave. As G. K. Chesterton said, whatever else is or is not true, this one thing is certain—man is not what he was meant to be.

But then the writer to the Hebrews goes still further on. Into this situation came Jesus Christ. He suffered and He died, and because He suffered and died, He entered into glory. And that suffering and death and glory are all for man, because Jesus Christ died to make man what he ought to be. Jesus Christ died to rid man of his frustration and his servitude and his bondage and his weakness and to give him the dominion he ought to have. Jesus Christ died to recreate man until man became the creature he was originally created to be.

So in this passage there are three basic ideas. (i) God created man, only a little less than Himself, to have the mastery over all things. (ii) Man through his sin entered into frustration and defeat instead of mastery and dominion. (iii) Into this state of frustration and defeat came Jesus Christ, in order that by His life and death and glory, He might make man what man was meant to be.

We may put it another way. The writer to the Hebrews in this passage shows us three things. (i) He shows us *the ideal of what man should be*—kin to God and master of the universe. (ii) He shows us *the actual state of man*—the frustration instead of the mastery, the failure instead of the glory. Man who was made for kingship has become a slave. (iii) And then he shows us *how the actual can be changed into the ideal.* That change is wrought by Christ. The writer to the Hebrews sees in Jesus Christ the One, who, by His sufferings and His glory, can make man what man was meant to be, and, without Him, could never be.

THE ESSENTIAL SUFFERING

Hebrews 2: 10-18

> For, in His work of bringing many sons to glory, it
> was fitting that He for whom everything exists and
> through whom everything exists, should make the
> pioneer of salvation fully adequate for His destined
> work through suffering.   For he who sanctifies and
> they who are sanctified must come of one stock.
> It is for this reason that He does not hesitate to call
> them brothers, as when He says: " I will tell your
> name to my brothers; I will sing hymns to you in
> the midst of the gathering of your people." And again:
> " I will put all my trust in Him." And again: " Behold
> me and the children whom God gave to me." ‾ The
> children then have a common flesh and blood and He
> completely shared in them, so that, by that death
> of His, He might bring to nothing him who has the
> power of death, and might set free all those who,
> for fear of death, were all their lives liable to a slave's
> existence.   For I presume that it is not angels that
> He helps; but it is the seed of Abraham that He helps.
> So He had in all things to be made like His brothers,
> so that He might become a merciful and faithful
> high priest in the things which pertain to God, to
> win forgiveness for the sins of His people. For in that
> He himself was tried and suffered, He is able to help
> those who are undergoing trial.

HERE the writer to the Hebrews uses one of the great
titles of Jesus. He calls him *the pioneer* (*archēgos*) *of glory*.
The same word is used of Jesus in Acts 3: 15; 5: 31;
Hebrews 12: 2.   At its simplest this word means *head* or
chief.   So Zeus is the *head* of the gods and a general is
the *head* of his army.   It can mean a *founder* or *originator*.
So it is used of the founder of a city, or of a family, or of a
philosophic school.   It can be used in the sense of *source*
or *origin*.   So a good governor is said to be the *archēgos* of
peace and a bad governor the *archēgos* of confusion.   One
basic idea clings to the word in all its uses.   An *archēgos*
is some one who begins something in order that others
may enter into it.   He begins a family that some day others
may be born into the family; he founds a city in order

that others may some day dwell in the city; he founds a philosophic school that others may follow him into the truth and the peace that he himself has discovered; he is the author of blessings, or of penalties, into which others will also enter. An *archēgos* is one who blazes the trail for others to follow. Someone has used this analogy. Suppose a ship was on the rocks, and suppose the only way to rescue was for someone to swim ashore with a line, in order that, once the line was secured, others might follow. The one who was first to swim ashore would be the *archēgos* of the safety of the others. That is what the writer to the Hebrews means when he says that Jesus is the *archēgos* of our salvation. Jesus was the pioneer who blazed the trail to God for us to follow.

How was He enabled to become such? The Authorised Version says that God made Him *perfect* through suffering. The verb which is translated *to make perfect* is *teleioun*. *Teleioun* is the verb which comes from the adjective *teleios* which is usually translated *perfect*. But in the New Testament this word *teleios* has a very special meaning. It has nothing to do with abstract and metaphysical and philosophic perfection. It is used, for instance, of an animal which is unblemished and fit to be offered as a sacrifice; of a scholar who is no longer at the elementary stage but who is mature; of a human being or an animal who is full grown; of a Christian who is no longer on the fringe of the Church but who is baptised. The basic meaning of *teleios* in the New Testament is always that the thing or person so described *fully carries out the purpose or the plan for which he or it was purposed and designed*. In the New Testament sense a person is *teleios* when he fully carries out the purpose for which God designed him and sent him into the world. Therefore the verb *teleioun* will mean in English, not so much *to make perfect*, as *to make fully adequate for, able for, the task for which the person is designed*. So, then, what the writer to the Hebrews is saying is that through suffering Jesus was made fully able for the task of being the pioneer of our salvation. It was His suffering which made Him able to blaze the trail to salvation for others.

Why should that be so?

(i) It was through His sufferings that He was reallv *identified* with men. The writer to the Hebrews quotes three Old Testament texts as forecasts of this identity with men—Psalm 22: 22; Isaiah 8: 17; Isaiah 8: 18. If Jesus had come into this world in a form in which He could never have suffered, He would have been quite different from men, and because He would have been quite different from men, He would have been no Saviour for men. As Jeremy Taylor said: " When God would save men, He did it by way of a man." It is, in fact, this very identification with men which is the very essence of the Christian idea of God. When the Greeks thought of their gods they thought of them as Tennyson pictures them in the *Lotus Eaters*:

> " For they lie beside their nectar, and the bolts
>   are hurl'd
> Far below them in the valleys, and the clouds
>   are lightly curl'd
> Round their golden houses, girdled with the
>   gleaming world:
> Where they smile in secret, looking over wasted
>   lands,
> Blight and famine, plague and earthquake,
>   roaring deeps and fiery sands,
> Clanging fights and flaming towns, and sinking
>   ships and praying hands."

The basis of the Greek idea of God was *detachment*; the basis of the Christian idea is *identity*. Through His sufferings Jesus Christ identified Himself with man.

(ii) Through this identity Jesus Christ *sympathises* with man. He literally *feels* with them. It is almost impossible to understand another person's sorrows and sufferings unless we have been through them. A person without a trace of nerves has no conception of the tortures of nervousness. A person who is perfectly physically fit has no conception of the weariness of the person who is easily tired and the pain of the person for whom life is never free of pain. It is often true that a person who is clever and who learns easily cannot understand why someone who is slow finds things so difficult. A person who has never sorrowed cannot understand the pain at the heart of the person into whose life grief has come. A person who has never loved can never understand either the sudden glory or the aching loneliness in the lover's heart. Before we can have sympathy we must go through the same things as the other person has gone through— and that is precisely what Jesus did.

(iii) And because He sympathises Jesus can really *help.* He knows our need; He has met our sorrows; He has faced our temptations. And because of that He knows exactly what help we need and He can give it. The supreme truth of Jesus is that because He went through things Himself He can help others who are going through them.

GREATER THAN THE GREATEST

Hebrews 3: 1-6

> Brothers who are dedicated to God, you who are sharers in heaven's calling, because of all this you must fix your attention on Him whom our creed holds to be the apostle and the high priest of God, I mean Jesus, for He was faithful to Him who appointed Him, just as Moses was in all His house. For He was deemed worthy of more honour than Moses, in so far as the man who builds and equips the house has more honour than the house itself. For every house is built and equipped by someone; but it is God who builds and equips all things. Moses was faithful in all His house, but his role was the role of a servant, and his purpose was to bear witness to the things which some day would be spoken. But Christ is over His house because He is a Son. We are His house if only we keep strong the confidence and pride of our hope to the end.

LET us again remember the conviction with which the writer to the Hebrews starts. The basis of his whole thought is that the full and supreme revelation of God comes through Jesus Christ, that only through Jesus Christ has a man real access to God. He began by proving that Jesus was superior to the prophets; he went on to prove that Jesus was superior to the angels; and now he proceeds to prove that Jesus is superior to Moses. It might at first sight seem that that is an anticlimax. But it was not so for a Jew. In the thought of the Jew, Moses held a place which was utterly and absolutely unique. He was the man with whom God had spoken face to face as a man speaks with his friend. He was the direct recipient of the Ten Commandments, the very Law of God. The greatest thing in all the world for the Jew was the Law, and Moses and the Law were one and the same thing. In the second century there was a Jewish teacher called Rabbi Jose ben Chalafta and he was commenting on this very passage which declared that Moses was faithful in all His house, and he said: " God calls Moses faithful in all His house, and thereby He ranked him higher than the ministering angels themselves." For a Jew the step that the writer to the Hebrews takes is the logical and inevitable step in the argument. He has proved that Jesus is greater than the angels; now he must prove that He is greater than Moses who was greater than the angels. In point of fact this very quotation which is used to tell of the greatness of Moses is proof of the unique position which the Jews assigned to Moses. " Moses was faithful in all His house." The quotation comes from Numbers 12: 6, 7. Now the point of the argument in *Numbers* is that Moses differs from all the prophets. To the prophets God makes Himself known in a vision; to Moses God speaks " mouth to mouth." To the Jew it would have been impossible to conceive that anyone ever stood closer to God than Moses did, and yet that is precisely what the writer of the Hebrews sets out to prove.

The writer to the Hebrews bids his hearers *to fix their attention* on Jesus. The word he uses is interesting and suggestive. It is the word *katanoein*. Now this word does not mean simply to look at or to notice a thing. Anyone can look at a thing or notice it without in any sense really seeing it. The word means to fix the attention on something in such a way that the inner meaning of the thing, the lesson that the thing is designed to teach, may be learned. In Luke 12: 24 Jesus uses the same word when He says: " *Consider* the ravens." He does not merely mean, " *Look* at the ravens." He means, " Look at the ravens and *understand and learn* the lesson that God is seeking to teach you through them." If we are ever to learn Christian truth, a lack-lustre, disinterested, detached glance is never enough; there must be a concentrated gaze in which we gird up the loins of the mind in a determined effort to see its meaning for us.

In a sense the reason for that is implicit when the writer to the Hebrews speaks to his friends as *sharers in heaven's calling*. The invitation, the summons, the call that comes to a Christian has a double direction. It is a calling *from* heaven, and it is a calling *to* heaven. It is a voice which comes *from* God and calls us *to* God. It is a call which demands concentrated attention because of both its origin and its destination, its source and its purpose. A man cannot afford to give a disinterested glance to an invitation *to* God *from* God.

So then, when we do fix our attention on Jesus what do we see? We see in Jesus two things. (i) We see the great *apostle*. Now no one else in the New Testament ever called Jesus an *apostle*. That the writer to the Hebrews does so deliberately is quite clear, because *apostle* is a title he never gives to any man. He does not use the word at all to describe any rank or place within the Church. He keeps the word for Christ. What does he mean when he so uses it? The word *apostolos* literally means *one who*

is sent forth. In Jewish terminology it was used to describe
the envoys of the Sanhedrin, the supreme court of the
Jews. The Sanhedrin sent out *apostoloi* who were clothed
with its authority and who were the bearers of its commands.
In the Greek world it can and does frequently mean an
ambassador. So then Jesus is the supreme ambassador of
God. What are the characteristics of an ambassador?
There are two supremely important and relevant characteristics. (*a*) The ambassador is clothed with all the power
and authority of the country and the king who sends him.
On one occasion the king of Syria, Antiochus Epiphanes,
invaded Egypt. Rome desired to stop him. Rome sent
an envoy called Popillius to tell Antiochus to abandon his
projected invasion. Popillius caught up with him on the
borders of Egypt. Antiochus and Popillius talked of this
and that for they had known each other in Rome. Popillius
had not the vestige of an army with him, not even a guard,
no force at all. Finally Antiochus asked him why he had
come. Quietly Popillius told him that he had come to tell
him that Rome wished him to abandon the invasion and
go home. " I will consider it," said Antiochus. Popillius
smiled a little grimly; he took his staff and drew a circle
in the earth round Antiochus. " Consider it," he said,
" and come to your decision before you leave that circle."
Antiochus thought for a few seconds and then he said:
" Very well, then. I will go home." Popillius himself had
not the slightest force available—but behind him was all
the power of Rome. The ambassador was clothed with the
authority of the empire from which he came. So Jesus
came from God, clothed with all the power of God. All
God's grace and mercy and love and power were in His
ambassador, His *apostolos*, Jesus Christ. (*b*) The voice
of the ambassador is the voice of the king or country
who sent him. In a foreign land the British ambassador
speaks for Britain. His is the voice of Britain. So Jesus
came with the voice of God; in Him God speaks; in listening
to Him we hear the voice of God.

(ii) Jesus is the great *High Priest*. What does that mean?
This is an idea to which the writer to the Hebrews is going
to recur again and again. Just now we can only set down
the fundamental basis of what he means. The Latin for
a priest is *pontifex*, which means a *bridge-builder*. The
priest is the person who builds a bridge between man and
God. To do that he must know two things—he must
know man and God. He must be able to speak to God
for men, and to speak to men for God. Jesus is the perfect
High Priest because He is perfectly man and perfectly
God; He can represent man to God and God to man.
In Him God approaches man and man approaches God.
Jesus is the one person through whom man comes to
God and God comes to man.

Wherein then lies the superiority of Jesus over Moses?
The picture in the mind of the writer to the Hebrews is
this. He thinks of the world as God's house and God's
family. We use the word house in a double sense. We
use it in the sense of a building and we use it in the sense of
a family of people. We speak of a house which an architect
built and we speak of the House of Hanover, when we
mean a family. The Greeks used *oikos* in the same double
sense. Therefore the world is God's house and men are
God's family. But he has already shown us the picture of
Jesus as the creator of God's universe. Now Moses was
only part of God's universe. He was a created man and
he worked in a created universe. He was part of the house,
involved in the house. But Jesus is the creator of the
house, and the creator of the house is bound to stand above
the house itself. Moses did not create the law; he only
mediated it. Moses did not create the house; he only
served in it. Moses did not speak of himself; all that he
ever said was only a pointer to the greater things that
Jesus Christ would some day say. Moses, in short, was
the *servant*; but Jesus was the *Son*. Moses knew a little
about God; Jesus *was* God. Therein lies the greatness of
Jesus and the secret of His unique superiority.

And now the writer to the Hebrews uses another picture. True, the whole world is God's house; but in a special sense the Church is God's House, for in a special sense God built the Church and created it and brought it into being. That is a picture the New Testament loves (cp. I Peter 4: 17; I Timothy 3: 15, and especially I Peter 2: 5). And that building of the Church will only stand indestructible and foursquare when every stone in it is firm; that is to say, when every member of it is strong in the proud and confident hope he has in Jesus Christ. Each one of us is like a stone in the Church. If one stone is weak the whole edifice is endangered. The Church only stands firm when each living stone in it is rooted and grounded in faith in Jesus Christ.

WHILE TO-DAY STILL LASTS

Hebrews 3: 7-19

So then, as the Holy Spirit says, " If to-day you will hear my voice, do not harden your hearts, as in the Provocation, as happened on the day of the Temptation in the wilderness, where your fathers tried to test me, and, in consequence, experienced for forty years what I could do. So my anger was kindled against that generation, and I said, ' Always they wander in their hearts; they do not know my ways.' So I swore in my anger, ' Very certainly they shall not enter in to my rest.' " Have a care, brothers, lest that evil and disobedient heart be in any of you in a state of rebellion against the living God. But keep on exhorting each other day by day, so long as the term " to-day " can be used, lest any among you be hardened in heart by the seductiveness of sin; for you have become participators in Christ, if indeed you hold fast the beginning of your confidence firm to the end. While it is still possible to hear it being said, " If *to-day* you will hear my voice," do not harden your hearts as at the Provocation. For who heard and provoked God? Was it not all who came forth from Egypt under the leadership of Moses? Against whom was God's anger kindled for forty

> years? Was it not against those who had sinned and whose bones lay in the desert? To whom did He swear that they should not enter into His rest, if not to those who were disobedient? Thus we see that it was through disobedience that they could not enter in.

THE writer to the Hebrews has just been striving to prove the unique supremacy of Jesus, and now he leaves argument for exhortation. He presses upon his hearers the inevitable consequence of this unique supremacy. If Jesus is so supremely and uniquely great, then it follows that complete trust and complete obedience must be given to Him. If they harden their hearts and refuse to hear His voice and to give Him their obedient trust the consequences are bound to be very terrible.

The way in which the writer to the Hebrews cements and buttresses his argument is for us very difficult for it is doubly allusive. He begins by making a quotation from Psalm 95: 7-11. That Psalm appeals to those who hear it to listen to the voice of God and not to be like the children of Israel " as in the *provocation* and as in *the day of temptation.*" Now the two phrases, *the provocation* and *the day of temptation* translate two words which in the Hebrew are *place names*—the names Massah and Meribah. The whole is a reference to the story which is told in Exodus 17: 1-7 and Numbers 20: 1-13. These two stories tell of a rebellious incident in the history of the pilgrimage of the children of Israel. They were thirsty in the desert and in their thirst they railed against Moses, they regretted that they had ever left Egypt, and they completely lost their trust in God. In the Numbers version of the story God told Moses to speak to the limestone rock and water would gush forth. But Moses in his anger and irritation did not *speak* to the rock; he *struck* it; the water came forth; but for this act of distrust and disobedience God declared that Moses would never be allowed to lead the people into the promised land. The act of distrust and disobedience debarred from entry into the land of

promise. " Very certainly you shall not enter in *my rest*,"
means, " Very certainly you will not enter into *the Promised
Land*." To nomads and wanderers in the desert the
Promised Land was the place of rest, and it was often
called *the rest* (cp. Deuteronomy 12: 9). The point is that
the disobedience and the distrust of Israel debarred them
from ever enjoying the blessings of God that they might
have enjoyed.

The writer to the Hebrews says to his people, " Beware
lest you show the same disobedience and distrust of God
that your forefathers showed, and that you do not for that
reason lose the blessings you might have had, just as they
lost them." In effect he says, " While there is yet time,
while you can still speak of ' to-day ' give God the trust
and the obedience that God must have." Of course for the
individual person the word " to-day " means " while
life lasts." And the writer to the Hebrews is saying, " While
you have the chance, while life lasts, give God the trust
and the submission you ought to give. Give it to Him
before your day closes, and before for you ' to-day ' is
for ever gone." There are certain great warnings here.

(i) God makes men an offer. Just as He offered the
Israelites the blessings of the Promised Land, He offers
to all men the blessings of a life which is far beyond the
life that men can live without God.

(ii) But to obtain the blessings of God two things are
necessary. (*a*) *Trust* is necessary. We must believe that
what God says and God offers is true. We must believe
that what God says He can do God will do. We must be
willing to stake our lives on the fact that God's promises
are true. (*b*) *Obedience* is necessary. It is just as if a doctor
were to say to us: " I can cure you if you obey my instructions implicitly." It is just as if a teacher were to say:
" I can make you a scholar if you follow my curriculum
with absolute fidelity." It is just as if a trainer were to
say to an athlete: " I can make you a champion if you
never deviate from the laws of discipline that I lay down."

In any realm of life success depends on obedience to the word of the expert. God, if we may put it so, is the expert in life, and real happiness in life depends on obedience to Him.

(iii) To the offer of God there is a limit. That limit is the limit of life. Now we never know when that limit will come. We speak easily about " to-morrow " but for us to-morrow may never come. All that we have got is to-day, this moment of time. Someone has said: " We should live each day as it were a lifetime." God's offer must be accepted to-day; the trust and the obedience must be given to-day—for we never know if for us to-morrow will ever come.

Here then we have the supreme offer of God, but it is an offer which is only made to perfect trust and full obedience, and it is an offer which must be accepted now—before it is impossible to accept it.

THE REST WE DARE NOT MISS

Hebrews 4: 1-10

It is true that the promise which offers entry into the rest of God still remains for us; but beware lest any of you be adjudged to have missed it. It is indeed true that we have had the good news preached to us, just as those of old had. But the word which they heard was no good to them, because it did not become woven into the very fibre of their being through faith. It is we who have made the decision of faith who are entering into the rest, for of them God said: " I swore in my anger, ' Very certainly they shall not enter into my rest.' " This He said although His works had been finished after the foundation of the world. For somewhere in scripture it speaks thus about the seventh day: " And God rested on the seventh day from all His labours." And it says in the same place: " Very certainly they shall not enter into my rest." Since then it remains that some people must enter into it, and since those who in former times did not enter into it because of their lack of

trust, He again defines a day, when in David, after
so long a lapse of time, He says, " To-day," just as
He had said before, " To-day if you will hear my voice
do not harden your hearts." If Joshua had actually
brought them into rest, God would not then after
that be speaking about another day. So a Sabbath rest
remains for the people of God. He who has entered
into this rest has rest from all his works, just as God
rested from His works.

IN a complicated passage like this it is better to try
to grasp the broad lines of the thought and of the argument
before we look at any of the details. The writer of the
Hebrews is really using the word *rest* (*katapausis*) in three
different senses in this passage. (i) He is using it as we
would use the phrase *the peace of God*. It is the greatest
and the most precious thing in the world to enter into
the peace of God. (ii) He is using it, as we already saw
that he used it in 3: 12, to mean *The Promised Land*.
To the children of Israel who had wandered so long in the
desert The Promised Land was indeed the rest of God after
their long wanderings. (iii) He is using it of *the rest of
God* after the sixth day of creation, when all God's work
was completed and done. This way of using a word in
two or three different ways, of teasing at it until the last
drop of meaning was extracted from it, was typical of
cultured, academic thought in the days when the writer
to the Hebrews wrote his letter.

Now let us see the steps of the argument. It will be
simpler if we enumerate them one by one.

(i) The promise of the rest, the peace of God for His
people still abides. The promise is there unchanged;
the danger is that we miss it and fail to reach it.

(ii) The Israelites in the long ago failed to enter into
the rest of God. Here the word *rest* is being used in the
sense of the rest and the peace and the settlement of
The Promised Land after the wilderness years. The
reference is actually to the passage in Numbers 14: 12-23.
That passage tells how the children of Israel came to the

borders of The Promised Land, how they sent out scouts to spy out the land, how ten of the twelve scouts came back with the verdict that it was a good land but that the difficulties of entering into it were completely insuperable, how Caleb and Joshua alone were for going forward in the strength of the Lord, how the people hearkened to the advice of the cowards, and how the result was that that generation of distrusting cowards were doomed for ever to wander in the wilderness and debarred for ever from entering into the rest and the peace of The Promised Land. These people failed to enter into the rest which they might have enjoyed because they had no faith in God. They did not trust God to bring them through the difficulties that lay ahead. They had no confidence, no faith, no trust in God; and therefore they never enjoyed the rest they could have had.

(iii) Now the writer to the Hebrews switches the meaning of the word *rest*. It is true that these people long ago missed the rest they might have had; but, although they missed it, *the rest remained*. Behind this argument there lies one of the favourite conceptions of the Rabbis. On the seventh day, the day after creation had been completed, God rested from His labours. Now in the creation story in Genesis 1 and 2 there is a strange and curious fact. On the first six days of creation it is said that morning and evening came; that is to say, each day had an end and a beginning. But on the seventh day, the day of God's rest, *there is no mention of evening at all*. From this the Rabbis argued that, while the other days came to an end, the day of God's rest had no ending; it was eternal and everlasting. The rest of God had no evening, no close to its day, it was for ever and ever. Therefore although long ago the Israelites may have failed to enter that rest, that rest still remained for it was an eternal rest.

(iv) Once again the writer goes back to the meaning of *rest* as The Promised Land. The day came, after the forty years wandering in the wilderness, when, under

Joshua, the people did enter into The Promised Land.
Now, The Promised Land was *the rest*, and therefore it
could be argued that then the promise was fulfilled and
that the people did enter into their rest. Under Joshua
they had come into The Promised Land. Is not then the
promise fulfilled?

(v) No; the promise is not fulfilled, because in Psalm
95: 7 David hears God's voice saying to the people that
if they do not harden their hearts they can enter into
His *rest*. That is to say, hundreds of years *after* Joshua had
led the people into the *rest* of The Promised Land, God is
still appealing to them to enter into His *rest*. There is
more to this *rest* than merely entry into The Promised
Land.

(vi) So the final appeal comes. God still appeals to men,
not to harden their hearts, but to enter into His peace and
rest. God's " to-day " still exists; the promise is still
open; but " to-day " does not last for ever; life comes to
an end; the promise can be missed; therefore, says the
writer to the Hebrews: " Here and now, through faith
enter into the peace of God, and know the very rest of
God Himself."

There is one very interesting question of meaning in verse
1. We have taken the translation: " Beware lest any of you
be *adjudged* to have missed the rest of God." That is to say:
" Beware lest your disobedience and your lack of faith
and response may mean that you have shut yourselves
out from the rest and the peace that God offers you.
Beware lest by your disobedience and lack of trust you
show yourself unworthy ever to enter into the rest and the
peace of God." That is a perfectly possible translation,
and it may very well be the correct one. But there is
another and most interesting possibility. The phrase
may mean: " Beware lest you think that you have come
too late to enter into the rest of God. Beware lest you
get the idea that you have arrived too late in history ever

to enjoy the rest and the peace of God." In that second translation there is a warning. It is very easy to think that the great days of religion are past; that the great eras of the Church's life lie behind. It is told that a child, on being told some of the great Old Testament stories, said wistfully: " God was much more exciting then." There is a continual tendency in the Church to look back; to think that the great manifestations of God are past; to believe, if we were honest enough to say so, that God's arm is shortened and that God's power is grown less, that the golden days lie behind. The writer to the Hebrews sounds forth a trumpet call. " Never think," he says, " that you have arrived too late in history; never think that the days of great promise and great achievement lie behind. This is still God's ' to-day.' There is a blessedness for you as great as the blessedness of the saints; there is an adventure for you as great as the adventure of the martyrs. God is as great to-day as ever He was."

There are two great permanent truths in this passage.

(i) A word, however great and noble and precious, is of no avail unless it becomes integrated into the person who hears it by faith. There are many different kinds of hearing in this world. There is indifferent hearing; there is disinterested hearing; there is critical hearing; there is sceptical hearing; there is cynical and mocking hearing. The hearing that matters is the hearing that listens eagerly, and then believes and then acts. The promises of God are not merely beautiful pieces of literature; they are not merely sweet sayings which mean nothing; they are promises on which a man is meant to stake his life and by which he is meant to dominate his action.

(ii) In the first verse the writer to the Hebrews bids his people to *beware* lest they miss the promise. The word which we have translated *beware* literally means *to fear* (*phobeisthai*). This Christian fear is not the fear which makes a man run away from a task; nor is it the fear which reduces him to paralysed inaction; it is the fear which makes him put out every ounce of strength he possesses in a great effort not to miss the one thing that is worth while.

THE TERROR OF THE WORD

Hebrews 4: 11-13

> Let us then be eager to enter into that rest, lest we follow the example of the Israelites and fall into the same kind of disobedience. For the word of God is instinct with life; it is effective; it is sharper than a two-edged sword; it pierces right through to the very division of soul and spirit, joints and marrow; it scrutinizes the desires and intentions of the heart. No created thing can ever remain hidden from His sight; everything is naked to Him, and is compelled to meet the eyes of Him with whom we have to reckon.

THE point of this passage is that the word of God has come to men and the word of God is such that it cannot possibly be disregarded. The Jews always had a very special idea about words. To the Jews once a word was spoken, it had an independent existence. A word was not only a sound with a certain meaning; a word was a power, a force which went forth and did things. When Isaiah heard God speak, he heard God say that the word which went out of His mouth would never be ineffective; it would always do that which God designed it to do. The Jew always regarded a word, not as a sound, but as a power. We can understand something of this if we think of the tremendous effect of words in history. A leader coins a phrase, and that phrase becomes a trumpet-call and a battle-cry which kindles men to crusades or to crimes. Some great man sends forth a manifesto and that manifesto produces action which can make or destroy nations. It is profoundly true that over and over again in history the spoken word of some leader or thinker has gone out and done things. If that be so of the words of men, how much more is it so of the word of God.

The writer to the Hebrews describes the word of God in a series of great phrases. *The word of God is instinct with life.* There are certain issues which are as dead as the dodo; there are certain books and words which have no living interest whatever. There are certain words which have a very great interest for a limited circle, but not for all men. Plato was one of the world's supreme thinkers, but it is unlikely that there would be any public for Daily Studies in Plato. The great fact about the word of God, the demand of God, the offer of God is that it is a living issue for all men for all time. Other things may pass quietly into oblivion; other things may acquire an academic or antiquarian interest; but the word of God to men is a living issue for every man. Its demand is something that every man must face; its offer is something which every man must accept or reject. The word of God is *effective*. Again it is one of the facts of history that wherever men have taken God's word seriously things have begun to happen. When the English Bible is laid bare and the word of God comes to the common people, the tremendous event of the Reformation inevitably follows. When people take God seriously they immediately realize that God's word is not only something to be studied; it is not only something to be read; it is not only something to be written about; *it is something to be done.* The word of God is *penetrating*. The writer to the Hebrews piles up phrases to show how penetrating it is. It penetrates to the division of *soul and spirit*. In Greek the *psuchē*, the *soul*, is the life principle. All living things possess *psuchē*. Animals and men alike possess *psuchē* for *psuchē* is physical life. In Greek the *pneuma*, the *spirit*, is that which is characteristic of man. Only man has *spirit*, *pneuma*. It is by spirit that man thinks and reasons and looks beyond the earth to God. It is as if the writer to the Hebrews said the word of God tests a man's earthly life and his spiritual existence. His bodily life and his spiritual life alike come under the scrutiny of the word of God.

He says that the word of God scrutinizes a man's *desires* and *intentions*. *Desire* (*enthumēsis*) is the *emotional* part of man, that part which is governed by his feelings and instincts and passions. *Intention* (*ennoia*) is the *intellectual* part of man, that part of him which is governed by his intellect and his will. It is as if he said: " Your emotional and intellectual life must alike be submitted to the scrutiny of God."

Finally the writer to the Hebrews sums things up. He says that everything is *naked* to God; and that everything is *compelled to meet God's eyes*. He uses two interesting words. The word he uses for *naked* is the literal word (*gumnos*). What he is saying is that as far as men are concerned we may be able to wear our outward trappings and our disguises; but in the presence of God these things are stripped away and we have to meet God as we are. The other word he uses is even more vivid. He says that *we are compelled to meet God's eyes*. The word he uses is *tetrachēlismenos*. Now this is not a common word and its meaning is not quite certain. It seems to have been used in three different ways. (i) It is a wrestler's word and was used for seizing an opponent by the throat in such a way that he could not move. We may escape God for long enough, but in the end God grips us in such a way that we cannot help meeting Him face to face. God is one issue that no man can finally evade. (ii) It was the word that was used for flaying animals. Animals were hung up and flayed. The skin, the hide was taken off them. Men may judge us by our outer conduct and our outer appearance, but God sees into the very inmost secrets of our hearts. It is as if to say that the very inmost recesses of our emotional and intellectual being are open to His sight. (iii) It appears that sometimes in ancient times, when a criminal was being led to judgment or to execution, a dagger, with point upwards, was so fixed below his chin that he could not bow his head in shame and in concealment, but that he had to keep his head up so that all would see his face and know his dishonour. When that was done to a man he was said to be *tetrachēlismenos*. It means that in the end we have got to meet the eyes of God. We may avert our gaze from people whom we are ashamed to meet. But in the end we cannot do that with God; we are *compelled* to look God in the face. Kermit Eby writes in *The God in You*: " At some time or other, a man must stop running from himself and his God—possibly because there is just no other place to run to." There comes a time to every man when he has to meet that God from whose eyes nothing is and nothing ever can be concealed.

THE PERFECT HIGH PRIEST

Hebrews 4: 14-16

> Since, then, we have a high priest, great in His nature, who has passed through the heavens, Jesus, the Son of God, let us hold fast to our creed. For we have not a high priest who is such that He cannot feel with us in our weaknesses; but one who has gone through every temptation, just in the same way as we have, and who is without sin. Let us then confidently approach His throne of grace, that we may receive mercy, and find grace to help as need demands.

HERE we are coming to closer grips with the great characteristic conception of the writer to the Hebrews—the conception of Jesus as the perfect high priest. Perfectly to fulfil his office a high priest must be fully in touch with men and fully in touch with God. His task is to bring the voice of God to man, to bring the very presence of God to man; and to usher men into the very presence of God. The high priest at one and the same time must perfectly know man and God. That is what this epistle claims for Jesus.

(i) First, this passage begins by stressing the sheer greatness, the absolute deity of Jesus. He is great in

His nature. He is not great by honours conferred by men, or by any external trappings; He is great in His own right, in His own essential being. He has passed through the heavens. That may mean one of two things. In the New Testament we can discern differing uses of this word *heaven*. It can mean the heaven of the sky and of the starry firmament; it can mean the heaven of the angels; and it can mean the highest of all heavens—the heaven of the presence of God. This may mean that Jesus has passed through every heaven that may be and is in the very presence of God. It can mean what Christina Rossetti meant when she said: " Heaven cannot hold Him." It could mean that Jesus is so wonderful and so great that even heaven itself is too small a place for Him. No one ever stressed the sheer greatness of Jesus like the writer to the Hebrews.

(ii) But then he turns to the other side. No one was ever surer of Jesus' complete identity with men. He went through everything that a man has to go through. He went through our human experience. He is like us in all things—except that He emerged from it all completely sinless. Now before we turn to examine more closely the precious meaning of this, there is one thing that we must note. The fact that Jesus was without sin necessarily means that He knew depths and tensions and assaults of temptation which we never know and never can know. So far from His battle being easier it was immeasurably harder. Why? For this reason—we fall to temptation long before the tempter has put out the whole of his power. We are easily vanquished; we never know temptation at its fiercest and its most terrible, because we fall long before that stage is reached. But Jesus was tempted as we are—and far beyond what we are. For in His case the tempter put everything he possessed into the assault, and Jesus withstood it. Think of it in terms of pain. There is a degree of pain which the human frame can stand— and then when that degree is reached a person faints and loses consciousness; he has reached his limit. There are agonies of pain he does not know, because there came collapse. It is so with temptation. We collapse before temptation; but Jesus went to our stage of temptation and far beyond it and still did not collapse. It is true to say that He was tempted in all things as we are; but it is also true to say that never was man tempted as He was.

(iii) This experience of Jesus had three effects. (*a*) It gave to Jesus *the gift of sympathy*. Here is something which we must understand, but which we find it very difficult to understand. The Christian idea of God as a loving Father is interwoven into the very fabric of our mind and heart; but *that was a new idea*. To the Jew God was *holy*; the root meaning of *holy* is *different*; the basic idea of God was that He was *different*, that He belonged to a completely different sphere of life and being from that to which we belong, that in no sense did He share our human experience. He was in fact incapable of sharing it just because He was God. It was even more so with the Greeks. The Stoics, the highest Greek thinkers, said the primary attribute of God is *apatheia*. By *apatheia* they meant essential inability to feel anything at all. They argued that if a person can feel sorrow or joy it means that some other person is able to influence that person. The other person can make him happy or glad, can affect him. Now if he can affect him, it must mean that, at least for that moment, he is greater than he is. He has been able to do something to him. So the Greeks argued no one must be able to do anything to God; no one must be able in any sense to affect God; no one can ever be greater than God; therefore God must be completely and essentially incapable of feeling joy or sorrow, gladness or grief. The Stoics argued that the very essence of God's being and nature was that God was beyond all feeling. The other great Greek school was the Epicureans. The Epicureans held that the gods lived in perfect happiness and blessedness. They lived out in what they called the *intermundia*, the spaces between the worlds; and there in complete detachment they were not even aware of the world. The Jews had their *different* God; the Stoics, their *feelingless* gods; the Epicureans, their completely *detached* gods. And into that world of thought there comes the Christian religion with its completely incredible conception of a God who has deliberately undergone every human experience. Plutarch, who was one of the most religious of the Greeks, declared that it was blasphemous to involve God in the affairs of this world. Christianity comes with its staggering conception of a God, not so much involved, as identified with the suffering of this world. It is almost impossible for us to realize the revolution that Christianity brought about in men's relationship to God. For century after century they had been confronted with the idea of the untouchable God; and now they discover a God who has gone through all that man must go through. (b) Now that had two results. It gave God *the quality of mercy*. It is easy to see why. It was because God *understands*. Some people have lived a sheltered life; the wind has never been allowed to blow on them. Some people have lived an easy life; they have been protected from the temptations that come to those for whom life has not been an easy way. Some people have a temperament and a nature which is easy to control; others have hot hearts and hot passions that make life a perilous thing. The person who has lived the sheltered life, the person who has the non-inflammable nature, finds it very hard to understand why the other person falls. They are faintly disgusted and repelled. They cannot help condemning what they cannot understand. *But God knows.* " To know all is to forgive all "—of no one is that truer than God. John Foster in one of his books tells a thing. He came into his home in this country one day in the thirties to find his daughter in tears before the radio set. He asked her why. He found that the news bulletin that day had contained one sentence—" Japanese tanks entered Canton to-day."

Most people must have heard that with at the most a faint feeling of regret. Statesmen may have heard it with a feeling of grim foreboding. But to most people it did not make so very much difference. Why then was John Foster's daughter in tears? Because she had been born in Canton. To her Canton meant a home, a nurse, a school, friends, a well-loved place. The difference was that *she had been there*. When you have been there it makes all the difference. And there is no part of human experience of which God cannot say: " I have been there." When we have a sad and sorry tale to tell, when life has drenched us with the tears of things, we do not go to a God who is quite incapable of understanding what has happened to us; we go to a God who has been there. That is why—if we may put it so—God finds it easy to forgive. (c) It makes God *able to help*. He knows our problems because He has come through them. The best person to give you advice and help on a journey is someone who has travelled the road before you. The best person to help you through an illness is someone who has come through it. God can help because He knows it all.

Here then is the tremendous truth. Jesus is the perfect high priest because He is perfectly God, and because He is perfectly man. Because He has known our life He can give us sympathy, mercy and power. He brought God to men, and He can bring men to God.

AT HOME WITH MAN AND GOD

Hebrews 5: 1-10

> Every high priest, who is chosen from among men, is appointed on men's behalf to deal with the things which concern God. His task is to offer gifts and sacrifices for sins, in that he himself is able to feel gently to the ignorant and to the wandering, because he himself wears the garment of human weakness. By reason of this very weakness it is incumbent upon him, just as he makes sacrifice for the people,

so to make sacrifice for sins on his own behalf also.
No one takes this honourable position to himself,
but he is called by God to it, just as Aaron was. So
it was not Christ Himself who gave Himself the glory of
becoming high priest; but it was He who said to
Him: " You are my beloved Son; to-day I have
begotten you." Just so, He says also in another passage:
" You are a priest for ever according to the order of
Melchizedek." In the days when He lived this
human life of ours, He offered prayers and entreaties
to Him who was able to bring Him safely through
death, with strong crying and with tears. And, when
He had been heard because of His reverence, although
He was a Son, He learned obedience from the sufferings
through which He passed. When He had been made
fully fit for His appointed task, He became the author
of eternal salvation to all who obey Him, for He had
been designated by God a high priest after the order
of Melchizedek.

Now the writer to the Hebrews comes to work out the
doctrine which is his special contribution to Christian
thought—the doctrine of the High Priesthood of Jesus
Christ. He has in this passage three great basic thoughts
about the office of a priest. These three fundamental
qualifications are not in the least local and temporary.
They are the essential qualifications of the priest in any
age and in any generation.

(i) A priest is appointed on men's behalf to deal with
the things concerning God. A. J. Gossip used to tell his
students how he felt when he was ordained to the ministry.
It was as if the people said to him: " We are for ever
involved in the dust and the heat of the day; we have to
spend our time getting and spending; we have to serve
at the counter, to toil at the desk, to make the wheels
of industry go round. We want you to be set apart so that
you can go in to the secret place of God and come back
every Sunday with a word from God to us." The real
priest is the link between God and man. Now in Israel
the priest had one special function. The priest was the
person whose function it was to offer sacrifice for the sins

of the people. Sin disturbs the relationship which should exist between man and God; it puts up a barrier between man and God; it estranges man and God. And the sacrifice is meant to restore the relationship which should exist, and to remove the barrier and the estrangement. But here again we must stop to notice one thing. The Jew was always quite clear, when he was thinking at his highest, that the sins which sacrifice could atone for were *sins of ignorance*. The deliberate, callous sin did not find its atonement in sacrifice. The writer to the Hebrews himself says: " For if we sin *wilfully* after that we have received the knowledge of the truth, *there remaineth no more sacrifice for sin* " (Hebrews 10: 26). This is a belief and a conviction that emerges again and again in the sacrificial laws of the Old Testament. Again and again they begin: " If a soul shall sin *through ignorance* against any of the command-ments of the Lord . . . " (Leviticus 4: 2, 13). Numbers 15: 22-31 is a key passage. There the requisite sacrifices are laid down " if ought be committed *through ignorance*." But at the end it is laid down: " The soul that doeth ought *presumptuously* . . . shall be cut off from among his people. Because he hath despised the word of the Lord . . . that soul shall utterly be cut off." Deuteronomy 17: 12 lays it down: " The man that will do *presumptuously* . . . even that man shall die." The sin of ignorance is pardonable; the sin of presumption is not. Nevertheless we must note what the Jews meant by the sin of ignorance. They meant more than simply lack of knowledge. They included the sins committed when a man was swept away in a moment of impulse or anger or passion, when a man was mastered by some overmastering temptation, when a man repented in sorrow for something that he had done. By the sin of presumption they meant the cold, deliberate, calcu-lated sin for which a man was not in the least sorry, the open-eyed disobedience of God, the time when a man, not in a moment of passion or impulse, but in cool detachment took his own way and disobeyed God. So, then, the priest existed to open the way for the sinner back to God—so long as the sinner wanted to come back.

(ii) The priest must be one with men. He must have gone through a man's experiences and all his sympathy must be with men. At this point the writer to the Hebrews stops to point out—he will later show that this is one of the ways in which Jesus Christ is superior to any earthly priest—that the earthly priest is so one with men that he is under the necessity of offering sacrifice for his own sin, before he offers sacrifice for the sins of other people. The priest must be a man; he must be completely involved in the human situation; he must be bound up with men in the bundle of life; he must live with them and feel with them and know their heights and their depths. In connection with this he used a wonderful word—the word *metriopathein*. We have translated it *to feel gently*; but it is really one of these untranslatable Greek words. The Greeks always defined a virtue as the mean between two extremes. On either hand there was an extreme into which a man might fall; in between there was the right thing and the right way. Virtue to the Greek was a balance, a mean, the right point between two extremes. So the Greeks defined *metriopatheia* (which is the corresponding noun) as the mean between extravagant grief and utter indifference. It was feeling about men in the right way. W. M. Macgregor defined it as " the mid-course between explosions of anger and lazy indulgence." Plutarch speaks of that *patience* which is the child of *metriopatheia*. He spoke of it as that sympathetic feeling which enabled a man to raise up and to save, to spare and to hear. Another Greek blames a man for having no *metriopatheia* and for therefore *refusing to be reconciled* with someone who had differed from him. It is a wonderful word. It means the ability to bear with people without getting irritated and annoyed; it means the ability not to lose one's temper with people when they are foolish and when they will not learn and when they do the same thing over and over again and when they seem to be senselessly blind. It describes the attitude to others which does not issue in anger at the fault and which does not condone the fault, but which to the end of the day spends itself in a gentle yet powerful sympathy, which by its very patience moulds a man back on to the right way. It is the attitude which never regards a man as a lost fool, but often sees in him a contrary child of God, who somehow must be gently led back to the right way. No man can ever deal with his fellow men unless **he** has this strong and patient, this God-given *metriopatheia*.

(iii) **The third essential** of a priest is this—no man appoints himself to the priesthood; his appointment is of God. The priesthood is not an office which a man takes; it is a privilege and a glory to which he is called. The ministry of God among men is neither a job nor a career; it is a vocation and a calling. A man ought to be able to look back and say, not, " I chose this work," but rather, " God chose me and gave me this work to do."

And now the writer to the Hebrews goes on to show how Jesus Christ fulfils the great conditions of the priesthood.

(i) He takes the last one first. Jesus did not choose His task. God chose Him for it. At the Baptism there came to Jesus the voice which said: " You are my beloved Son; this day I have begotten you " (Psalm 2: 7).

(ii) Jesus has gone through the bitterest experiences of men and understands manhood in all its strength and its weakness. The writer to the Hebrews has four great thoughts about Jesus. (*a*) He remembers Jesus in Gethsemane. That is what he is thinking of when he speaks of Jesus' prayers and entreaties, His tears and His cry. The word he uses for *cry* is very significant. It is the word *kraugē*, and *kraugē* is a cry, which a man does not choose to utter, but which is wrung from him even involuntarily in the stress and the agony of some tremendous tension or some searing pain. So, then, the writer to the Hebrews says that there is no agony of the human spirit through which Jesus has not come. The rabbis had a saying: " There are three kinds of prayers, each loftier than the preceding—prayer, crying and tears. Prayer is made in silence; crying with raised voice; but tears overcome all things." There is no door through which tears do not pass. Jesus Christ knew even the desperate prayer of tears. (b) Jesus learned from all the experiences of life through which He passed, because He met them all with reverence. The Greek phrase for " He learned from what He suffered " is a linguistic jingle—*emathen aph' hōn epathen*. And this is a thought which keeps recurring in the Greek thinkers. They are always connecting *mathein*, to learn, and *pathein*, to suffer. Aeschylus, the earliest of the great Greek dramatists, had as a kind of continual text: " Learning comes from suffering " (*pathei mathos*). He calls suffering a kind of *savage grace* from the gods. Herodotus declared that his sufferings were *acharista mathēmata*, ungracious ways of learning. A modern poet says of the poets:

" We learned in suffering what we teach in song."

God speaks to a man in the many experiences of life, and not least in the experiences which try men's hearts and souls. But we can only hear that voice of God when we accept what comes to us in reverence. If we accept it with resentment, then the rebellious cries of our own heart make us deaf to the voice of God. (c) Through the experiences through which He passed, the Authorised Version says that Jesus *was made perfect* (*teleioun*). The verb *teleioun* is the verb of the adjective *teleios*. It is quite true that *teleios* can quite correctly be translated *perfect*, so long as we remember what the Greek meant by that perfection. To the Greek a thing was *teleios* if it perfectly carried out the purpose for which it was made and designed. When he used the word he was not thinking in terms of abstract and metaphysical perfection; he was thinking in terms of *function*. What the writer to the

Hebrews is saying is that all the experiences, the sufferings, through which Jesus passed perfectly fitted Him to become the Redeemer and the Saviour of men. He was able to save men because He came through every dark valley of life through which the human spirit must pass. (*d*) Finally, the writer to the Hebrews says that the salvation which Jesus brought is an *eternal salvation*. It is something which keeps a man safe in time and in eternity. It is something which keeps a man safe in this life or in any life that there may ever be. With Christ a man is safe for ever and for ever. There are no circumstances, conceivable or inconceivable, that can pluck a man from the hand of Christ.

THE REFUSAL TO GROW UP

Hebrews 5: 11-14

> The story which has been laid upon me to tell you about this matter is a long story, difficult to tell and difficult to grasp, for your ears have become dull. For, indeed, at a stage when you ought to be teachers because of the length of time that has passed since you first heard the gospel, you still need someone to tell you the simple elements of the very beginning of the message of God. You have sunk into a state when you need milk and not solid food; for when anyone is at the stage of participating in milk feeding, he does not really know what Christian righteousness is, for he is only a child. For solid food is for those who have reached maturity, those who, through the development of the right kind of habit, have reached a stage when their perceptions are trained to distinguish between good and evil.

HERE the writer to the Hebrews deals with the difficulties which confront him in attempting to get across an adequate conception of Christianity to his hearers.

He is confronted with two difficulties. First, the full orb of the Christian faith is by no means an easy thing to grasp, nor can it be learned in a day. It takes time to teach, and it takes effort to learn. Second, the hearing

of his hearers is dull. The word he uses is full of meaning.
The word he uses for *dull* is *nōthros*. In Greek it means
slow-moving in mind; it means torpid in understanding;
it means dull of hearing; it means witlessly and senselessly
forgetful. It can be used of the numbed limbs of an animal
which is ill. It can be used of a person who has the
imperceptive and lethargic nature of a stone. Now here
is something which has something to say to everyone whose
business and whose duty it is to preach and to teach;
in fact, it has something to say to everyone whose business
it is to think, and that is to say, that it has something to
say to everyone who is a real person. It often happens
that we dodge teaching something because it is difficult;
we never face trying to explain it because exposition and
explanation are hard. It often happens that we defend
ourselves by saying that our hearers or our congregation
or our pupils would never grasp or understand that. It is,
in fact, one of the tragedies of the Church that there is
so little attempt to teach people new knowledge, new
approaches, and new thought. It is true that the task of
such teaching is difficult. It is true that often to try to
teach in such a way is to meet the lethargy of the lazy
mind and the embattled prejudice of the shut mind. But
the task remains. The writer to the Hebrews did not
shirk to bring to men his message, even if his message was
difficult and the minds of his hearers were slow to learn.
He regarded it as his supreme responsibility to pass on
the truth he knew.

His complaint is that his hearers have been Christians
for many years now, and they are still babes and no
nearer maturity. The contrast between the immature
Christian and the child, between milk and solid food often
occurs in the New Testament (I Peter 2: 2; I Corinthians
2: 6; 3: 2; 14: 20; Ephesians 4: 13ff). He says that
by now they should be teachers. It is not necessary to
take that literally. To say that a man was able to teach
was the Greek way of saying that he had a real and mature

grasp of a subject. He says that they still need someone to teach them *the simple elements of Christianity*. The word he uses for elements is *stoicheia*. This word has a variety of meanings. In grammar it means the letters of the alphabet, the A B C; in physics it means the four basic elements of which the world is composed; in geometry it means the elements of proof like the point and the straight line; in philosophy it means the first elementary principles with which the students begin. It is the sorrow of the writer to the Hebrews that, after many years of Christianity, his people have never got past the elements; they are like children who do not know the difference between right and wrong.

Here the writer to the Hebrews is face to face with a problem which haunts the Church in every generation. He is face to face with the problem of *the Christian who refuses to grow up*.

(i) The Christian can refuse to grow up in knowledge. He can be guilty of what someone called " the culpable incapacity resulting from the neglect of opportunity." There are people who keep on saying that what was good enough for their fathers is good enough for them. There are Christians in whose faith there has been no development for thirty or forty or fifty or sixty years. There are Christians who have deliberately refused to try to understand the advances that Biblical scholarship and theological thought have made. They are grown men and women and yet they insist on remaining content with the religious development of a child. They are like a surgeon who refused to use the new techniques of surgery, who refused to use the new and wonderful anaesthetics, who refused to use any new equipment, who might say: " What was good enough for Lister is good enough for me." They are like physicians who refuse to use penicillin or the sulphonamides or any of the new drugs, and who might say: " What I learned as a student fifty years ago is good enough for me." In religious things it is still worse. God is infinite; the riches of Christ are unsearchable; and to the end of the day we should be going on.

(ii) There are people who have never grown up in behaviour. It may be forgivable in a child to sulk, to be liable to fits of uncontrolled temper, to refuse to play if he does not get his own way. And there are many adults— and in the Church—who are as childish in their behaviour as any child. Physically they are men and women; in matters of conduct they have never grown up.

A case of arrested development is always a pathetic thing; and the world is full of people whose religious development has been arrested. They refuse to grow up. They stopped learning years ago; their thought is still the thought of a child; their conduct is still the conduct of a child. It is true that Jesus said that the greatest thing in the world is the *childlike* spirit; but there is a world of difference between the *childlike* and the *childish* spirit. Peter Pan, the boy who would not grow up, makes a charming play on the stage; but Peter Pan, the man and the woman who will not grow up, make a tragedy in real life. Let us have a care lest we are still in the religion of childhood when we should have reached the faith of maturity. Let us have a care that we are not still behaving like children when we should be behaving like men and women full grown.

THE NECESSITY OF PROGRESS

Hebrews 6: 1-3

So, then, let us leave elementary teaching about Christ behind us, and let us be borne onwards to full maturity; for we cannot go on laying the foundations all the time and teaching about repentance from dead works, and giving information about washings, about the laying on of hands, about the resurrection from the dead, and upon that sentence which lasts to all eternity. God willing, this very thing we will do.

THE writer to the Hebrews was very certain of the necessity of progress in the Christian life. No teacher would ever get anywhere if he had to lay the foundations all over again every time he began to teach. Progress would be impossible if we had to start all over again at the beginning every time. The writer to the Hebrews says that his people must be going on to what he calls *teleiotēs*. The Authorised Version translates this word *perfection*. But in Greek *teleios*, which is the adjective, and its kindred words have a special, technical meaning. Pythagoras divided his students into *hoi manthanontes*, which means *the learners*, and *hoi teleioi*, which means *the mature*. Philo classified his students into three different classes—*hoi archomenoi*, which means *those just beginning*, *hoi prokoptontes*, which means *those making progress*, and *hoi teleiōmenoi*, which means *those beginning to reach maturity*. *Teleiotēs* does not imply complete knowledge and complete perfection; what it does imply is a certain maturity in the Christian faith.

What does the writer to the Hebrews mean by this *maturity*? He means two things. (i) He means something which has got to do with *the mind*. He means that as a man gets older he should more and more have thought things out for himself. He should, for instance, be able to say better who he believes Jesus to be. He should have a deeper grasp, not only of the facts, but also of the significances of the Christian faith. (ii) He means something that has got to do with *life*. As a man grows older there should be more and more of the reflection of Christ upon him. All the time he should be ridding himself of old faults and getting to himself new virtues. Life, as it grows older, should be growing more lovely and more strong and more fine. Daily a new serenity and a new nobility should be breaking upon life. As the nameless poet has it:

> " Let me grow lovely, growing old;
>   The many fine things too,
> Laces and Ivory and Gold and Silks,
>   Need not be new.
> And there is healing in old trees,
>   Old streets and glamour old,
> Why may not I, as well as these,
>   Grow lovely, growing old? "

There can be no standing still in the Christian life. It is told that on his pocket Bible Cromwell had a motto written in Latin—*qui cessat esse melior cessat esse bonus*—he who ceases to be better ceases to be good.

What then are the elementary truths of the Christian life? This passage is interesting because it enables us to see what the Early Church regarded as, what we might call, basic Christianity.

(i) There is *repentance from dead works*. The Christian life begins with repentance; and repentance (*metanoia*) is literally *a change of mind*. The Christian begins with a new attitude to God, to men, to life, to self. It is a repentance from *dead works*. What does the writer to the Hebrews mean by this strange phrase? There are many things that he may mean, and each of them is relevant and suggestive. (*a*) Dead works may be *deeds which bring death*. They may be deadly deeds. They may be the immoral, the selfish, the godless, the loveless, the soiled actions which lead to death. (*b*) They may be *defiling deeds*. For a Jew to touch a dead body was the greatest defilement; to do so rendered him unclean and barred him from the worship of God until he was cleansed. Dead works may be the works which defile a man and separate him from God. (*c*) They may be *works which have no connection with character*. For the Jew life was ritual; if he did the right external things at the right time, if he offered the correct animal sacrifices, he was a good man. But none of these things had any effect upon the character, the man himself. It may be that the writer to the Hebrews means that the Christian has broken away from the meaningless rituals and conventions of life, to give himself to the things which deepen his character and develop his soul.

(ii) There is *faith which looks to God*. The first essential in the Christian life is the godward look. The Christian looks to God, not to men, for approval. He determines his actions, not by the verdict of men, but by the verdict of God. He looks, not to his own achievement for salvation, but to the grace of God. He looks to God, and to God alone, as the Guide of his life and the Saviour of his soul.

(iii) There is *teaching about washings*. This means that the Christian must realise what baptism really means. The first book of Christian instruction for those about to enter the Church, and the first service order book is a little book called *The Didachē, The Teaching of the Twelve Apostles*. It was written about the year A.D. 100. It lays down the regulations for Christian Baptism. Now it must be remembered that at this time infant baptism had not yet emerged. Men were coming straight from heathendom, and baptism was reception into the Church and confession of faith. *The Didachē* begins with six short chapters on the Christian faith and the Christian life. It begins by telling the candidate for baptism what he ought to believe and how he ought to live. Then in the seventh chapter it goes on like this:

"Concerning Baptism, baptise in this way. When you have instructed the candidate in all these things, baptise in the name of the Father and of the Son and of the Holy Spirit in running water. If you do not have running water, baptise in any other kind of water. If you cannot baptise in cold water, baptise in warm. If both of these are unobtainable, pour water three times upon the head of the candidate in the name of the Father and of the Son and of the Holy Spirit. Before baptism, let him who is to baptise and him who is to be baptised fast, and let any others who can do so do the same. You must bid him who is to be baptised to fast for two or three days before the ceremony."

That is interesting. It shows that baptism in the early Church was, if possible, by total immersion. It shows that the person to be baptised was either immersed or affused with water three times, in the name of the Father, of the Son and of the Holy Spirit. It shows that baptism was instructed baptism, for the account of the Christian faith and life is to be rehearsed before the sacrament of baptism is carried out. It shows that the candidate for baptism had to prepare, not only his mind, but also his spirit, for he had to fast beforehand as a preparation. In the early days no one slipped into the Church without knowing what he was doing. So the writer to the Hebrews says: " At your baptism you were instructed in the basis of the Christian faith. There is no need to go back to that. You must erect a fuller faith on the basis you have already learned."

(iv) There was *the laying on of hands*. In Jewish practice the laying on of hands had three significances. (*a*) It was the sign of the transference of guilt. The sacrificer laid his hands upon the head of the victim to symbolise the fact that he transferred his guilt to the animal which was being offered. (*b*) It was the sign of the transference of blessing. When a father blessed his son he laid his hands on the son's head as a token of that blessing. (*c*) It was the sign of setting apart to some special office. A man was ordained to office by the laying on of hands. In the early Church it always accompanied baptism and was the way in which the Holy Spirit was conveyed to the person newly baptised (Acts 8: 17; 19: 6). This is not to be thought of in a material way. In those days the apostles were regarded with reverence because they had actually been the friends of Jesus when they were with Him on this earth. It was a thrilling thing to be touched by a man who had actually touched the hand of Jesus. The effect of the laying on of hands depends, not on the office of the man who lays on the hands, but on his character and his nearness to Christ.

(v) There was *the resurrection from the dead*. Christianity from the beginning was a religion of immortality. It gave a man two worlds in which to live; it taught him that the best was yet to be and thereby it made this world the training school for eternity.

(vi) There was *the sentence which lasts to all eternity*. Christianity was from the beginning a religion of judgment. No Christian was ever allowed to forget that in the end he must face God, and that what God thought of him was infinitely more important than what men thought of him. He was presented with a life in which he must always seek to please, not men, but God.

CRUCIFYING CHRIST AGAIN

Hebrews 6: 4-8

> For it is impossible to renew to repentance those who were once enlightened, those who tasted the free gift from heaven, those who were made sharers in the Holy Spirit, those who tasted the fair word of God and the powers of the age to come, and who then became apostates, for they are crucifying the Son of God again for themselves, and are making a mocking show of Him. For when the earth has drunk the rain that comes often times upon it, and when it brings forth herbage useful to those who cultivate it, it receives a share of blessing from God; but if it produces thorns and thistles it is rejected and is in imminent danger of a curse, and its end is to be appointed for burning.

THIS is one of the most terrible passages in scripture. It begins with a kind of list of the privileges of the Christian life. The Christian has been *enlightened*. The idea of enlightenment is a favourite New Testament idea. No doubt it goes back to the picture of Jesus as the Light of the World, the Light that lighteth every man that cometh into the world (John I: 9; 9: 5). As Bilney, the martyr said, " When I heard the words, ' Christ Jesus came into the world to save sinners,' it was as if day suddenly broke in the midst of a dark night." The light of knowledge, the light of joy, the light of guidance breaks in upon a man with Christ. So entwined with the idea of enlightenment did Christianity become that the word *enlightenment* (*phōtismos*) became a synonym for *baptism,* and the verb *to be enlightened* (*phōtizesthai*) became a synonym for *to be baptised.* That is, in fact, the way that many people have read this word here; and they have taken this passage to mean that there is no possibility of forgiveness for sins which have been committed after baptism; and there have been times and places in the Church when baptism has been postponed to the moment of death, in order to be safe. That idea we shall discuss later. The Christian has tasted *the free gift that comes from heaven.* It is only in Christ that a man can be at peace with God. Forgiveness is not something he can ever deserve or merit or win; it is a free gift. It is only when he comes up to the Cross that his burden is rolled away. The Christian is a man who knows the immeasurable relief of experiencing the free gift of the forgiveness of God. Something has been done for him that he could never have done for himself. The Christian is *a sharer in the Holy Spirit.* The Christian is a man who has in his life a new directive and a new power and a new presence. He has discovered the presence of a power that can both tell him what to do and enable him to do it. He has found the promise of the Holy Spirit fulfilled. The Christian has *tasted the fair word of God.* That is another way of saying that he has discovered the truth. It is characteristic of men that instinctively they do follow truth as blind men long for light; it is part of the penalty and the privilege of being a man that we can never rest content until we have learned the meaning of life. In God's word we find the truth; in God's word we find the meaning of life. The Christian is a man who *has tasted the powers of the world to come.* Jew and Christian alike divided time into two ages. There was this present age (*ho nun aiōn*), and they believed that this present age was wholly bad and sunk in sin; there was the age to come (*ho mellōn aiōn*), which would be wholly good and wholly God's. Some day God would break in and intervene; there would come the shattering destruction and the terrible judgment of the Day of the Lord and then this present age would end and the age to come would begin. But the Christian is a man who here and now is tasting the joys, the blessedness, the peace, the power of the age which is God's. Even in time he has a foretaste of eternity.

" Heaven above is softer blue,
    Earth around is sweeter green;
Something lives in every hue,
    Christless eyes have never seen;
Birds with gladder songs o'erflow,
    Flowers with deeper beauties shine,
Since I know, as now I know,
    I am His, and He is mine."

So the writer to the Hebrews sets out the shining catalogue of Christian blessedness; and then at the end of it there comes the word like a sudden knell, *and who then have become apostates, who then have fallen away.*

What does he mean when he says that it is impossible that those who have become apostates can ever be renewed to repentance? Many thinkers have tried to find a way round this word *impossible*. Erasmus held that the word impossible (*adunaton*) was to be taken in the sense of *difficult*, difficult almost to the point of impossibility. Bengel held that what was impossible for man was possible for God, and that we must leave those who have fallen away to the mercy of God's singular love and singular influence. But when we read this passage we must remember one thing—*it was written in an age of persecution*: and in any age of persecution apostasy is the supreme sin. In any age of persecution a man can save his life by denying Christ; but every person who, to save his life or comfort, denies Christ, aims a body-blow at the Church, for it means

that his life and comfort are dearer to him than his religion;
it means that Jesus Christ is not really his Lord; it means
that there is something more precious to him than Jesus
Christ. This particular way of putting things has always
emerged during and after persecutions. Two hundred
years after this there came the terrible persecution of the
Emperor Diocletian. When peace came after the storm
the one test that some wished to apply to every surviving
member of the Church was: " Did you deny Christ and
so save your life? " And if he had denied his Lord they
would have shut the door on him once and for all. Kermit
Eby tells of a French churchman, who, when asked what
he did during the French Revolution, whispered: " I
survived." This is the condemnation of the man who
loved life more than he loved Christ. It was never meant
to be erected into a doctrine and a theology that there is
no forgiveness for post-baptismal sin. Who is any man to
say that any other man is beyond the forgiveness of God?
What it is meant to show is the terrible seriousness of
choosing existence instead of Christ.

The writer to the Hebrews goes on to say a tremendous
thing. He says that those who fall away, those who deny
Christ, *crucify Christ again*. This is the point of the great
Quo vadis legend. It tells how in the Neronic persecution
Peter was caught in Rome, and Peter's courage failed.
He fled for life. Down the Appian Way he fled, all courage
lost. Suddenly there was a figure standing in his path.
Peter looked up. It was Jesus Himself. " *Domine*," said
Peter, " *quo vadis*? Lord, where are you going? " Back
came the answer: " Peter, I am going back to Rome to
be crucified again, this time in your stead." And Peter,
shamed into heroism, turned and returned to Rome and
died a martyr's death. Late on in Roman history there
was an Emperor who tried to put the clock back. His name
was Julian; he wished to destroy Christianity and to bring
back the old ways and the old gods. His attempt ended
in defeat. Ibsen makes him say: " Where is He now?

Has He been at work elsewhere since *that* happened at Golgotha? . . . Where is He now? What if *that*, at Golgotha, near Jerusalem, was but a wayside matter, a thing done, as it were, in the passing? What if He goes on and on, suffers and dies and conquers again and again, from world to world?" There is a certain truth there. At the back of the thought of the writer to the Hebrews there is one of the most tremendous conceptions in all Christian thought. He saw the Cross as an event which opened a window into the heart of God. He saw the Cross as showing in a moment of time that which was happening in God's being throughout all eternity. The Cross showed in one moment of time the suffering love which is for ever and for ever in the heart of God. The Cross said to men: "That is how I have always loved you and always will love you. This is what your sin does to me and always has done to me and always will do to me. This is the only way I can ever redeem men. Men's sins have always done this to me and always will do it to me until men sin no more." There is something tremendous there. In God's heart there is for ever and for ever, so long as there is sin, this agony of suffering and redeeming love. When we sin we crucify Christ again. Sin does not only break God's law; again and again it breaks God's heart. It is true that when we fall away, when we sin, we crucify Christ again.

And further, the writer to the Hebrews says that when we fall away we make a mocking show of Christ, we put Him to open shame. How is that? When we sin the world will say: "So that is all that Christianity is worth. So that is all this Christ can do. So that is all the Cross achieved." It is bad enough when a Church member falls into sin in that he brings shame to himself and discredit on his Church; but what is worse is that he draws men's taunts and jibes and jeers on *Christ*. He shames His Lord and makes men laugh at the Cross.

We may note one final thing. It has been pointed out that in the letter to the Hebrews there are four impossible

THE LETTER TO THE HEBREWS

things. There is the impossibility of this passage. The
other three are: (I) It is impossible for God to lie (6: 18).
(ii) It is impossible that the blood of sheep and goats
should take away sin (10: 4). (iii) Without faith it is
impossible to please God (11: 6).

THE BRIGHTER SIDE

Hebrews 6: 9-12

> Beloved, even if we do speak like this, we are persuaded
> better things for you, yes, things that are bound
> up with salvation. For God is not unjust to forget
> your work and the love that you displayed, in, that
> you have been and still are active in the service of
> God's dedicated people. We hope with all our hearts
> that each one of you will display the same zeal to
> make your hope come true, and that you will go on
> doing so until the end, so that you may not become
> lazily lethargic, but that you may copy those who
> through faith and patience inherit the promises.

ONE thing stands out here. This is the only passage in
the whole letter where the writer to the Hebrews addresses
his people as *beloved*. It is precisely after the sternest
passage of all that he uses the address of love. It is as
if he said to them: " If I did not love you so much I
would not speak with such severity." Chrysostom para-
phrases the thought this way: " It is better that I should
scare you with words than that you should sorrow in
deeds." He speaks the truth, but, however stern that
truth may be, he speaks it in love.

Further, his very form of speaking shows how individual
his love is. " We hope," he says, " that *each one of you*
will display the zeal that will make your hope come true."
He is not thinking of them as a crowd; he is thinking
of them as individual men and women whom he knows
and loves. Dr. Paul Tournier, in his book, *A Doctor's
Casebook*, has a paragraph on what he calls *the personalism*
of the Bible. " God says to Moses, ' I know thy name '

60

(Exodus 33: 17). He says to Cyrus, ' I am the Lord which call thee by thy name ' (Isaiah 45: 3). These texts express the essence of the personalism of the Bible. One is struck, on reading the Bible, by the importance in it of personal names. Whole chapters are devoted to long genealogies. When I was young I used to think that they could well have been dropped from the Biblical Canon. But I have since realised that these series of proper names bear witness to the fact that, in the Biblical perspective, man is neither a thing nor an abstraction, neither a species nor an idea, that he is not a fraction of the mass, as the Marxists see him, but that he is a person." When the writer to the Hebrews wrote with sternness he was not rebuking a Church; he was yearning over individual men and women, for that is what God Himself does.

There are two interesting things implicit in this passage.

(i) From it we learn that even if these people to whom he is writing have failed to grow up in Christian faith and knowledge, even if they have been falling away from their first enthusiasm and their first love, they have never given up their practical service and their practical help to their fellow Christians. They have been and still are active in the service of God's dedicated people. There is a great practical truth here. Sometimes in the Christian life we come to times which are arid. Sometimes the Church services have nothing to say to us. Sometimes the teaching that we do in Sunday School, or the singing that we do in the choir, or the service we give on a board or court or committee becomes a labour without joy. At such a time there are two things we can do. We can give up our attendance and our work. If we do that we are lost. We can go on grimly with it, and the strange thing is that if we do, the light and the romance and the joy will certainly come back again. In the arid times, the best thing to do is to go on with the habits and the routine of the Christian life and the life of the Church. If we do, we can be sure that the sun will shine again.

(ii) He tells his people to be imitators of those who through faith and patience inherited the promise. What he is saying to them is: " You are not the first to launch out on the glories and the perils of the Christian faith. Others braved the dangers and endured the tribulations before you and won through." He is telling them to go on in the realisation that others have gone through their struggle and won their victory; that others have dared their voyage and come safe to harbour. The Christian is not treading an untrodden pathway. He is treading where the saints have trod.

THE SURE HOPE

Hebrews 6: 13-20

When God made His promise to Abraham, since He was not able to swear by anyone greater, He swore by Himself. " Very certainly," He said, " I will bless you, and very certainly I will multiply you." When Abraham had thus exercised patience he received the promise. Men swear by someone who is greater than themselves; and an oath serves for a guarantee beyond all possibility of contradiction. But, on this occasion, God, in His quite exceptional desire to make clear to the heirs of the promise the unalterable character of his intention, interposed with an oath, so that by two unalterable things, in which it is impossible that God should lie, we, who have fled to Him for refuge, might be strongly encouraged to lay hold upon the hope that is set before us. This hope is to us like an anchor, safe and sure, and it enters with us into the inner court beyond the veil, where Jesus already entered as a forerunner for us, when He had become a High Priest for ever after the order of Melchizedek.

God made more than one promise to Abraham. Genesis 12: 7 tells us of the promise that God made to Abraham when He called him out of Ur and sent him into the unknown to the promised land. Genesis 17: 5, 6 is the promise of many descendants who would be blessed in

him. Genesis 18: 18 is a repetition of that promise. But
the promise in which God swore with an oath to keep it
comes in Genesis 22: 16-18. The real meaning of this
first sentence is: " God made many a promise to Abraham,
and in the end He actually made a promise which He
confirmed with an oath." That was a promise which was
as it were doubly binding. It was God's word, and that
in itself made it sure; it was actually confirmed by an
oath; God became His own witness and guarantor, and
that made it doubly sure. It was in a double sense an
unchangeable promise. Now that promise was a promise
that all Abraham's descendants would be blessed; therefore
that promise was to the Christian Church, for the Church
is the true Israel and the true seed of Abraham. That
blessing came true in Jesus Christ. It is true that Abraham
had to exercise patience before he received the promise.
It was not till twenty-five years after he had left Ur that
the son Isaac was born to Abraham. Abraham was old;
Sarah was barren; the wandering was long; but Abraham
never wavered from his hope and trust in the promise
of God.

In the ancient world the *anchor* was the symbol of hope.
Epictetus says: " A ship should never depend on one
anchor, or a life on one hope." Pythagoras said: " Wealth
is a weak anchor; fame is still weaker. What then are the
anchors which are strong? Wisdom, great-heartedness,
courage—these are the anchors which no storm can shake."
The writer to the Hebrews insists that the Christian
possesses the greatest hope in the world.

What is that hope? He says that it is a hope which
enters into the inner court beyond the veil. What does
he mean by that? In the Temple the most sacred of all
places was the Holy of Holies. The veil was the covering
which covered it. Within the Holy of Holies there was
held to abide the very presence of God. Into that place
only one man in all the world could go, and that one man
was the High Priest; and even the High Priest might

enter that Holy Place on only one day of the year, the Day of Atonement. And even on that day it was laid down that he must not linger in it for it was a dangerous and a terrible thing to enter into the presence of the living God. Now what the writer to the Hebrews says is this: " Under the old Jewish religion no one might enter into the presence of God but the High Priest, and he might only enter in on one day of the year; but now, Jesus Christ has opened a way to the presence of God for every man at every time. The way that was closed is open. The presence of God is there for all." The writer to the Hebrews uses a most illuminating word about Jesus. He says that Jesus entered the presence of God as our *forerunner*. The word is *prodromos*. It has three stages of meaning. (i) It means *one who rushes on.* (ii) It means *a pioneer.* (iii) It means a scout, a member of the reconnaissance corps of an army, the advance guard who goes ahead to see that it is safe for the body of the troops to follow. Jesus went into the presence of God to make it safe for all men to follow. That presence so long hidden and barred is now open to every man.

Let us put it very simply in another way. Before Jesus came, God was the distant stranger, whom only a very few might approach and that at peril of their lives. But because of what Jesus was and did, God has become the Friend of every man. Once men thought of God as barring the door; now they think of the door to God's presence as thrown wide open to all.

A PRIEST AFTER THE ORDER OF MELCHIZEDEK

Hebrews 7

WE have come now to a passage which is of such paramount importance for the writer of the Letter to the Hebrews, and which in itself is so difficult to understand that we must deal with it in a special way. Chapter 6 ended with

the statement that Jesus had been made a priest for ever
after the order of Melchizedek.   This priesthood after
the order of Melchizedek is the most characteristic thought
of the writer to the Hebrews.   Behind it there lie ways of
thinking, and of arguing, and of using scripture which
are quite strange to us, and which we must yet try to
understand.   It will be best first to collect together all
that the writer to the Hebrews has to say about the priesthood after the order of Melchizedek, and to read it
as a whole before we divide it into shorter passages to
study it in detail.   After we have done that we shall then
try to understand what the writer to the Hebrews was
getting at when he used this idea as a whole, before we
study this chapter in detail.   So then, we first collect the
passages which deal with this idea.   The first of them is
in *Hebrews* 5: 1-10.

> Every high priest who is chosen from among men,
> is appointed on men's behalf to deal with the things
> which concern God.   His task is to offer gifts and
> sacrifices for sins, in that he himself is able to feel
> gently to the ignorant and to the wandering, because
> he himself wears the garment of human weakness.
> By reason of this very weakness it is incumbent
> upon him, just as he makes sacrifice for the people,
> so to make sacrifice for sins on his own behalf also.
> No one takes this honourable position to himself,
> but he is called by God to it, just as Aaron was.   So
> it was not Christ Himself who gave Himself the glory
> of becoming high priest; but it was He who said to
> Him:
>
>> " You are my beloved Son; to-day I have
>> begotten you."
>> " You are a priest for ever according to the
>> order of Melchizedek."
>
> In the days when He lived this human life of ours,
> He offered prayers and entreaties to Him who was
> able to bring Him safely through death, with strong
> crying and with tears.   And, when He had been heard
> because of His reverence, although He was a Son, He
> learned obedience from the sufferings through which

He passed.   When He had been made fully fit for
His appointed task, He became the author of eternal
salvation to all who obey Him, for He had been
designated by God *a high priest after the order of
Melchizedek.*

The second passage which deals with this idea is the whole
of *Hebrews* 7. So then, first, let us set it down as a whole,
remembering that the last verse of Hebrews 6 has already
said that Jesus had become *a high priest for ever after the
order of Melchizedek.*

Now this Melchizedek was King of Salem and priest
of the most high God.   He met Abraham when he
was returning from the smiting of the kings, and blessed
him, and set apart for him a tenth part of the spoils.
In the first place, the interpretation of his own name
means King of Righteousness, and, in the second place,
King of Salem means King of Peace.   His father is
never mentioned, nor his mother; nor is there any
record of his descent;   there is no mention of the
beginning of his days, nor any of the end of his life;
he is exactly like the Son of God;   and he remains a
priest for ever.

Just see how great this man was—Abraham gave
him the tenth part of the spoils of victory—and
Abraham was no less than the founder of our nation.
Now look at the difference—when the sons of Levi
receive their priesthood, they receive an injunction
laid down by the law, to exact tithes from the people.
Now, that is to say, they exact tithes from their own
brothers, even although they are descendants of
Abraham.   But this man, whose descent is not traced
from them at all, exacted tithes from Abraham, and
actually blessed the man who had received the promises.
Beyond all argument, the lesser is blessed by the
greater.   Just so, in the one case, it is a case of men
who die receiving tithes; but in this case, it is the
case of a man whom the evidence proves to live.
Still further—if I may put it this way—through
Abraham, Levi, too, the very man who receives
the tithes, had tithes exacted from him, for he was
in his father's body when Melchizedek met him.

If then the desired effect could have been achieved
by the Levitical priesthood—for it was on the basis
of that priesthood that the people became a people

of the law—what further need was there to set up
another priest, and to call him a priest after the order
of Melchizedek, and not to call him a priest after
the order of Aaron? Once the priesthood was altered,
of necessity, there follows an alteration of the law
too, for the person of whom the statements are made
belongs to another tribe altogether, from which no
one ever served at the altar. It is obvious that it was
from Judah that our Lord sprang, and, with regard
to that tribe Moses said nothing about priests. And
certain things are still more abundantly clear—if a
different priest is set up, a priest after the order of
Melchizedek, a priest who became so, not according
to the law of a mere human injunction, but according
to the power of a life that is indestructible—for the
witness of scripture in regard to this is: " You are a
priest for ever after the order of Melchizedek."—if
all that is so, two things emerge. On the one hand
there emerges the cancellation of the previous injunction, because of its own weakness and uselessness
(for the law never achieved the effect which it was
designed to produce), and, on the other hand, there
emerges the introduction of a better hope, through
which we can come near to God.

And inasmuch as it happened with an oath—for the
Levitical priests are made priests without an oath,
but He with an oath, because scripture says of Him:
" The Lord swore and will not repent of it, ' You
are a priest for ever ' "—in so far Jesus has become
the surety of a better covenant. Further, of the
Levitical priests more and more were made priests,
because they were prevented from continuing permanently by death, whereas He has a priesthood
which will never pass away, because He remains for
ever. For that very reason it is in every possible
way and for all time that He, who is for ever alive,
can save those who come to God through Him.

We needed such a high priest—one who is holy,
one who has never hurt any man, one who is stainless,
one who is different from sinners, one who has become
higher than the heavens. He does not need, as the
high priests do, daily first to offer sacrifices for His
own sins, and then thereafter for the sins of the people.
For He did this once and for all when He offered
Himself. For the law appointed as high priests men
subject to weakness; but the word of the oath, which

came after the law, appointed one who is a Son who is fully equipped to carry out His office for ever.

THESE, then, are the passages in which the writer to the Hebrews describes Jesus as *a priest after the order of Melchizedek*. Now let us see just what he is trying to say when he uses that conception.

We must begin by understanding the general position from which the writer to the Hebrews starts. He starts with the basic idea that *religion is access to God*. The essence of religion, to the writer to the Hebrews, is that it takes a man, without fear and without barriers, into the presence of God. Now it was to make that access to God possible that two things existed. First, it was to give that access that *the law* existed. The basic idea of the law is that so long as a man faithfully and obediently observes the commandments of the law, he is in a position of friendship with God, and the door to God's presence is open to him. But men do not and cannot keep the law, and therefore their fellowship with God, their access to God's presence, is interrupted. It was exactly to deal with that situation of estrangement that the second thing existed. The second thing was *the priesthood and the whole sacrificial system*. The Latin word for *priest* is *pontifex* which means a *bridge-builder*; the priest was a man whose function it was to build a bridge between men and God. How? By means of the sacrificial system. A man broke the law; his fellowship with God was interrupted and his access to God was barred; by the offering of the correct sacrifice that breach of the law was atoned for; the fellowship was restored and the barrier was removed. That was the theory of the matter. But in practice all life showed that that was precisely what the priesthood and the sacrificial system could not do. There was no escaping the human estrangement from God which followed sin; and the problem was that not all the efforts of the priesthood and not all the sacrifices could restore that lost relationship and could make sinning man feel at home with God.

Therefore, it is the argument of the writer to the Hebrews, what is needed is a new and a different priesthood, and a new and effective sacrifice. Otherwise the road to God's presence can never be opened up. The writer to the Hebrews sees in Jesus Christ the only High Priest who can open the way to God; and he calls the priesthood of Jesus a priesthood *after the order of Melchizedek.*

Where did he get that idea? He got it from two passages in the Old Testament. The first was Psalm 110: 4 where it is written:

> " The Lord hath sworn and will not repent, ' Thou art a priest for ever after the order of Melchizedek'. "

The second is Genesis 14: 17-20 where the story of the original Melchizedek is told.

> " And the king of Sodom went out to meet Abram after his return from the slaughter of Chederlaomer and of the kings that were with him, at the valley of Shaveh, which is the king's dale. And Melchizedek king of Salem brought forth bread and wine; and he was the priest of the most high God. And he blessed him and said: ' Blessed be Abram of the most high God, possessor of heaven and earth; and blessed be the most high God, which hath delivered thine enemies into thy hand.' And Abram gave him tithes of all."

It is from these two passages that the writer to the Hebrews gets his picture of the priesthood after the order of Melchizedek and of what that priesthood means. But before we can understand what he is doing we must first understand the Jewish method of interpreting scripture. In point of fact the writer to the Hebrews is here doing what any skilled Jewish Rabbi might do. He is following rabbinic methods of interpretation. To understand that method of interpretation we must understand two things. (i) To the scholarly Jew any passage of scripture had *four* meanings to which he gave four different names. (*a*) First, there was *Peshat*, which is the literal and factual

meaning. (*b*) Second, there was *Remaz*, which is the suggested meaning. (*c*) Third, there was *Derush*, which is the
meaning arrived at after long and careful investigation.
(*d*) Fourth, there is *Sod*, which is the allegorical or the
inner meaning. Now it is the fact that to the Jew the
most important meaning by far was the fourth, *Sod*, the
inner, allegorical, mystical meaning. The Jew was not
nearly so much interested in the literal, historical, factual,
obvious meaning of a passage, as he was in the allegorical
and mystical meaning which could be extracted from it.
The most important meaning was the meaning which
could be read into the passage, and obviously that inner
meaning might have no connection whatever with the
literal meaning of the passage. It was quite permissible,
in fact it was the regular practice, to take things right out
of their context and to read into them meanings which
we would consider quite fantastic and quite unjustified.
That is what the writer to the Hebrews is doing here.
(ii) Second, for the interpretation which the writer to the
Hebrews gave to this passage, it is essential to note that
the Jewish interpreters considered themselves completely
justified in arguing not only from the *utterances*, but also
from the *silences* of scripture. In other words, an argument
could be built, not only on what scripture said, but also
on what scripture did not say. In point of fact, the writer
to the Hebrews bases his argument in this passage at
least as much on what scripture did not say about Melchizedek as on what scripture did say about him.

Now let us see wherein the quality of the priesthood
after the order of Melchizedek differs from the quality
of the ordinary, existing Aaronic priesthood.

(i) *Melchizedek has no genealogy*; he is without father
and without mother (*Hebrews* 7: 3). Now, note straight
away that this is one of the arguments drawn from the
silence of scripture. Scripture does not provide Melchizedek with any genealogy. This was unusual for two
reasons. (*a*) It is the very reverse of the habitual practice

of *Genesis*. Genealogies are a feature of *Genesis*; long lists of a man's ancestors constantly occur. But Melchizedek arrives on the scene, as it were, from nowhere. That in itself is quite unusual. *(b)* But far more important— this is the reverse of the rules which governed the Aaronic priesthood. The Aaronic priesthood depended entirely on descent. Under Jewish law a man could not under any circumstances become a priest unless he could produce an unbroken and certificated pedigree going back to Aaron. If he had not that genealogy, nothing in the world could make him a priest. Character and ability had nothing to do with it. The one and the only essential was that pedigree. When the Jews came back from exile to Jerusalem we find that certain priestly families could not produce their genealogical records and were therefore debarred from the priesthood for ever (Ezra 2: 61-63; Nehemiah 7: 63-65). On the other hand, if a man could produce a pedigree reaching back to Aaron, apart only from certain specified physical blemishes, nothing on earth could stop him being a priest. Genealogy was literally everything. So then the first difference between the Aaronic priesthood and the priesthood after the order of Melchizedek was this—*the Aaronic priesthood depended on genealogical descent; the priesthood of Melchizedek depended on personal qualification and on personal qualification alone.* Melchizedek's priesthood was based in what *he was*, not on what *he had inherited*. As one scholar puts it— it is the difference between a claim based on *legality*, and a claim based on *personality*. First and foremost then, the new priesthood is based on personal qualification and personal qualification alone.

(ii) *Hebrews* 7: 1-3 collects further qualities about Melchizedek. The name *Melchizedek* literally means *King of Righteousness*. The word *Salem* means *peace*; therefore he was also *King of Peace*. We have seen that he was without father and without mother, that he has no genealogy. But again the writer to the Hebrews draws

71

THE LETTER TO THE HEBREWS

on the silence of scripture. We are told of no time when Melchizedek began his priesthood, and of no time when he ended it; we are told of no time when he was born and of no time when he died. Therefore it is to be deduced that Melchizedek had no beginning and has no end; and that his priesthood lasts for ever and ever. From this we can collect five great qualities in the priesthood of Melchizedek. (a) It is a priesthood of *righteousness*. (b) It is a priesthood of *peace*. (c) It is a *royal* priesthood, for Melchizedek was a king. (d) It is *personal and not inherited* because he has neither father nor mother nor genealogy. (e) It is *eternal*, because he has no birth or death, and his priesthood has no beginning or end. These, then, are the qualities which differentiate the priesthood after the order of Melchizedek from the ordinary priesthood.

(iii) Suppose all this to be true, how, then, can it be proved that the priesthood of Melchizedek is superior to and greater than the Aaronic priesthood? To prove this the writer to the Hebrews seizes on two points in the Genesis story about Melchizedek. First, there is the saying that *Abraham gave Melchizedek tithes of all*. Now the priests also exact tithes. But there are two differences. The priests tithe their brethren, their fellow Jews; and they tithe them as a result of legal enactment; the law gives them the right to tithe. But Melchizedek tithed Abraham who had no racial connection with him whatsoever and who was in fact the founder of the Jewish nation; further, he exacted the tithes not because the law gave him the right to do so; but because of an unquestionable personal right. He did not need a law to give him the right to exact tithes; he *had* the right. Obviously that sets him far above the ordinary priesthood. Second, there is the saying that *Melchizedek blessed Abraham*. Now it is always the superior who blesses the inferior; therefore Melchizedek was superior to Abraham, and Abraham was the founder of the Jewish race and the unique recipient of the promises of God. That indeed gives Melchizedek a place than which none could be higher.

A. B. Bruce thus sums up the points in which Melchizedek is superior to the ordinary Levitical priesthood. (a) He tithed Abraham and was therefore superior to Abraham. Abraham was one of the patriarchs; the patriarchs are superior to their descendants; therefore Melchizedek is greater than the descendants of Abraham; the ordinary priests are the descendants of Abraham; therefore Melchizedek is greater than they. (b) Melchizedek is greater than the sons of Levi because they can exact tithes by legal enactment; he did it as a right he personally possessed and which was given to him by no man. (c) The Levites receive tithes as mortal men who are dying; he received them as one who lives and lives for ever (*Hebrews* 7: 8). (d) In point of fact, Levi, to whom the Israelites paid tithes, may be said to have paid tithes to Melchizedek, because Levi was Abraham's grandson and was therefore in the body of Abraham at the time Abraham paid tithes. On all these counts Melchizedek was superior to the Levitical priesthood.

(iv) From Hebrews 7: 11 onwards the writer to the Hebrews goes on to show *wherein the superiority of the new priesthood lay.*

(a) *The very fact that a new priesthood was promised* (*Hebrews* 7: 11) *shows that the old priesthood was inadequate.* If the old priesthood had fulfilled the function of bringing men to the presence of God there would have been no need for any priesthood after the order of Melchizedek. And further, the introduction of the new priesthood is a revolution. According to the law, all priests must belong to the tribe of *Levi*; but Jesus is from the tribe of *Judah*. This shows that the whole old system is superseded. The law is wiped out. Something greater than the law has come. The law is a dead letter now.

(b) *The new priesthood is for ever* (*Hebrews* 7: 15-19). Under the old system the priests died and kept on dying;

there was no permanency; but now there has come a priest who lives for ever.

(c) *The new priesthood is introduced by an oath of God.* Psalm 110: 4 says: "The Lord swore and will not repent 'Thou art a priest for ever after the order of Melchizedek'." Clearly God does not swear lightly. He never introduced the ordinary priesthood like that. This is something new.

(d) *The new priest offers no sacrifice for himself* (*Hebrews* 7: 27). The ordinary priest always had to make sacrifice for *his own* sin before he could make sacrifice for the sins of the people. But Jesus Christ, the new High Priest, is sinless and needs no sacrifice for himself.

(e) *The new priest does not need endlessly to repeat sacrifices* (*Hebrews* 7: 27). He makes the one perfect sacrifice, which never needs to be made again, because it has for ever opened the way to the presence of God.

We may now sum up very briefly the ideas which were in the mind of the writer to the Hebrews when he thought of Jesus in terms of the High Priest after the order of Melchizedek. To make it clearer we set out only the great salient ideas without the side-lines.

(i) Jesus is the High Priest, whose priesthood depends not on any genealogy, but on Himself and Himself alone.

(ii) Jesus is the High Priest who lives for ever and who never dies.

(iii) Jesus is the High Priest who Himself is sinless and never needs to offer any sacrifice for His own sin.

(iv) Jesus is the High Priest who in the offering of Himself made the perfect sacrifice. No more need sacrifice be made every day. Once and for all the sacrifice has been made which opens the way to God.

The function of the priest is to open the door of access to God; once and for all Jesus did that, achieving for ever that which the ordinary and the earthly priesthood could never do.

We have now seen what the general ideas in the mind of the writer to the Hebrews are when he thinks of Jesus as a priest after the order of Melchizedek. Now we must turn to this passage in detail, and study it in sections, always keeping the general conception in our minds.

THE TRUE KING AND THE TRUE PRIEST

Hebrews 7: 1-3

> Now this Melchizedek was King of Salem and priest of the most high God. He met Abraham when he was returning from the smiting of the kings, and blessed him, and Abraham set apart for him a tenth part of the spoils. In the first place, the interpretation of his own name means King of Righteousness, and, in the second place, King of Salem means King of Peace. His father is never mentioned, nor his mother; nor is there any record of his descent; there is no mention of the beginning of his days, nor any of the end of his life; he is exactly like the Son of God; and he remains a priest for ever.

As we have seen, the two passages on which the writer to the Hebrews founds his argument are Psalm 110: 4 and Genesis 14: 18-20. In the old Genesis story Melchizedek is a strange and almost eerie figure. He arrives out of the blue; there is nothing about his life, his birth, his death or his descent. He simply arrives. He gives Abraham bread and wine, which to us, reading the passage in the light of what we know, sounds so sacramental. He blesses Abraham. And then he vanishes from the stage of history with the same unexplained suddenness as he arrived upon it. There is little wonder that in the mystery of this story the writer to the Hebrews found a type and forecast and symbol of Christ.

Melchizedek, from his name, was King of Righteousness; Melchizedek, from his realm, was King of Peace. The order is at once significant and inevitable. *Righteousness must always come before peace*. Without righteousness there can be no such thing as peace. As Paul has it in Romans 5: 1: " Therefore being *justified* by faith, we have *peace* with God." As he has it again in Romans 14: 7: " The kingdom of God is . . . *righteousness, peace* and joy." The order is always the same—first righteousness, and then peace.

It may well be said that all life is a search for peace, and it may also well be said, that men persist in looking for peace in the wrong place.

(i) Men look for peace in *escape*. But the trouble about escape is that it is always necessary to return. A. J. Gossip somewhere draws a picture of a slatternly woman who lived in a slatternly house, lazy, untidy, dirty. She leaves her home on an afternoon and she goes to a picture house. For an hour or two she escapes into the glamour and the luxury of the world of the film—and then she must go back. It is escape all right—but there is the inevitable return. W. M. Macgregor tells of an old woman who lived in a terrible slum in Edinburgh called the Pans. Every now and again she would grow disgusted with the surroundings in which she lived, and she would make a tour of her friends, extracting a penny or two from each. With the proceeds she would get helplessly drunk. And when others remonstrated with her she would answer: " Do you grudge me my one chance to get out of the Pans with a sup of whisky?" Again it was escape—but she had to return. It is always possible to find some kind of peace by the route of escape, but it is never a lasting peace. Dr. Johnson used to insist that a man should have a hobby, let it be chemistry or anything like that, for he held that a man should have as many retreats for his mind as possible. But, even there, there is still the necessity to return. Escape is not wrong; sometimes it is necessary if health and sanity are to be preserved; but escape is always a palliative and never a cure.

(ii) There is the peace of *evasion*. Many a man seeks peace by refusing to face his problems. He delays facing them; or he pushes them into the back of his mind and seeks to draw down the blind on them. There are two things to be said about that. The first is that no one ever solved a problem by refusing to look at it. However much we evade the problem, the problem is still there. And problems are like diseases—the longer we refuse to face them the worse they get; and we may well come to a stage when the disease is incurable and the problem insoluble. The second thing is maybe even more serious. Psychology tells us that there is a part of the mind which never stops thinking. With our conscious minds we may be evading a problem, but our subconscious mind is teasing away at it. The thing is there like a piece of hidden shrapnel in the body; and it can ruin life. So far from bringing peace, evasion is the thing in this world most destructive of peace.

(iii) There is the way of *compromise*. It is possible to arrive at some kind of peace by arriving at some kind of compromise. It is in fact one of the commonest methods of the world. We can seek peace by toning down some principle; we can seek peace by an uneasy agreement in which neither party is fully satisfied. Kermit Eby says that we can compromise for long enough but the time comes when a man must stand up and be counted, if he wants to sleep at nights. Compromise means the loose ends of things unsolved. Compromise, therefore, inevitably means tension, even if a more or less hidden tension. Tension inevitably means a gnawing worry; and therefore compromise is the enemy of peace.

(iv) There is the way of *righteousness*. There is another way of putting that. There is the way of *the will of God*. There is no peace for any man until he has said: "Thy will be done." But once he has said that, peace floods his soul. It happened even to Jesus. Jesus went into the Garden with a soul under tension, such a tension that He sweated blood. In the Garden He accepted God's will, and He came out a man at peace. To take the way of righteousness, to accept God's will is to remove the root of dispeace. It is the final way to lasting peace.

The writer to the Hebrews piles up words to show that Melchizedek has no descent. He did that to contrast the new priesthood of Jesus Christ with the old Aaronic priesthood. A Jewish priest could not be a priest unless he could trace an unbroken descent from Aaron; and if a man could trace such a descent nothing could stop him being a priest. If a priest married, if his bride-to-be was the daughter of a priest, she must produce her pedigree for four generations back; if she was not the daughter of a priest, she must produce her pedigree for five generations back. It is the odd and almost incredible fact that the whole Jewish priesthood was founded on genealogy. Personal qualities did not enter into it at all. But Jesus Christ is the true priest, not because of what He inherited but because of what He is. His priesthood is in Himself.

As we have said, the writer to the Hebrews piles up words to stress this, and some of them are amazing words. He says that Jesus was *without descent*. The Greek word is *agenealogētos*. That is a word that, so far as we know, no Greek writer ever used before. It may well be that, in his eagerness to stress the fact that Jesus' power did not depend on descent, he invented it. It is very likely a new word to describe a new thing. He says that Melchizedek was without father and without mother. The words he uses are *apatōr and amētōr*. Now these words are very interesting. They have certain uses in secular Greek. They are the regular description of waifs and strays and of people of low pedigree. They contemptuously dismiss a man as having no ancestry. But more, the word *apatōr*, *without father*, has a technical legal use in the contemporary Greek of the papyri. It is the word which is used on legal documents, especially on birth certificates, for *father unknown*, and, therefore, *illegitimate*. So, for instance, there is a papyrus which speaks of : " Chairēmōn, *apatōr*, father unknown, whose mother is Thasēs." It is an amazing thing that the writer to the Hebrews took words like this to stress his meaning. The Christian writers have a strange way of redeeming words as well as redeeming men and women. No phrase seemed too strong to the writer to the Hebrews to insist upon the fact that Jesus' authority was in Himself, and came to Him from no man.

THE GREATNESS OF MELCHIZEDEK

Hebrews 7: 4-10

> Just see how great this man was—Abraham gave him the tenth of the spoils of victory—and Abraham was no less than the founder of our nation. Now look at the difference—when the sons of Levi receive their priesthood, they receive an injunction laid down by the law to exact tithes from the people. Now, that is to say, they exact tithes from their own brothers, even although they are descendants of Abraham. But this man, whose descent is not traced through them at all, exacted tithes from Abraham, and actually blessed the man who had received the promises. Beyond all argument the lesser is blessed by the greater. Just so, in the one case, it is the case of men who die receiving tithes; but in this case, it is the case of a man whom the evidence proves to live. Still further, if I may put it this way, through Abraham, Levi too, the very man who receives the tithes, had tithes exacted from him, for he was in his father's body when Melchizedek met him.

THE writer to the Hebrews is here concerned to prove the superiority of the priesthood after the order of Melchizedek to the ordinary priesthood. He proceeds on the matter of tithes, because Abraham had given to Melchizedek a tithe, a tenth part of the spoils of his victory. The law of tithes is laid down in Numbers 18: 20, 21. There Aaron is told that the Levites will have no actual territory in the promised land laid down for them, but that they are to receive a tenth part of everything for their services in the tabernacle. " And the Lord spake unto Aaron, ' Thou shalt have no inheritance in their land, neither shalt thou have any part among them: I am thy part and thine inheritance among the children of Israel. And behold I have given the children of Levi all the tenth in Israel for an inheritance, for their service which they serve, even the service of the tabernacle of the congregation.' " By law, then, it was laid down that the Levites had the right to receive one tenth, the tithe, of the produce of all their brother Israelites. So now in a series of contrasts the writer to the Hebrews works out the superiority of Melchizedek over the Levitical priests. He makes five different points. (i) The Levites receive tithes from the people, and that is a right that only the Levites enjoy. Melchizedek received tithes from Abraham, and he was not a member of the tribe of Levi. Now, it could be argued that that puts Melchizedek on a level with the Levites, but it does not prove that he was superior to them. So our writer adds four other points. (ii) The Levites tithe their brother Israelites; but Melchizedek was not an Israelite; he was a stranger; and it was no ordinary Israelite from whom he received tithes; it was from no less a person than Abraham, the founder of the nation. (iii) It was due to a legal enactment that the Levites had the right to exact tithes; but Melchizedek received tithes for the sake of what he was personally, and not because of any legal enactment. He had such an essential and personal greatness that he needed no legal enactment to entitle him to receive tithes. (iv) The Levites receive tithes as dying men; but Melchizedek lives for ever. (v) Finally he produces a strange and curious argument for which he apologises before he states it. Levi was a direct descendant of Abraham and Levi was the only man legally entitled to receive tithes. Now, if Levi was a direct descendant of Abraham it means that Levi was already in Abraham's body. It was Abraham who begat Isaac; and Isaac begat Jacob; and Jacob begat Levi; therefore it can be argued that even at this time Levi was potentially in Abraham's body. Therefore when Abraham paid tithes to Melchizedek, Levi also paid them, because he was included in Abraham's body; therefore Levi, the one man who was entitled to receive tithes, actually paid tithes to Melchizedek, which is the final proof that Melchizedek was superior to Levi. It is an extremely odd argument. As a rabbinic argument it was no doubt convincing enough to those to whom it was addressed, however fantastic it may sound to us.

But, strangely enough, this argument enshrines one great truth. It does enshrine the fact and the truth that what a man does reacts on his descendants. If a man commits some sin, he may transmit to his descendants, either the tendency to sin or some actual physical handicap, or both of these things. If a man builds up excellence and purity of character, he transmits a fine inheritance to those who come after. Levi, on the argument of the writer to the Hebrews, was affected by what Abraham did. Therein, amidst the fantastics of the rabbinic argument, there remains the truth that no man lives to himself, but that he transmits something of himself to those who follow after.

THE NEW PRIEST AND THE NEW WAY

Hebrews 7: 11-20

> If, then, the desired effect could have been achieved by the Levitical priesthood—for it was on the basis of it that the people became a people of the law—what further need was there to set up another priest, and to call him a priest after the order of Melchizedek, and not to call him a priest after the order of Aaron? Once the priesthood was altered, of necessity there follows an alteration of the law too, for the person of whom the statements are made belongs to another tribe altogether, from which no one ever served at the altar. It is obvious that it was from Judah that our Lord sprang, and with regard to that tribe Moses said nothing about priests. And certain things are still more abundantly clear—if a different priest is

set up, a priest after the order of Melchizedek, a priest who has become so, not according to the law of a mere human injunction, but according to the power of a life that is indestructible—for the witness of scripture in regard to this is: " You are a priest for ever after the order of Melchizedek "—if all that is so two things emerge. On the one hand there emerges the cancellation of the previous injunction because of its own weakness and uselessness (for the law never achieved the effect it was designed to produce), and, on the other hand, there emerges the introduction of a better hope through which we can come near to God.

As we read this passage we have to remember the basic idea of religion which never leaves the mind of the writer to the Hebrews. To him religion is access to God's presence; religion is that which allows us to come to God as God's friends, with nothing between us and Him. It was that fellowship which the old Jewish religion was designed to produce. It was designed to produce it in two ways. First, it was designed to produce it by obedience to the law. Let a man obey the law and that man was the friend of God. Let a man be for ever obedient to God's commandments and that man had for ever the right of access to God. But second, it was recognised that such perfect obedience was out of the question for any man; therefore the whole sacrificial system came in. When a man was guilty of a breach of the law, the requisite sacrifice was made and the breach was supposed to be healed by that sacrifice. That is what the writer to the Hebrews means by saying that the people became a people of the law on the basis of the Levitical priesthood. He means that without the Levitical sacrifices to atone for breaches of the law, the law would have been completely impossible. But, in point of fact, the system of Levitical sacrifices had proved ineffective to restore the lost fellowship between God and man. It did not, in fact, restore the lost access to God. So then a new priesthood was necessary, the priesthood after the order of Melchizedek. Now he says that that

priesthood differed from the old priesthood in that it
was not dependent on merely human—*fleshly* is the word
in the Greek—injunctions, but on the power of a life that
is indestructible. What he means is this—every single
regulation that governed the old priesthood had to do
with the priest's physical body. To be a priest he must be
a pure descendant of Aaron—that is physical descent.
Even then there were one hundred and forty-two physical
blemishes which might disqualify him; some of them are
detailed in Leviticus 21: 16-23. The disqualification is
purely physical. The ordination ceremony is outlined in
Leviticus 8. (i) He was bathed in water so that he would
be ceremonially clean. (ii) He was clothed in the four
priestly garments—the linen knee breeches, the long linen
garment woven in one piece, the girdle round the breast,
and the bonnet or turban. (iii) He was anointed with oil.
(iv) He was touched on the tip of the right ear, his right
thumb and his right great toe with the blood of certain
sacrifices which had been made. Every single item in
the whole ceremony is a physical thing, affecting the
priest's body. Once he was ordained he had to observe
so many washings with water, so many anointings with
oil; he had to cut his hair in a certain way. The whole
programme was purely physical. From beginning to end
the Jewish priesthood was dependent on physical things.
Character, ability, personality had nothing to do with it.
But the new priesthood is dependent on *a life that is indestructible.* Christ's priesthood depends not on physical
things, but on His character, His personality, His being,
what He was in Himself. Here was a revolution; it is
no longer outward ceremonies and observances that make
a priest; it is inward worth.

But further, there is another great change which has
fundamental implications. The law was definite that all
priests must belong to the tribe of *Levi*; they must be
descendants of Aaron; but Jesus belonged to the tribe of
Judah. Therefore, the very fact that He is the supreme

priest means that the law is cancelled; it is wiped out. The word that is used for cancellation is *athetēsis*; that is the word that is used for annulling a treaty, for abrogating a promise, for scoring a man's name off the register, for rendering a law or regulation inoperative. The whole paraphernalia of the sacrificial and ceremonial law is wiped out in the priesthood of Jesus.

Finally, Jesus can do what the old priesthood never could do—He can give us access to God. How does He do that? What is it that keeps a man from having access to God? What is it that puts the barriers up? Two things do that. (i) There is *fear*. So long as a man is terrified of God he can never be at home with God. Jesus came to show men the infinite tender love of the God whose name is Father—and the awful fear is gone. We know now that the one thing God wants us to do is to come home, not to punishment, but to the welcome of His open arms. (ii) There is *sin*. But Jesus on His Cross made the one perfect sacrifice which atones for sin. Fear is gone; sin is conquered; the way to God is open to men.

THE GREATER PRIESTHOOD

Hebrews 7: 21-25

And in so far as it happened with an oath—for the Levitical priests are made priests without an oath, but He with an oath, because scripture says of Him, " The Lord swore and will not repent of it, ' You are a priest for ever ' "—in so far Jesus has become the surety of a better covenant. Further, of the Levitical priests more and more were made priests because they were prevented from continuing permanently by death, whereas He has a priesthood which will never pass away, because He remains for ever. For that very reason, it is in every possible way and for all time that He who is for ever alive to make intercession for us can save those who come to God through Him.

THE writer to the Hebrews is still accumulating his proofs that the priesthood after the order of Melchizedek, the priesthood of Jesus, is superior to the old Levitical priesthood. Here he brings forward other two proofs.

First, he stresses the fact that the institution of the priesthood after the order of Melchizedek was confirmed by the oath of God, while the ordinary priesthood was not. The reference is to Psalm 110: 4: " *The Lord hath sworn, and will not repent, ' Thou art a priest for ever after the order of Melchizedek.' *" Now the very idea of God taking an oath is startling. Long ago Philo saw this. Philo pointed out that the only reason for taking an oath is because a man's bare word may be disbelieved; and he takes an oath in order to guarantee that his word is true. God never needs to do that, because it is impossible that God's word should ever be disbelieved. If, therefore, God ever confirms a statement by an oath, that statement must be of unique and extraordinary importance. A thing which God confirms by an oath must be something so utterly unchangeable that it is woven into the very fibre of the universe and must remain for ever. So then it is possible that the ordinary priesthood can pass away; but the priesthood after the order of Melchizedek can never pass away; that is, the priesthood of Jesus Christ can never pass away, because God did not only institute it; He followed the amazing and unique course of confirming it with an oath.

Because this priesthood has been confirmed by an oath, Jesus is *the surety of a better covenant.* Now let us remember the function of the priest, the function of all true religion— the function of the priest and of all religion is to open a way of access to God, to enable men to enjoy the intimate friendship of God. Now here we come upon the word *covenant.* We shall soon have to examine this word more closely and in more detail. It is sufficient at the moment to say that a covenant is in essence an agreement between two people. It is an agreement that if one faithfully performs certain undertakings, the other will respond in a certain way. There was an ancient covenant, an ancient agreement between Israel and God. That agreement was that if the Israelites faithfully obeyed God's law, then the way of access to the friendship of God would always be open to them. We see the nation entering into that covenant in Exodus 24: 1-8. We see Moses taking the book of the law and reading it to the people; and we see the people responding with the words: " All that the Lord hath said will we do and be obedient " (Exodus 24: 7). That is to say the old agreement was based on obedience to the law; and the agreement could only be kept open when the priests kept on making sacrifices for every breach of the law. But Jesus is the surety of a new and a better covenant. That is to say, Jesus is the surety of a new kind of agreement, a new kind of relationship between man and God. Wherein was the difference? Wherein is the new and better relationship of the new covenant? The difference is this—the old covenant was based on law and justice and obedience; the new covenant is based entirely on love and on the perfect sacrifice of Jesus Christ. Under the old covenant access to God was dependent on man's obedience; under the new covenant access to God is based only on the welcoming love of God. The old covenant was based on man's achievement; the new covenant is based on God's love. And what does the writer to the Hebrews mean by saying that Jesus is the *surety* of this new covenant? The word he uses for *surety* is *egguos*, which is an interesting word. An *egguos* was one who gave security, who was surety, who stood guarantor. It is used, for instance, for a person who guarantees someone else's overdraft at a bank. He is surety that the money will be paid. It is used for someone who goes bail for a prisoner. He guarantees that the prisoner will appear at the trial. The *egguos* is the one who guarantees that something will be paid, that someone will be produced, that some undertaking will be assuredly honoured. So, then, what the writer to the Hebrews means is this. Someone might say: "How do you know that the old covenant, the old agreement between God and man is no longer operative? How do you know that access to God, friendship with God now depends, not on man's achievement of obedience, but simply and solely on the welcoming love of God?" The answer is: "Jesus Christ guarantees that it is so. Jesus is the guarantor of the love of God. Jesus is the surety who promises that God's love will be forthcoming, if only we take Him at His word." To put it in the simplest possible way—we must believe that when we look at Jesus in all His love and mercy and kindness, we are seeing what God is like.

But the writer to the Hebrews then introduces a second proof of the superiority of the new priesthood, the priesthood of Jesus. There was no permanency about the old priesthood. Death came, and those who were priests died and had to be replaced. None of the old order of priests lasted for ever. But the priesthood of Jesus is for ever and ever. Now the thing that matters in this passage is the overtones and the implications of the almost untranslatable words the writer to the Hebrews uses. He says that the priesthood of Jesus is a priesthood *that will never pass away.* The word that he uses is the word *aparabatos.* *Aparabatos* is a legal word. It means *inviolable.* A judge lays down that his decision must remain *aparabatos.* It must remain *unalterable.* It means *non-transferable.* It describes something which belongs to one person and cannot ever be transferred to anyone else. Galen, the medical writer, uses it to describe absolute, scientific law which can never be violated, the principles on which the very universe is built and holds together. So then the writer to the Hebrews says that the priesthood of Jesus, the power of Jesus to give men access to God, the power of Jesus to enable men to become the friends of God is something which can never be taken from Him, is something that no one else can ever possess, is something that

is as lasting as the laws which hold the universe together.
Jesus can never be surpassed; there can never be any
substitute for Him. He is and will always remain the only
way to God. But the writer to the Hebrews uses another
wonderful word about Jesus. He says of Jesus that *He
remains for ever*. The verb he used for *to remain* is the verb
paramenein. Now that verb does mean *to remain*, but it
has two characteristic flavours. First, it means *to remain
in office*. No one can ever take the office of Jesus from Him.
To all eternity He remains the introducer of men to God.
Second, it means *to remain in the capacity of a servant*,
to remain with a person in such a way that the person
who remains continues always to render service to the
person with whom he does remain. Gregory of Nazianzen
provides in his will that his daughters will *remain (paramenein)* with their mother so long as she is alive. They
are to stay with her and be her help and her support.
The papyri talk of a girl who must *remain (paramenein)*
in a shop for three years in order to discharge by her work
a debt that she cannot pay. She has to *remain* and to
serve. There is a papyrus contract which says that a boy,
who is being bound as an apprentice, must *remain (paramenein)* with his master for as many days extra as he has
played truant. He has to *remain* in order *to complete
his service*. So when the writer to the Hebrews says that
Jesus *remains for ever*, there is wrapped up in that phrase
the amazing thought that *Jesus is for ever at the service of
men*. For ever and ever, in eternity as He was in time,
Jesus exists as the one who remains to be of service to
mankind. That is why He is the complete Saviour. On
earth He served men; He gave His life for them; in
Heaven He still exists to make intercession for them.
He lived and died for them on earth; He lives in Heaven
to plead their cause. He is the priest for ever, the one who
is for ever opening the door to the friendship of God, the
one who is for ever and ever the great servant of mankind.

THE LETTER TO THE HEBREWS

THE HIGH PRIEST WE NEED

Hebrews 7: 26-28

> We needed such a high priest—one who is holy,
> one who never hurt any man, one who is stainless,
> one who is different from sinners, one who has become
> higher than the heavens. He does not need, as the
> high priests do, daily first to offer sacrifices for his
> own sins, and thereafter for the sins of the people.
> For He did this once and for all when He offered
> Himself. For the law appointed as high priests men
> subject to weakness, but the word of the oath, which
> came after the law, appointed one who is a Son who
> is fully equipped to carry out His office for ever.

STILL the writer to the Hebrews is filled with the thought
of Jesus as high priest. He begins this passage by using
a series of great words and phrases to describe Jesus.

(i) He says that Jesus is *holy*. The word which he uses
is the word *hosios*. This word in the New Testament is
used of Jesus in Acts 2: 27 and 13: 35; it is used of the
Lord in Revelation 15: 4 and 16: 5. It is used of the
Christian bishop in Titus 1: 18. It is used of the hands
that a man must present to God in prayer in I Timothy
2: 18. Behind it there is always one special idea. It always
describes the man who faithfully and meticulously does
his duty to God. It describes a man, not so much as he
appears before his fellow men, but as he appears before
God. *Hosios* is a word that has in it the greatest of all
goodnesses, the goodness which is pure in the sight of God.

(ii) He says that Jesus *never hurt any man*. In the
Greek this is one adjective, the word *akakos*. *Kakia* is
the Greek word for evil; and this word describes the man
who is so cleansed of evil that there is nothing left in
him but good. It describes a man in his effect upon
his fellow men. Sir Walter Scott claimed for himself
as a writer that he never corrupted any man's morals
or unsettled any man's faith. The man who is *akakos* is
the man who is so cleansed that his presence is like an

antiseptic and in his heart there is nothing but the loving kindness of God.

(iii) He says that Jesus is *stainless*. The Greek word is *amiantos*, which describes the man who is absolutely free from any of the blemishes or defilement which might make it impossible for him to draw near to God. The blemished victim cannot be offered to God; the defiled man cannot approach God. But the one who is *amiantos* is fit to enter into the presence of God.

(iv) He says that Jesus is *different from sinners*. This is a phrase whose meaning we must understand. It does not mean that Jesus was not really a man; it does not in any way try to take away the full humanity of Jesus. Jesus was different from sinners in that, although He was fully man and underwent all a man's temptations, He never fell to any temptation, but conquered them all, and emerged without sin. The difference between Him and other men lies not in the fact that He was not fully man, but in the fact that He was true manhood at its highest and its best, man without sin.

(v) Finally he says that Jesus *was made higher than the heavens*. In this phrase he is thinking of the Ascension and the exaltation of Jesus. If the last phrase stresses the perfection of the manhood of Jesus, this phrase stresses the perfection of His godhead. He who was a man amongst men is also He who is exalted to the right hand of God.

The writer to the Hebrews now introduces still another aspect in which the priesthood of Jesus Christ is far superior to the Levitical priesthood. Before the High Priest could offer sacrifice for the sins of the people, he had first to offer sacrifice *for his own sin*, for he was a sinful man. It is of the Day of Atonement that the writer is specially thinking. That was the great day when atonement was made for all the sins of the people. That was the day on which the High Priest performed his supreme function. Usually it was the only day in the year when he personally carried out the sacrifices. On ordinary days the sacrifices were left to the subordinate priests, but on the Day of Atonement the High Priest himself officiated. Now the very first item on the ritual of that day was a sacrifice for the sins of the High Priest himself. He washed his hands and his feet; he put off his gorgeous robes; he clothed himself in spotless white linen. There was brought to him a bullock which he had purchased with his own money. He laid both hands on the bullock's head to transfer his sin to it; and thus he made confession: " Ah, Lord God, I have committed iniquity; I have transgressed; I have sinned, I and my house. O Lord, I beseech Thee, cover over the sins and transgressions which I have committed, transgressed and sinned before Thee, I and my house." The greatest of all the Levitical sacrifices began with a sacrifice for the sin of the High Priest himself. That is a sacrifice that Jesus never needed to make, for He was without sin. The Levitical High Priest was a sinful man offering animal sacrifices for sinful people; Jesus was the sinless Son of God, offering Himself for the sin of all men. It was the law which had appointed the Levitical High Priest; it was the very oath of God which gave Jesus His office; and, because He was what He was, the sinless Son of God, Jesus was perfectly equipped for His office as no human High Priest could ever be.

And then the writer to the Hebrews does what in his letter he so often does. He drops a marker to indicate the direction in which he is going to go. He says of Jesus that *He offered himself*. Two things were necessary in a sacrifice. There was the priest who offered the sacrifice and there was the sacrifice itself. With long and intricate argument the writer to the Hebrews has proved that Jesus is the perfect High Priest; and now he is going to move on to another thought. Not only was Jesus the perfect High Priest, *He was also the perfect offering*. The writer to the Hebrews is going to go on to show that Jesus alone can open the way to God because He is the

perfect High Priest and He offered the one perfect sacrifice
—even the sacrifice of Himself.

There is much in this argument which for us is difficult
to understand. It speaks and thinks in terms of ritual
and ceremony which are long since forgotten; but one
eternal thing remains. Man seeks the presence of God;
man's sin has erected a barrier between him and God;
man is restless until he rests in God; and Jesus alone is
the priest who can bring the only offering that can open
the way back to God for men.

THE WAY TO REALITY

Hebrews 8: 1-6

> The pith of what we are saying is this—it is just such a
> high priest we possess, a priest who has taken His
> seat at the right hand of the throne of majesty in
> the heavens, a high priest who is a minister of the
> sanctuary and of the real tabernacle, which the
> Lord, and not man, founded. For every high priest is
> appointed to offer gifts and sacrifices. It is therefore
> necessary that He should have something which He
> might offer. If then He had been upon earth, He
> would not even have been a priest, for there already
> exist those who offer the gifts the law lays down,
> men whose service is but a shadowy outline of the
> heavenly order, just as Moses received instructions
> when he was about to complete the tabernacle—
> " See," it says, " that you do everything according
> to the pattern that was shown to you on the mountain."
> But, as things are, He has obtained a more excellent
> ministry, in so far as He is also the mediator of a
> better covenant, a covenant which was enacted on
> the basis of superior promises.

THE writer to the Hebrews has finished describing the
priesthood after the order of Melchizedek in all its glory.
He has described it as the priesthood which is for ever
without beginning and without end; the priesthood that
God confrmed with an oath; the priesthood that is founded
on personal greatness and not on any legal appointment

or racial qualification; the priesthood which death cannot touch; the priesthood which is able to offer a sacrifice that never needs to be repeated; the priesthood which is so pure that it has no necessity to offer sacrifice for any sins of its own. Now he makes and underlines his great claim. " It is," he says, " a priest precisely like that that we have in Jesus Christ." Jesus alone fulfils the conditions of the perfect priest. He goes on to say two things about Jesus. (i) Jesus took His seat at the right hand of the throne of majesty in the heavens. That is the final proof of *the glory* of Jesus.

> " The highest place that heaven affords
> Is His, is His by right,
> The King of kings, and Lord of lords,
> And heaven's eternal light."

There can be no glory greater than the glory of the ascended and exalted Jesus. His glory is nothing less than the glory of the majesty of God. (ii) He says that Jesus is a minister of the sanctuary. That is the proof of *the service* of Jesus. He is unique both in majesty and in service. Jesus never looked on majesty as something to be selfishly enjoyed. He did not look on majesty as something to be conferred on Him for His own sake. One of the very greatest of the Roman Emperors was Marcus Aurelius. As an administrator he was unsurpassed; he died at fifty-nine, having worked himself to death in the service of his people. He was one of the Stoic saints. When he knew that he was chosen to succeed in due time to the imperial power, as his biographer Capitolinus tells us: " He was appalled rather than overjoyed, and when he was told to move to the private house of Hadrian, the Emperor, it was with reluctance that he departed from his mother's villa. And, when the members of the household asked him why he was sorry to receive the royal adoption, he enumerated to them the toils which sovereignty involved." Marcus Aurelius saw kingship in terms of service and not of majesty. The motto of the Prince of

Wales was: " I serve." Jesus is the unique example of divine majesty and divine service combined. He knew that He had been given His supreme position, not jealously to guard it in splendid isolation, but rather to enable others to attain to it and to share it. He had received glory to enable others to enter into glory. In Him the supreme majesty and the supreme service met.

And now there enters into the picture a thought that was never far from the mind of the writer to the Hebrews. Let us remember what he considered religion to be. Religion to him was *access to God*; it was fellowship with God; it was the right to enter into the presence of God. Therefore the supreme function of any priest is to open the way to God for men. The priest removes the barriers between God and man. He builds that bridge across which a man can go into the presence of God. But we can put this another way. Instead of talking about *access to God* we might talk about *access to reality*. We must remember that every religious writer has to search for terms which the people to whom he is writing will understand. He has to present his message in language and in thoughts which will get home because they are familiar to his readers, or at least because they strike a chord in the reader's mind. Now the Greeks had a basic thought which was ever in their thinking about the universe. They thought in terms of two worlds. One was the real world and one the unreal world. They believed that somewhere there was a world of reality; but they believed that this world of space and time was only a world of shadows, of pale copies, of unreal reflections of the real world. That was the basic doctrine of Plato, the greatest of all the Greek thinkers. He believed in what he called *forms*. Somewhere there was a world where there was laid up the perfect patterns, the perfect archtypes, the perfect forms of which everything in this world is an imperfect copy or an imperfect reflection. Sometimes he called the forms *ideas*. Somewhere there is the idea of a chair of which all actual chairs are imperfect copies. Somewhere there is an idea of a horse of which all actual horses are inadequate reflections. The Greeks were fascinated by this conception of a real world of which this world is only a flickering, impermanent, imperfect copy. In this world we walk in shadows; somewhere there is reality. And the great problem in life is how to pass from this world of shadows to the other world of realities. That is the idea of which the writer to the Hebrews makes use. The earthly Temple is a pale copy of the real Temple of God; earthly worship is a remote reflection of real worship; the earthly priesthood is an inadequate shadow of the real priesthood, which can really bring men to God. All these things point beyond themselves to the reality of which they are the shadows. The writer to the Hebrews even finds that idea in the Old Testament itself. When Moses had received from God instructions about the construction of the tabernacle and all its furnishings, God said to him: " And look that thou make them after their pattern, which was shewed thee in the mount " (Exodus 25: 40). God had shown Moses the real and eternal pattern of which all earthly worship is the ghost-like copy. So then the writer to the Hebrews says that the earthly priests have a service which is but a *shadowy outline* of the heavenly order. For *shadowy outline* he combines two Greek words. The one is *hupodeigma*, which means *a specimen*, or, still better, a sketch-plan. He uses the word *skia*, which means *a shadow*, a reflection, a phantom, a silhouette. The earthly priesthood is unreal and cannot lead men into reality. But Jesus *can* lead men into reality. His is the real priesthood which alone can lead men out of this world of shadows into the real unseen world. We can say that Jesus leads us into the presence of God; we can say that Jesus leads us into reality; it means the same thing. When the writer to the Hebrews spoke of *reality* he was using language that his contemporaries used and understood.

In the highest that this world can offer there is some

imperfection. It never quite reaches to what we know the thing might be. In the greatest love on earth there is still some imperfection; in the highest knowledge on earth there is still some ignorance; in the greatest human achievement there is still some haunting element of something not achieved. Nothing we ever do, or experience, or achieve here quite reaches the ideal that haunts us. The real world is beyond. As Browning had it: " A man's reach should exceed his grasp, or what's a heaven for? " Call it heaven, call it reality, call it the idea or the form, call it God—it all means the same. Reality is beyond.

As the writer to the Hebrews saw it, only Jesus can lead us into that haunting reality; only He can lead us out of the frustrating actuality into the all-satisfying real. So the writer to the Hebrews calls Jesus by a great title. He calls Him the *mediator*, the *mesitēs*. The word *mesitēs* comes from the word *mesos*, which, in this case, means *in the middle*, and a *mesitēs* is *one who stands in the middle between two people and who brings them* together. When Job is desperately anxious that somehow he should be able to put his case to God, he cries out hopelessly: " Neither is there any daysman, *mesitēs*, between us " (Job 9: 33). Paul calls Moses the *mesitēs* (Galatians 3: 19) in that Moses was the one between who brought the law from God to men. In Athens in classical times there were a body of men—all citizens in their sixtieth year—who could be called upon to act as mediators when there was a dispute between two citizens, and their first duty was to effect a reconciliation. In Rome there were *arbitri*. The judge settled points of actual law; but the *arbitri* settled matters of equity; and it was their duty to bring disputes to an end. Further, in legal Greek a *mesitēs* was a *sponsor*, a *guarantor* or a *surety*. He went bail for a friend who was on trial; he guaranteed a debt or an overdraft. The *mesitēs* was the man who was willing to pay his friend's debt to make things right again. The *mesitēs* is the man who stands between and brings together two other parties in reconciliation. Jesus is our perfect *mesitēs*. He stands between the unreality of this world and the reality of the real world; He stands between us and God. He opens the way to reality and to God. He is the only person who can effect this union, this reconciliation between man and God, between the real and the unreal. That is, in effect, to say that Jesus is the only person who can bring us real life. A character in a novel says to another: " I never knew what life was till I saw it in your eyes." There is no one in this universe except Jesus who can introduce us to real life, by introducing us to reality and to God.

THE NEW RELATIONSHIP

Hebrews 8: 7-13

> For, if the first covenant, which is so well known to you, had been faultless there would have been no need to seek any place for a second one. It is to censure them that He says: " Look you the days are coming, says the Lord, when I will consummate a new covenant with the house of Israel and with the house of Judah. It will not be the same as the covenant which I made with their fathers, when I laid my hand on them to lead them forth from the land of Egypt; this must be so because they did not abide by my covenant, and I let them go their own way, says the Lord. It will be different because this is the covenant which I will make with the house of Israel after these days, says the Lord. I will put my laws into their mind and I will inscribe them upon their hearts. I will be to them all that a God should be to them, and they will be to me all that a people should be to me. And no one will teach his fellow citizen and no one will teach his brother, saying, ' Know the Lord,' for all will know me, small and great alike, because I will graciously forgive their iniquities and I will not remember their sins any more." In that He calls the covenant *new*, He has rendered the first covenant out of date; and that which is out of date and ageing into decay is near to final obliteration.

HERE the writer to the Hebrews begins to deal with one of the great basic Biblical ideas—the idea of *a covenant*. In the Bible the word that is always used for a covenant is the Greek word *diathēkē*, and, as we shall see, there was a special reason for the choice of that rather unusual word. Ordinarily a covenant is an agreement entered into by two people. The agreement is dependent on conditions on which they mutually agree; and if either should break the conditions the covenant becomes void. It is sometimes used in that simple sense in the Old Testament. For instance, it is used of the *league* that the Gibeonites wished to make with Joshua (Joshua 9: 6); of the forbidden *league* with the Canaanites (Judges 2: 2); and of David's *covenant* with Jonathan (I Samuel 23: 18). But its distinctive use is to describe the relationship between Israel and God. " Take heed unto yourselves, lest ye forget the *covenant* of the Lord your God " (Deuteronomy 4: 23). In the New Testament the word is also used to describe the relationship between God and man. But there is one strange point which requires explanation. For all normal uses the Greek word for an agreement is *sunthēkē*. *Sunthēkē* is the word for a marriage covenant or bond; it is the word for an agreement between two states. Always in ordinary Greek any kind of bond or agreement or covenant is *sunthēkē*. Further, in all normal Greek *diathēkē* means not an agreement, but *a will*. Why should the New Testament use this unusual word for a covenant? The reason is this—*sunthēkē* always describes an agreement entered into on equal terms. The parties to a *sunthēkē* are on the one level, and each can bargain with the other and propose terms to the other. But God and man do not meet on equal terms. And, in the Biblical sense of a covenant, the whole approach, the whole offer comes from God. It is God who comes to man and who offers this relationship with Himself and who states the terms on which this relationship will remain effective. Man cannot bargain with God; man cannot argue about the terms and conditions of the covenant; man can only accept or reject the offer that God makes; he cannot in any way alter it or alter its terms. Now the supreme example of such an agreement is in fact *a will*. The conditions of a will are not made on equal terms. They are made entirely by one person, the testator, and the other party cannot alter them, and could not even have made them. The will is made by one person, and the other person can only accept or refuse the inheritance as it is offered. That is why our relationship to God is described as a *diathēkē*, a covenant for the terms of which only one person is responsible. Our relationship with God is given to us solely on the initiative and solely on the grace of God. As Philo said: " It is fitting for God to give and for a wise man to receive." When we use the word convenant, and when we think of it in terms of an agreement, we must always remember that it does not and cannot mean that man made a bargain with God on equal terms. It always means that the whole initiative is with God; the terms are God's terms, and man cannot alter them in the slightest.

Now the ancient covenant, which was so well known to the Jews, was the covenant made with the people after the giving of the law. God graciously approached the people of Israel. He offered them a unique and special relationship to Himself; but that relationship was entirely dependent on one thing—it was dependent on the keeping of the law. We see the Israelites accepting that condition in Exodus 24: 1-8. God's covenant with His people offered them a special relationship to Himself, but it was made quite clear that that relationship would only obtain so long as the people obeyed the law of God. The argument of the writer to the Hebrews is that that old covenant is done away with, and Jesus has brought a new covenant, a new relationship with God.

In the thought of this passage we can distinguish certain marks of the new covenant which Jesus brought.

(i) The writer to the Hebrews begins by pointing out that the idea of a new covenant is not something revolutionary. It is already there in the Old Testament in Jeremiah 31: 31-34 which he quotes in full. The idea of a new covenant is not some new and strange heresy which he has invented. It was there in Jeremiah hundreds of years ago. Further, the very fact that scripture itself speaks of the new covenant shows that the old covenant was not fully satisfactory, because if the old covenant had been fully satisfactory a new covenant would never need to have been mentioned. So he begins by pointing out that scripture itself looked to a new covenant, and that therefore scripture itself indicated that the old covenant was not by any means perfect.

(ii) This covenant will not only be new; *it will be different in quality and in kind*. In Greek there are two words for *new*. There is *neos* which describes a thing as being new in point of time. A thing which is *neos* might be a precise copy of its predecessors, but if it is new in point of time, if it has been made since the others, it is *neos*. There is *kainos*, and *kainos* means, not only new in point of time, but new in point of quality. A thing which is simply a reproduction of what went before is new in the sense that it is *neos*, but it is not new in the sense that it is *kainos*. Now this covenant which Jesus introduces is *kainos*, not merely *neos*; it is different in quality from the old covenant. In point of fact the writer to the Hebrews uses two words to describe the old covenant. He says that it is *gēraskōn*, which means, not only *ageing*, but *ageing into decay*. He says that it is near to *aphanismos*. Now *aphanismos* is the word that is used for wiping out a city, obliterating an inscription, or completely abolishing a law. It indicates a complete obliteration or wiping out. So the covenant which Jesus brings is new in quality and it completely obliterates and cancels the old covenant.

(iii) Wherein is this covenant new? *It is new in its scope*. It is going to include *the house of Israel and the house of*

Judah. Now one thousand years before this, in the days of Rehoboam, the kingdom had split into two; it had split into Israel with the ten tribes, and Judah with the two; and these two sections had never come together again. The new covenant is a covenant which is going to unite that which has been divided. It is going to close the schisms; in it the old enemies will be at one.

(iv) *It is new in its universality.* All men will know God from the least to the greatest. That was something quite new. In the ordinary life of the Jews there was a complete cleavage. On the one hand there were the Pharisees and the orthodox who kept the law; on the other hand there were what were contemptuously called The People of the Land. They were the ordinary common people who did not fully observe all the details of the ceremonial law. They were completely despised. It was forbidden to have any fellowship with them; to marry one's daughter to them was as bad, and worse, than to throw her to a wild beast; it was forbidden to go on a journey with them; it was even forbidden, as far as it was possible, to have any trade or business dealings with them. To the rigid observers of the law the ordinary people were beyond the pale. But in the new covenant these breaches would no longer exist. All men would be under it. There would be no specially privileged class. All men, wise and simple, great and small, would know the Lord. The doors which had been shut were thrown wide open.

(v) But there was one even more fundamental difference. The old covenant depended on obedience to an externally imposed law. *The new covenant was to be written upon men's hearts and minds.* We may put it in another way— men would obey God, not because of the terror of punishment, but because they loved God in their hearts. Men would obey God, not because the law ordered them unwillingly to do so, but because the desire to obey Him was written on their very hearts. It would not be an

external law which would effect an unwilling obedience.
The desire to obey would be in a man's own heart.

(vi) It would be a covenant *which would really effect
forgiveness.* Now see how that forgiveness was to come.
*God said that He would be gracious to their iniquities and
would forget their sins.* Now it is all of God. The new
relationship is based entirely on the love of God. Under
the old covenant a man could keep this relationship to
God only by obeying the law; that is, he must keep it
by his own efforts. Now everything is dependent, not
on man's efforts, but solely on the grace and the love and
the mercy of God. The new covenant puts men into
relationship with a God, who is still a God of justice. but
a God whose justice has been swallowed up in His love.
The most tremendous thing about the new covenant
was that it made man's relationship to God no longer
dependent on man's obedience. It became entirely dependent on God's love.

One thing remains to say. In Jeremiah's words about the
new covenant there is no mention of sacrifice at all. It
would seem that Jeremiah believed that in the new age
sacrifice would be abolished as irrelevant; but the writer
to the Hebrews cannot think except in terms of the sacrificial system; and very shortly, as we shall see, he will go
on to speak of Jesus as Himself the perfect sacrifice, whose
death alone made the new covenant possible for men.

THE GLORY OF THE TABERNACLE

Hebrews 9: 1-5

So, then, the first tabernacle too had its ordinances
of worship, and its holy place which was an earthly
symbol of the divine realities. For the first tabernacle
was constructed and in it there was the lampstand
and the table with the shewbread, and it was called
the Holy Place. Behind the second curtain there was
that part of the tabernacle which was called the
Holy of Holies. It was approached by means of the

golden altar of incense, and it had in it the ark of the covenant, which was covered all over with gold. In the ark there was the golden pot with the manna, and Aaron's rod which budded, and the tables of the covenant. Above it there were the cherubim of glory, overshadowing the mercy seat; but this is not the place to speak about all these things in detail.

THE writer to the Hebrews has just been thinking of Jesus as the one who leads us into reality. He has been using the idea that in this world we have only shadows and pale copies of that which is truly real. The worship that men can offer is only a pale copy and ghostlike shadow of the real worship, which Jesus, the real High Priest, alone can offer. But even as he thinks of that his mind goes back to the Tabernacle. We must remember that it is the Tabernacle and not the Temple that he is thinking of. Lovingly he remembers its beauty and its loveliness; lovingly he lingers on it and its priceless possessions. And the thought that is in his mind is this—if this earthly worship was as lovely, as beautiful, as moving as this, what must the true worship be like? If all the loveliness of the Tabernacle was only a shadow of reality, how surpassingly lovely reality must be. He does not tell of the Tabernacle in detail; he only alludes to certain of its treasures. He did not need to tell of it in detail, because his readers knew its glories and had them printed on their memories. But we do not know them; therefore, let us see what the beauty of the earthly Tabernacle was like, always remembering that all this was only a pale, shadowy copy of reality.

The main description of the Tabernacle in the wilderness is in Exodus 25-31 and 35-40. God said to Moses: " Make me a sanctuary that I may dwell among them " (Exodus 25: 8). It was made and constructed out of the freewill offerings of the people (Exodus 25: 1-7), and the people gave with such open-hearted and lavish generosity that they gave so much that a halt had to be called to their giving (Exodus 36: 5-7). *The Court of the Tabernacle* was 150 feet long and 75 feet wide. It was surrounded by a curtain-like fence of fine, twined linen 7½ feet high. The white linen stood for the wall of holiness that surrounds the presence of God. The curtain was supported by twenty pillars on the north and south sides, and by ten on the east and west sides, and the pillars were set in sockets of brass and had tops of silver. There was only one gate. It was on the east side and it was 30 feet wide and 7½ feet high. It was made of fine, twined linen wrought with blue and purple and scarlet. In the court itself there were two things. There was the *Brazen Altar*. The altar was 7½ feet square and 4½ feet high. It was made of acacia wood sheathed in brass. Its top was a brazen grating on which the sacrifice was laid; and it had four horns to which the offering was bound. There was *The Laver*. The laver was made from the brass mirrors of the women (glass mirrors did not exist at that time). Its dimensions are not given. The priests bathed themselves in the water in it to cleanse themselves before they carried out their sacred duties.

The Tabernacle itself was constructed of forty-eight acacia beams, 15 feet high and 2 feet 3 inches wide. They were overlaid with pure gold, and rested in sockets of silver. They were bound together by outside connecting rods and by a wooden tie-beam which ran through the centre of them. The Tabernacle was divided into two parts. The first part—two-thirds of the whole—was *The Holy Place*; the inner part, one-third of the whole, a cube 15 feet on each side, was *The Holy of Holies*. The curtain which hung in front of *The Holy Place* was supported on five brass pillars and was made of fine linen wrought in blue, purple and scarlet. *The Holy Place* contained three things. (i) There was *The Golden Lampstand*. It stood on the south side; it was beaten out of a talent of solid gold, whose value would be £5,000; the lamps were fed with pure olive oil, and were always lit. (ii) On the north side stood *The Table of the Shewbread*. It was made of acacia wood covered with gold; it was 3 feet long, 1½ feet wide and 2 feet 3 inches high. On it there were laid every Sabbath twelve loaves made of the finest flour, in two rows of six. Only the priests could eat these loaves when they were removed. They were changed every Sabbath. (iii) There was *The Altar of Incense*. It was of acacia wood sheathed in gold; it was 1½ feet square and 3 feet high. On it incense, symbolising the prayers of the people rising to God, was burned every morning and every evening.

In front of *The Holy of Holies* there was *The Veil* which was made of fine, twined linen, embroidered in scarlet and purple and blue, and with the cherubim upon it. Into *The Holy of Holies* no one but the High Priest might enter, and he might enter only once a year, on the Day of Atonement, and only after the most elaborate preparations. Within The Holy of Holies there stood *The Ark of the Covenant*. It contained three things—the golden pot of the manna, Aaron's rod that budded, and the tables of the law. It was made of acacia wood sheathed outside and lined inside with gold. It was 3 feet 9 inches long, 2 feet 3 inches wide, and 2 feet 3 inches high. The lid of it was called *The Mercy Seat*. On The Mercy Seat there were the two Cherubim of solid gold with their over-arching wings. It was there that the very presence of God rested, for God had said: " I will commune with thee from above the mercy seat, from between the two cherubim which are upon the ark of the testimony " (Exodus 25: 22).

It was of all this beauty that the writer to the Hebrews was thinking—and this beauty was only a shadow of reality. And in his mind there was another thing of which he will speak again—the ordinary Israelite could come only to the gate of the Tabernacle court; the priests and the Levites might enter the court; the priests alone might enter the Holy Place; and none but the High Priest might enter the Holy of Holies. There was beauty but it was a beauty in which the common man was barred from the inner presence of God. Jesus Christ took that barrier away, and opened the way to the secret of God's presence to every man. In Christ the shut door had become wide open.

THE ONLY ENTRY TO THE PRESENCE OF GOD

Hebrews 9: 6-10

> Since these preparations have been made, the priests continually enter into the first tabernacle as they perform the various acts of worship. But into the second tabernacle the High Priest alone enters, and that once a year, and not without blood which he offers for himself and for the errors of the people. By this the Holy Spirit is showing that the way into the Holy Place was not yet opened up, so long as the first tabernacle stood. Now the first tabernacle stands for this present age, and according to its services sacrifices are offered which cannot perfect the conscience of the worshipper, but which, since they are based on food and drink and various kinds of washings, are human regulations, laid down until the time of the new order should come.

WE have seen that the priests could enter into the court and the Holy Place of the Tabernacle, but that only the High Priest could enter into the Holy of Holies. The one day of all the year when he could enter in was *The Day of Atonement,* and it is of the ceremonies of that day that the writer to the Hebrews is here thinking. He did not need to describe them to his readers for they knew them. To them they were the most sacred religious ceremonies in all the world; but we do not know them, and if we are to understand the thought in the mind of the writer to the Hebrews we must have a picture of them in our minds. The main description of them is in Leviticus 16.

First, we must ask, What was the idea which lay behind The Day of Atonement? As we have seen, the relationship between Israel and God was the covenant relationship.

Sin on Israel's part broke that relationship, and the whole
system of sacrifice existed to make atonement for sin, and
to restore the broken relationship. But what if there were
some sins which were still not atoned for? What if there
were some sins of which a man was not conscious because
of his own sinfulness? What if, by some chance, the altar,
the Temple, the Holy Place itself had become tainted and
defiled? What if that were so and men were not even
aware of it? That is to say, what if the whole sacrificial
system was not performing the function that it should
perform? What then? The summary of the whole Day
of Atonement is given in Leviticus 16: 33:

> And he shall make an atonement for the holy
> sanctuary; and he shall make an atonement for the
> tabernacle of the congregation, and for the altar;
> and he shall make an atonement for the priests and
> for all the people of the congregation.

The Day of Atonement was one great comprehensive
act of atonement for all sin and for all uncleanness. It
was one grand day in which all things and all people were
cleansed, in which all uncleanness and all sin were wiped
out, so that the relationship between Israel and God should
continue unbroken. To that end it was a day of humiliation.
" Ye shall afflict your souls " (Leviticus 16: 29). The Day
of Atonement was not a *feast*; it was a *fast*. The whole
nation fasted all day, even the boys and girls; and the
really devout Jew prepared himself for it by fasting for the
ten days which went before. The Day of Atonement comes
ten days after the opening of the Jewish New Year, that
is, about the beginning of September in our calendar.
The Day of Atonement was the greatest of all days in the
life of the High Priest. It was for that day and for its
ceremonies and sacrifices that he really existed.

Let us then see what happened. Very early in the
morning the High Priest cleansed himself by washing.
He donned his gorgeous robes of office, worn only on that
day. There were the white linen breeches and the long

white undergarment reaching down to the feet, woven in one piece. There was *The Robe of the Ephod.* It was dark blue. It was a long robe with at the foot a fringe of blue, purple and scarlet tassels made in the form of pome-granates, interspersed with an equal number of little golden bells. Over this robe he put *The Ephod* itself. The Ephod was probably a kind of linen tunic, embroidered in scarlet and purple and gold, with an elaborate girdle. On the shoulders of it there were two onyx stones. The names of six of the tribes were engraved on one, and six on the other. On the tunic was *The Breastplate,* a span square. On it it had twelve precious stones which had the names of the twelve tribes engraved upon them. So the High Priest carried the people to God on his shoulders and on his heart. In the breastplate there was the *Urim and the Thummim,* which means *lights and perfections* (Exodus 28: 30). What exactly the Urim and the Thummim was is not known. It is known that the High Priest consulted it when he wished to know the will of God. It may be that it was a precious and costly diamond inscribed with the consonants IHWH which are the consonants of the name *Jahweh,* the name of God. On his head the High Priest put the tall *Mitre,* of fine linen; and on the mitre there was a gold plate bound by a band of blue ribbon, and on the plate were the words: " Holiness unto the Lord." It is easy to imagine what a dazzling figure the High Priest must have presented on this his greatest day.

The High Priest began by doing the things that were done every day. He burned the morning incense, made the morning sacrifice, and attended to the trimming of the lamps on the seven-branched lampstand. Then came the first part of the special ritual of the day. Still dressed in his gorgeous robes, the High Priest sacrificed a bullock and seven lambs and one ram (Numbers 29: 7). Then the High Priest removed his gorgeous robes, cleansed himself again in water, and dressed himself in the simple purity of white linen. There was brought to him a bullock bought with his own resources. He placed his hands on the bullock's head, and, standing there in the full sight of the people, confessed his own sin and the sin of his house:

> " Ah, Lord God, I have committed iniquity: I have transgressed: I have sinned—I and my house. O Lord, I entreat Thee, cover over (atone for) the iniquities, the transgressions, and the sins, which I have committed, transgressed, and sinned before Thee, I and my house, even as it is written in the law of Moses, Thy servant, ' For in that day, He will cover over (atone) for you to make you clean. From all your transgressions before the Lord you shall be cleansed.' "

For the moment the bullock was left before the altar. And then followed one of the unique ceremonies of the Day of Atonement. Two goats were standing by, and beside the goats an urn with two lots in it. One lot was marked *For Jehovah*; the other was marked *For Azazel*, which is the phrase which the Authorised Version translates *The Scapegoat*. The lots were drawn and laid one on the head of each goat. A tongue-shaped piece of scarlet was tied to the horn of the scapegoat. And for the moment the goats were left. Then the High Priest turned to the bullock which was beside the altar, and killed it. Its throat was slit and the blood caught by a priest in a basin. The basin was kept in motion so that the blood would not coagulate for soon it was to be used. Then came the first of the great moments. The High Priest took coals from the altar and put them in a censer; he took incense and put it in a special dish; and then he walked into the Holy of Holies to burn incense in the very presence of God. It was laid down that he must not stay too long " lest he put Israel in terror." The people literally watched with bated breath; and when he came out from the presence of God still alive, there went up a sigh of relief like a gust of wind.

When the High Priest came out from the Holy of Holies, he took the basin of the bullock's blood and he went back into the Holy of Holies. He took the blood and sprinkled the blood seven times up and seven times down within the Holiest of Holies. He came out; he killed the goat that was marked *For Jehovah*. Once again, with its blood, he re-entered the Holy of Holies and sprinkled again. Then he came out and mingled together the blood of the bullock and the goat and seven times he sprinkled the horns of the altar of the incense and the altar itself. What remained of the blood was laid at the foot of the altar of the burnt offering. Thus the Holy of Holies, the Holy Place, the altar were cleansed by blood from any defilement that might be on them. Atonement was made by blood.

Then came the most vivid ceremony. The scapegoat was brought forward. The High Priest laid his hands on it and confessed his own sin and the sin of the people, and the goat was led forth into the desert, " into a land not inhabited," laden with the sins of the people and there it was killed. The sins of the people had been laid upon the scapegoat.

The priest then turned to the slain bullock and goat and prepared them for sacrifice. Still in his linen garments he read scripture—Leviticus 16; 23: 27-32, and repeated by heart Numbers 29: 7-11. He then prayed for the priesthood and the people. Once again he cleansed himself in water and rearrayed himself in his gorgeous robes. He sacrificed, first, a kid of the goats for the sins of the people; then he made the normal evening sacrifice; then he sacrificed the already prepared parts of the bullock and the goat. Then once again he cleansed himself; took off his robes; and put on the white line again; and for the fourth and last time he entered the Holy of Holies to remove the censer of incense which still burned there. Once again he cleansed himself in water; once again he put on his vivid robes; then he burned the evening offering of incense; trimmed the lamps on the golden lampstand; and his work was done. In the evening he held a feast because he had been in the presence of God and had come out alive.

Such was the ritual of the Day of Atonement. That was the day which was designed to cleanse all things and all people from sin. That was the picture which was in the mind's eye of the writer to the Hebrews. He will make much of it. But there were certain things which were in his mind. Every year this ceremony had to be done again and again. Everyone but the High Priest was barred from the presence and even he entered in in terror. The cleansing was the purely external cleansing by baths of water. The sacrifice was the sacrifice of bulls and goats and animal blood—and the whole thing failed because such things cannot atone for sin. In it all the writer to the Hebrews sees a pale copy of the reality, a ghostly pattern of the one true sacrifice—the sacrifice of Christ. It was a noble ritual; it was a thing of dignity and beauty; but it was only an unavailing shadow. The only priest and the only sacrifice which can open the way to God for *all* men is Jesus Christ.

THE SACRIFICE WHICH OPENS THE WAY TO GOD

Hebrews 9: 11-14

> But when Christ arrived upon the scene, a High Priest of the good things which are to come, by means of a tabernacle which was greater and better able to produce the results for which it was meant, a tabernacle not made by the hands of men—that is, a tabernacle which did not belong to this world order—and not by the blood of goats and bullocks, but by His own blood, He entered once and for all into the Holy Place, because He had secured for us an eternal redemption. For, if the blood of goats and bulls and the ashes of a heifer, could by sprinkling cleanse those that were unclean so that their bodies became pure, how much more will the blood of Christ, who, through the eternal Spirit, offered Himself spotless to God, cleanse your conscience, so that you will be able to leave the deeds that make for death in order to become the servants of the living God?

WHEN we try to understand the meaning of this passage, we must begin by remembering three things which are basic and fundamental to the thought of the writer to the Hebrews. These three things are always in his mind and in his thought. The three things are: (i) Religion is access to God. The whole function of all religion is to bring a man into the presence of God. (ii) This world is a world of pale shadows and imperfect copies; beyond this world there is the world of realities. The function of all worship is to bring men into contact with the eternal realities. That was what the worship and ritual of the Tabernacle was meant to do; but the earthly Tabernacle is a pale copy of the real and the heavenly Tabernacle; the earthly worship is a remote reflection of the real worship; and it is only the real Tabernacle and the real worship which can give access to reality. (iii) There can be no religion without sacrifice. Purity is a costly thing; the access to God demands purity; man's sin must somehow be atoned for; man's uncleanness must somehow be cleansed. Until that happens there can be no access for men to God. With these ideas in his mind the writer to the Hebrews goes on to show that Jesus is the only High Priest who can bring men to God; that He alone brings a sacrifice which can open the way to God; and that that sacrifice is Himself.

So, to begin with, the writer to the Hebrews refers to certain of the great sacrifices which the Jews were in the habit of making under the old covenant with God. (i) There was the sacrifice of *bullocks* and of *goats*. In this he is referring to two of the great sacrifices on The Day of Atonement—the sacrifice of the bullock which the High Priest made for his own sins, and the sacrifice of the scapegoat which was led away to the wilderness bearing the sins of the people upon it (Leviticus 16: 15, 21, 22). We have already seen the part that these sacrifices played in the ritual of The Day of Atonement. (ii) There was the sacrifice of the *red heifer*. This strange ritual is described in Numbers 19. Under Jewish ceremonial law, if a man touched a dead body, he was unclean. He was barred from the worship of God, and everything and everyone he touched became unclean. To deal with this there was a method of cleansing of which the ritual was as follows. A red heifer was slaughtered outside the camp. The priest sprinkled the blood of the heifer before the Tabernacle seven times. The body of the beast was then burned, together with cedar and hyssop and a piece of red cloth. The resulting ashes were laid up outside the camp in a clean place, and they constituted a purification for sin. Both the origin and the meaning of this ritual are quite obscure. It must have been very ancient, so ancient that it was wrapped in obscurity. The Jews themselves told that once a Gentile questioned Rabbi Jochanan ben Zakkai on the meaning of this rite, and declared that it sounded like pure superstition and magic; the Rabbi's answer was that it had been appointed by the Holy One and that men must not enquire into His reasons and that the matter must be left there without explanation. In any event, although the meaning and the origin are beyond explanation, the fact remains that it was one of the great and sacred rites of the Jews.

The writer to the Hebrews tells of these sacrifices and then declares that the sacrifice that Jesus brings is far greater and far more effective. We must first ask, What does the writer to the Hebrews mean by the greater and the better and the more effective tabernacle, the tabernacle not made with hands, the tabernacle which really brought men into the presence of God? That is a difficult question, and a question to which no one can give an answer which is beyond dispute. But the ancient scholars nearly all took it in one way; they said that this new tabernacle which brought men into the very presence of God was nothing else than the body of Jesus. He came here in a body, in a tabernacle. And by so coming He brought God to men and He brought men into the presence of God.

It would be another way of saying what John said: " He who has seen me has seen the Father " (John 14: 9). The worship of the ancient tabernacle was designed to bring men into the presence of God. That it could do only in the most shadowy and imperfect way. The coming of Jesus really and truly brought men into the presence of God, because in Him God entered this world of space and time in a human form. To see Jesus is to see what God is like.

Now we must ask, Wherein lay the great superiority of the sacrifice which Jesus brought? It lay in three things. (i) The ancient sacrifices cleansed a man's body from ceremonial uncleanness; the sacrifice of Jesus cleansed men's souls. We must always remember one thing—in theory all sacrifice cleansed from sins against the ritual law and the legal requirements of the law; it did not cleanse from sins of the presumptuous heart and the high hand. Take the case of the red heifer. It was not *moral* uncleanness that sacrifice wiped out; it did not cleanse from *sin*; what it did cleanse from was the cere-monial, bodily uncleanness consequent upon touching a dead body. A man's body might be clean in the cere-monial sense; but his heart might be torn with remorse and anguished with regret; he might feel that he could enter the tabernacle and was yet far away from the presence of God. He might feel that the barrier to ritual worship was removed, but that the door to God's presence was still shut. The sacrifice of Jesus takes the load of guilt from a man's *conscience*. Jesus by living and by dying so brought to men the picture of the love of God, that they knew that the way to a God who loves like that is always wide open. The animal sacrifices of the old covenant might well leave a man in estrangement from God; the sacrifice of Jesus shows us a God whose arms are always outstretched to us and in whose heart is only love. (ii) The sacrifice of Jesus brought eternal redemption. The idea is that men were under the dominion of sin; they were under the slavery of sin; and just as the purchase price has to be paid to free a man from slavery, so the purchase price has to be paid to free a man from sin. Man is so involved in sin that he cannot free himself from it; it takes the power of Christ to give him liberty. (iii) The sacrifice of Christ enables a man to leave the deeds of death and to become the servant of the living God. That is to say, Jesus does not only win forgiveness for a man's past sin; He enables him in the future to live a godly life. The sacrifice of Jesus does not only look backwards; it looks forwards too. It does not only make a man a forgiven man; it makes a man a good man too. It is not only the paying of a debt; it is the giving of a victory. What Jesus did puts a man right with God and what Jesus does enables a man to stay right with God. The act of the Cross brings to men the love of God in a way that takes their terror of God away; the presence of the living Christ brings to men the power of God so that they can win a daily victory over sin.

Westcott finely lays down four ways in which Jesus's sacrifice of Himself differs from the animal sacrifices of the old covenant.

(i) The sacrifice of Jesus is *voluntary*. An animal dies because it has to die; Jesus chose to die. An animal's life is taken from it; Jesus *gave* His life. The sacrifice of Jesus was not forcibly extracted from Him. He willingly laid down His life for His friends.

(ii) The sacrifice of Jesus was *spontaneous*. An animal sacrifice was made because the regulations and ordinances of the law laid it down that it should be made. Animal sacrifice was entirely *the product of law*; the sacrifice of Jesus is entirely *the product of love*. We pay our debts to a tradesman because we have to; we give a gift to our loved ones because we want to. It is not law but love that lies behind the sacrifice of Christ.

(iii) The sacrifice of Jesus was *rational*. The animal victim did not know what was happening or what it was doing. It did not think and reason. Jesus all the time knew what He was doing. He died, not as an ignorant victim caught up in circumstances over which He had no control and did not understand; He died open-eyed and knowing whence He had come, whither He was going, and what He was doing.

(iv) The sacrifice of Jesus was *moral*. Animal sacrifice is mechanical. The ritual was carried out in the prescribed way. The wheels of the regulations ground out their routine. But Jesus' sacrifice was made, as the writer to the Hebrews says, through *the eternal Spirit*. It was not legal mechanism that was working in the sacrifice of Jesus; it was the Spirit of God. This thing on Calvary was not done because of any prescribed ritual mechanically carried out. It was done because the will of Jesus obeyed the will of God, for the sake of men. Behind it there was not the mechanism of law, but the choice of love.

THE ONLY WAY IN WHICH SINS CAN BE FORGIVEN

Hebrews 9: 15-22

It is through Him that there emerges a new covenant between God and man; and the purpose behind this new covenant is that those who have been called might receive the eternal inheritance which has been promised to them; but this could only happen after a death had taken place, the purpose of which was to rescue them from the consequences of the trans-gressions which had been committed under the conditions of the old covenant. For where there is a will, it is necessary that there should be evidence of the death of the testator before the will is valid. It is in the case of dead people that a will is confirmed, since surely it cannot be operative when the testator is still alive. That is why even the first covenant was not inaugurated without blood. For, after every commandment which the law lays down had been announced by Moses to all the people, he took the blood of calves and goats, together with water and scarlet and hyssop, and sprinkled the book itself, and all the people. And, as he did so, he said: " This is the blood of the covenant whose conditions God commanded you to observe." In like manner he sprinkled with blood the tabernacle also, and all the instruments used in its worship.   Under the conditions which the law lays down it is true to say that almost everything is cleansed by blood. Without the shedding of blood there is no forgiveness.

THIS is one of the most difficult passages in the whole letter to the Hebrews. It would not be difficult to those who read the letter for the first time, for it is using methods of argument and expression, and categories of thought which were familiar to them, although they are quite alien to us.

As we have seen, the idea of the *covenant* is basic to the thought of the writer of the letter to the Hebrews; by a *covenant* he meant a relationship between God and man. Now the first covenant was dependent on man's keeping of the law. As soon as he broke the law the covenant became ineffective. Let us remember the basic idea of our writer of the meaning and the function of religion. *Religion means access to God.* Therefore, the basic meaning of the *new covenant*, which Jesus brought and inaugurated, is that men should have access to God, that, to put it in another way, we should have *fellowship* with God.   But here is the difficulty.   Men come to the new covenant already stained with the sins and the disobediences committed under the old covenant. They come already guilty of breaches of the law.   They come as already having committed sins for which the old sacrificial system was powerless to atone.   So, then, the writer to the Hebrews has a tremendous thought—he says that the sacrifice of Jesus Christ is retroactive.   That is to say, the sacrifice of Christ is effective to wipe out the consequences of the sins of men committed under the old covenant, and to inaugurate the fellowship which is promised under the new covenant.

Now all that seems very difficult and complicated, but, at the back of it, and at the heart of it, there are two great eternal truths. First, the sacrifice of Jesus gains for us forgiveness for our past sins. We ought to be punished for what we have done; we ought to be shut out from God because of all our sins and disobediences; but because of what Jesus did the past is cancelled, the debt is wiped out, God has put our sins behind His back, the breach is forgiven and the barrier is taken away. Second, the sacrifice of Jesus opens to us a new life for the future. It opens for us the way to fellowship with God. The God whom our sins had made a stranger, the sacrifice of Christ has made a friend. Through Jesus Christ it is now open to us to live life in the daily friendship and fellowship of God. Because of what Jesus Christ did and is, the burden of the past is rolled away, and life in the future becomes life with God.

But it is the next step in the argument which appears to us a fantastic way in which to argue. The question in the mind of the writer to the Hebrews is this—Why should this new relationship with God involve the *death* of Christ? Why had He to *die* before the new relationship became effective and operative? He answers that question in two ways.

(i) His first answer is—to us almost incredibly—founded on nothing other than a pun on words. We have seen that the word for *covenant* is *diathēkē*. But we have also seen that the use of *diathēkē* in the sense of *covenant* is characteristically Christian, and that the normal secular use of *diathēkē* was in the sense of *will* or *testament*. Now up to verse 16 the writer to the Hebrews has been using *diathēkē* in the normal Christian sense of *covenant*, and then, suddenly and with no warning and with no explanation of what he is doing, he switches to the sense of *will*. Now a **will** does not become operative and effective until the testator dies; the death of the testator is a prerequisite without which the will cannot come into operation. So the writer to the Hebrews says that no *diathēkē, will,* can be operative until the death of the testator, therefore the new *diathēkē, covenant,* cannot become operative apart from the death of Jesus Christ. Clearly that is a merely verbal argument, and equally clearly it is quite unconvincing to a modern mind; but it must be remembered that this founding of an argument on a play between two meanings of a word was actually a favourite method of the Alexandrian scholars in the time when this letter was written. In fact this very argument which seems so fantastic and unconvincing to us would have been considered in the days when the letter to the Hebrews was written an exceedingly clever piece of exposition. Such an argument would have been greeted with admiring respect and not with incredulous surprise.

(ii) His second answer is to go back to the Hebrew sacrificial system. He goes back to a very basic verse in Leviticus 17: 11: " The life of the flesh is in the blood; and I have given it to you upon the altar to make an atonement for your souls; *for it is the blood that maketh an atonement for the soul."* " Without the shedding of blood there can be no atonement for sin," was actually a well-known and definitely stated Hebrew principle. So the writer to the Hebrews goes back to the inauguration of the first covenant under Moses, the occasion when the people accepted the law as the condition of their special relationship with God. There we are told how sacrifice was made and how Moses " took half of the blood and put it in basons; and half of it he sprinkled on the altar." And after the book of the law had been read and the people had signified their acceptance of it, Moses " took the blood and sprinkled it on the people, and said, ' Behold the blood of the covenant which the Lord hath made with you concerning these words ' " (Exodus 24: 1-8). It is quite true that the memory of the writer to the Hebrews of that passage was not strictly accurate. He introduces calves and goats and scarlet and hyssop which come from the ritual of The Day of Atonement, but that is because that day is so much in his mind. He talks about the sprinkling of the Tabernacle, which at that time had not yet been built; but again the Tabernacle is much in his mind. His basic idea is that there can be no cleansing and purifying, there can be no ratification of any covenant without the shedding of blood. *Why* that should be so, he does not know and does not need to think. Scripture says that it is so and that is enough for him and for his argument. The probable reason is that blood is life, as the Hebrew saw it, and life is the most precious thing in the world; and man must offer life's most precious thing to God.

Now all that goes back to a ritual which is only of antiquarian interest. But at the back of it there is one eternal principle which will be valid as long as the world lasts. The principle is—*Forgiveness is a costly thing. Human forgiveness* is costly. A son or a daughter may go wrong; a father or a mother may forgive; but that forgiveness has brought tears; it has brought whiteness to the hair, lines to the face, a cutting anguish and then a long dull ache to the heart. It did not cost nothing. There was the price of a broken heart to pay. *Divine forgiveness* is costly. God is love, but God is *holiness*. God, least of all, can break the great moral laws on which the universe is built. Sin must have its punishment or the very structure of life disintegrates. And God alone can pay the terrible price that is necessary before men can be forgiven. Forgiveness is never a case of saying: " It's all right; it doesn't matter." Forgiveness is the most costly thing in the world. Without the shedding of heart's blood there can be no remission and forgiveness of sins. There is nothing which brings a man to his senses with such arresting violence as to see the effect of his sin on someone who loves him in this world, or on the God who loves him for ever, and to say to himself: " It cost *that* to forgive *my* sin." Where there is forgiveness someone must be crucified on a cross.

THE PERFECT PURIFICATION

Hebrews 9: 23-28

> So, then, if it was necessary that the things which
> are copies of the heavenly realities should be cleansed
> by processes like these, it is necessary that the heavenly
> realities themselves should be cleansed by finer
> sacrifices than those of which we have been thinking.
> It is not into a man-made sanctuary that Christ has
> entered—that would be a mere symbol of the things
> which are real. It is into heaven itself that He entered,
> now to appear on our behalf before the presence of
> God. It is not that He has to offer Himself repeatedly,
> as the High Priest year by year enters into the Holy
> Place with a blood that is not his own. Were that so
> He would have had to suffer again and again since
> the world was founded. But, now as things are, once
> and for all, at the end of the ages, He has appeared
> with His sacrifice of Himself, so that our sins should
> be cancelled. And just as it is laid down for men to
> die once and for all, and then to face the judgment,
> so Christ, after being once and for all sacrificed, to
> bear the burden of the sins of many, will appear a
> second time, not this time to deal with sin, but for
> the salvation of those who are waiting for Him.

HERE the writer to the Hebrews is still thinking of the
supreme efficacy of the sacrifice which Jesus made; and
he begins with a flight of thought, which, even for so
adventurous a writer as he was, is amazing. Let us remember again the basic thought of the letter. The worship
of this world is a pale copy of the real worship. In this
world there is a worship which can give a man a shadow
of real fellowship with God; in the world to come there
is a worship whereby a man will really know God. Now the
writer to the Hebrews says that in this world the Levitical
sacrifices were designed to purify the means of worship.
For instance, the sacrifices of the Day of Atonement
purified the tabernacle and the altar and the Holy Place;
and now he goes on to say that the work of Christ purifies
not only earth but heaven. He has the tremendous thought
that the work of Christ had its effect on heaven and earth

alike. It is the picture of a kind of cosmic redemption that purified the whole universe, seen and unseen.

So he goes on to stress again the way in which the work and the sacrifice of Christ are supreme.

(i) Jesus Christ entered into no human, man-made Holy Place; He entered into the presence of God in heaven. What Jesus gives us is not entry to a Church, but entry to the presence of God. We are to think of Christianity not in terms of Church membership, but in terms of intimate fellowship with God.

(ii) Christ entered into the presence of God, not only for His own sake, but for ours. His entry into the presence of God was not only for His own glory and exaltation; it was to open the way for us; it was so that He could stand in the very presence of God and plead our cause. In Christ there is the greatest paradox in the world, the paradox of the greatest glory and the greatest service, the paradox of one for whom the world exists and who exists for the world, the paradox of the eternal King and the eternal Servant.

(iii) The sacrifice of Christ has been made and never needs to be made again. Year after year the ritual of the Day of Atonement had to go on. Year after year the things that blocked the road to God had to be atoned for; but Christ's sacrifice never needs to be made again. The road to God is for ever open and can never be closed again. Men were always sinners and always will be, but that does not mean that Christ must go on offering Himself again and again. The road is open once and for all. We can have a faint analogy of that. Some things need only be done once and a new road, never to be closed, is opened up. Take the case of a surgical technique. For long a certain surgical operation may be impossible. Then some surgeon finds a way round the difficulties. From that day that same road is open to all surgeons; that same cure is open to all sufferers from that disease; once and for all the road is open. We may put it this way—nothing need ever be added to what Jesus Christ has done to open and to keep open the way to God's love for sinning men.

Finally, the writer to the Hebrews draws a parallel between the life of man and the life of Christ.

(i) Man dies and then comes the judgment. Now that itself was a shock to the Greek. On the whole the Greek believed that man died, and that was final. " When earth once drinks the blood of a man," said Aeschylus, " there is death once and for all and there is no resurrection." Euripides says: " It cannot be the dead to light shall come." " For the one loss is this that never mortal maketh good again—the life of man though wealth may be re-won." As Homer makes Achilles say when he reaches the shades: " Rather would I live upon the soil as the hireling of another, with a landless man whose livelihood was small, than bear sway among all the dead who are no more." Mimnermus writes with a kind of despair:

> " O Golden love, what life, what joy but thine?
>   Come death, when thou art gone, and make an
>   end ! "

There is a simple Greek epitath:

> " Farewell, tomb of Melitē; the best of women lies here, who loved her loving husband, Onesimus; thou were most excellent, wherefore he longs for thee after thy death, for thou wert the best of wives. Farewell thou too, dearest husband, only love my children."

As G. Lowes Dickinson points out, in the Greek, in the face of death, the first and last word of that epitaph is " Farewell ! " Death was the end. When Tacitus is writing the tribute of biography to the great Agricola all that he can finish with is an " if."

> " If there be any habitation for the spirits of just men, if, as the sages will have it, great souls perish not with the body, mayest thou rest in peace."

" If " is the only word. Marcus Aurelius can say that when a man dies, and his spark goes back to be lost in

God, all that is left is " dust, ashes, bones, and stench."
The significant thing about this passage of *Hebrews* is
the basic assumption that a man will rise again; that is
part of the certainty of the Christian creed; and the basic
warning is that he rises to judgment.

(ii) With Christ it is different—Christ dies and Christ
rises and Christ comes again, and He comes, not to be
judged, but to judge. The early Church never forgot the
hope of the Second Coming. It throbbed through their
belief. But we must note one thing—for the unbeliever
that was a day of terror. As *Enoch* had it of the Day of the
Lord, when he wrote before Christ came: " For all you
who are sinners there is no salvation, but upon you all
will come destruction and a curse." In some way the
consummation must come. If in that day Christ comes
as a friend, it can only be a day of glory; if He comes as a
stranger or as one whom we have regarded as an enemy,
it can only be a day of judgment. A man can look to the
end of things with joyous expectation or with shuddering
terror. What makes the difference is—" How is your heart
with Christ? "

THE ONLY TRUE SACRIFICE

Hebrews 10: 1-10

> Because the law is only a pale shadow of the blessings
> which are to come, and not a real image of these
> things, it can never really fit for the fellowship of
> God those who seek to draw near to His presence,
> with the sacrifices which have to be brought year
> by year and which go on for ever. For if these sacrifices
> could achieve that, would they not have stopped being
> brought, because the worshipper had been once
> and for all brought into a state of purity and no
> longer had any consciousness of sin? So far from that,
> in them there is a year by year reminder of sin. For
> it is impossible for the blood of bulls and goats to
> take away sin. That is why He says as He enters
> the world: " You did not desire sacrifice and offering;
> it is a body you have prepared for me. You took

no pleasure in whole burnt-offerings and in sin-offerings. So, then, I said: ' So then I come—in the roll of the book it is written of me—to do, O God, your will.' " At the beginning of this passage He says: " You did not desire sacrifices and offerings and whole burnt-offerings and sin-offerings and you took no pleasure in them," and it is such offerings as these that the law prescribes. Then He went on to say: " Behold, I come to do your will." He abolishes the kind of offerings referred to in the first quotation in order to establish the kind of offering referred to in the second. It is by this way of " the will " that we have been purified through the once and for all offering of the body of Christ.

To the writer to the Hebrews the whole business of sacrifice was only a pale copy of what true and real worship ought to be. The whole business of religion was to bring a man into a close and intimate relationship with God, to give him free and full access to the presence of God. That is what these sacrifices could never do. The best that they could do was to give a man a distant and spasmodic contact with God. He uses two words to indicate what he means. He says that these things are a *pale shadow*; the word he uses is *skia*, which is the Greek word for *a shadow*; it means a pale, nebulous reflection, a mere outline or silhouette, a form without reality and without substance. He says that they do not give a *real image*; the word he uses is *eikōn*, which means a *complete representation, a detailed reproduction*. It actually does mean a *portrait*, and would mean a *photograph*, if there had been such a thing in these days. In effect he is saying: " Without Christ you cannot get beyond the shadows of God." He brings proof of that. Year by year and for ever the sacrifices of the Tabernacle, and especially the sacrifices of the Day of Atonement, go on. They are for ever repeated. Now an effective thing does not need to be done again; it is done and the effect is produced, and there is no need of repetition. The very fact of the daily and yearly repetition of these sacrifices is the final proof that they are *not* purifying men's souls, and that they are *not* giving full and uninterrupted access to God. In fact our writer goes further—he says that all that they are is *a reminder of sin*. So far from purifying a man from his sin, all that they do is remind him that he is not purified and that his sins still stand between him and God. Let us take a man as an analogy. Suppose a man is ill. A bottle of medicine is prescribed for him. If that medicine is efficacious and effects a cure, thereafter every time he looks at the bottle, he will say: " That is what cured me; that is what gave me back my health." On the other hand, if the medicine is ineffective and if he is in as bad a state as ever, every time he looks at the bottle he will simply be reminded that he is ill and that the recommended cure was useless and powerless. So the writer to the Hebrews says with prophetic vehemence: " The sacrifice of animals is powerless to purify a man, to take away a man's sin, to give him access to God; all that such sacrifices can do is to go on reminding a man that he is still an uncured sinner, and that the barrier of his sin is still between himself and God." So far from erasing his sin, they underline it.

The only effective sacrifice is the sacrifice of Jesus Christ. Why should that be? To make his point and to explain what is in his mind, the writer to the Hebrews takes a quotation from Psalm 40: 6-9. In the Authorised Version, which is close to the original Hebrew in its translation, the passage runs:

> " Sacrifice and offering Thou didst not desire;
> Mine ears hast Thou opened.
> Burnt-offering and sin-offering hast Thou not
> required.
> Then said I: Lo I come;
> In the volume of the book it is written of me.
> I delight to do Thy will, O God."

The writer to the Hebrews quotes the passage differently; in the second line he has:

> " A body you have prepared for me."

The explanation of the difference is that the writer to the Hebrews was not quoting from the original Hebrew of the Old Testament; he was quoting from the Septuagint, which is the Greek translation of the Old Testament. About 270 B.C. the task of translating the Old Testament from Hebrew into Greek was begun in Alexandria in Egypt. Obviously far more people in the ancient world read Greek than Hebrew. Very likely the writer to the Hebrews did not know any Hebrew at all; and therefore it is the Septuagint, the Greek version, that he uses. In any event the meaning of the two phrases is the same. " Mine ears hast Thou opened," means, " Thou hast so touched me that everything I hear I obey." It is the open, the obedient ear of which the psalmist is thinking. " A body you have prepared for me," really means, " You created me that in my body and with my body, I should do your will." In essence the meaning is the same.

What, then, is the argument of the writer to the Hebrews? He has taken the words of that psalm and he has put them into the mouth of Jesus. What that psalm says is that God does not want animal sacrifices; *He wants obedience to His will.* The only sacrifice God desires from man is *obedience.* In its essence sacrifice is a noble thing. Sacrifice meant that a man was taking something that was dear or precious or valuable to him and giving it to God to show his love. But human nature being what it is it was fatally easy for the idea of sacrifice to degenerate. It was easy for sacrifice to be thought of as a way of buying the forgiveness of God. Essentially sacrifice ought to be a token and pledge of love and of devotion; in fact it often became simply a way in which a man thought that he was paying the price for God's forgiveness. Now the writer to the Hebrews was not saying anything new when he said that obedience is the only true sacrifice. Long before him the prophets had seen how sacrifice had degenerated and they had told the people that what God wanted was not the blood and the flesh of animals, but the obedience of a man's life. That is precisely one of the noblest of the thoughts of the Old Testament men of God.

> "And Samuel said, Hath the Lord as great delight in burnt-offerings and sacrifices, as in obeying the voice of the Lord? Behold, to obey is better than sacrifice, and to hearken than the fat of rams" (I Samuel 15: 22).
>
> "Offer unto God thanksgiving; and pay thy vows unto the Most High" (Psalm 50: 14).
>
> "For thou desirest not sacrifice; else would I give it; Thou delightest not in burnt-offering. The sacrifices of God are a broken spirit; a broken and a contrite heart, O God, Thou wilt not despise" (Psalm 51: 16, 17).
>
> "For I have desired mercy and not sacrifice; and the knowledge of God more than burnt-offerings" (Hosea 6: 6).
>
> "To what purpose is the multitude of your sacrifices unto me? saith the Lord: I am full of the burnt-offerings of rams, and the fat of fed beasts; and I delight not in the blood of bullocks or of lambs or of goats. . . . Bring no more vain oblations. . . . Incense is an abomination unto me. . . . And when you spread forth your hands I will hide my eyes from you; yea, when you make your prayers, I will not hear; your hands are full of blood. . . . Cease to do evil; learn to do well" (Isaiah 1: 10-20).
>
> "Wherewith will I come before the Lord, and bow myself before the high God? Shall I come before Him with burnt-offerings, with calves a year old? Will the Lord be pleased with thousands of rams, or with ten thousands of rivers of oil? Shall I give my first-born for my transgression, the fruit of my body for the sin of my soul? He hath showed thee, O man, what is good; and what doth the Lord require of thee, but to do justly, and to love mercy, and to walk humbly with thy God?" (Micah 6: 6-8).

Always there had been voices crying out for God that the only sacrifice is the sacrifice of obedience. Nothing but obedience can open the way to God. Disobedience, self-will, rebellion sets up a barrier that no animal sacrifice can ever take away. That is why Jesus is the perfect sacrifice—*because He perfectly did God's will.* He took Himself; He took His body; He said to God: " Do with me as you will; your will be done." He said that it was His meat and drink to do His Father's will. He did for men what no man had ever been able to do; He brought for men the sacrifice that no man had been able to bring. He brought the perfect, complete obedience, and therefore the perfect, complete sacrifice.

If we are ever to have fellowship with God, if we are ever to have access into His familiar presence, the way of obedience is the only way. What man could not do, this Jesus did. What man could not offer, this Jesus offered. Jesus came to this earth and became man, and, in His perfect manhood, offered the perfect obedience. The perfect sacrifice has been offered and the way is once and for all opened up for us.

THE FINALITY OF CHRIST

Hebrews 10: 11-18

> Again, every priest stands every day engaged upon his service; he stands offering the same sacrifices over and over again, and they are sacrifices of such a kind that they can never take away sins. But He offered one single sacrifice for sin, and then took His seat for ever at the right hand of God, and, for the future, He waits until His enemies are made the footstool of His feet. For, by one offering, and for all time, He perfectly gave us that cleansing we need to enter into the presence of God. And, to this the Holy Spirit is our witness, for, after He has said: " This is the covenant I will make with them after these days, says the Lord. I will put my laws upon their hearts; and I will write them upon their minds," He goes on to say: " And I will not remember any more their sins and their breaches of the law." Now, where there is forgiveness of these things, a sacrifice for sin is no longer necessary.

ONCE again in this passage the writer to the Hebrews is drawing a series of implicit contrasts between the sacrifice that Jesus offered and the animal sacrifices that the priests offer.

(i) He stresses *the achievement of Jesus*. The sacrifice of Jesus was made once, and is effective for ever; the animal sacrifices of the priests must be made over and over again, every day in life; and even then they are not effective in any real way. Every day in life, so long as the Temple stood, the following sacrifices had to be carried out both morning and evening (Numbers 28: 3-8). Every morning and every evening a male lamb of one year old, without spot and blemish, was offered as a *burnt-offering*. Along with it there was offered a *meat-offering*, which consisted of one tenth of an ephah of fine flour mixed with a quarter of a hin of pure oil. In addition, there was a *drink-offering*, which consisted of a quarter of a hin of wine. In addition to that there was *the daily meat-offering of the High Priest*; it consisted of one tenth of an ephah of fine flour, mixed with oil, and baked in a flat pan; half was offered in the morning and half in the evening. In addition to that there was an offering of *incense* before these offerings in the morning, and after them in the evening. Ever since there was a Temple, and so long as the Temple continued to exist, this routine of sacrifice went on. There was a kind of priestly tread-mill of sacrifice. Moffatt speaks of " the levitical drudges " who, day in day out, kept offering these sacrifices. There was no end to this process, and, when all was said and done, it still left men conscious of their sin, and alienated from God.

In contrast with that, Jesus had made His sacrifice, and that sacrifice neither could be nor needed to be repeated. (*a*) It *could* not be repeated. There is something unrepeatable about any great work. It is possible to repeat the music of jazz tunes *ad infinitum*. Such music has a family resemblance; to a very great extent the one tune repeats and echoes the other; but it is not possible to repeat the Fifth or the Ninth Symphony of Beethoven. No one else will ever write anything like them. They stand alone.

It is possible to repeat the kind of poetry that is written in sentimental journals and on Christmas cards, but it is impossible to repeat the blank verse of Shakespeare's plays or the hexametres of Homer's *Iliad*. These things stand alone. There are certain things which can be copied, reproduced, repeated; other people can produce something which is very similar and which is just as good. But all works of genius have a certain unrepeatable quality; that is what makes them works of genius; they are once and for all productions. They can be admired; they can be studied; they can be used as inspiration; but they can never be repeated. It is so with the sacrifice of Christ. It is *sui generis*; it is unique; it is one of these masterpieces which have been done once and can never be done again. (b) It *need* not be repeated. Why should that be? For two reasons. First, *the sacrifice of Jesus perfectly shows the love of God*. In that life of service, and in that death of love, there stands fully displayed the heart of God. As we look at Jesus loving men in life and loving men unto death, we can say: " That is what God is like." In the life and the death of Jesus we see the complete revelation of God. Second, *the life and death of Jesus was one act of perfect obedience, and was, therefore, the only perfect sacrifice*. All scripture, at its deepest, declares that the only sacrifice God desires is obedience; and in the life and death of Jesus that is precisely the sacrifice that God received. Perfection cannot be improved upon; it stands lonely and unique. In Jesus there is at one and the same time the perfect revelation of God and the perfect offering of obedience. Therefore the sacrifice of Jesus cannot and need not ever be made again. The priests must go on with their weary routine of animal sacrifice ; but the sacrifice of Christ was made once and for all.

(ii) He stresses *the exaltation of Jesus*. It is with care that the writer to the Hebrews picks his words. The priests *stand* offering sacrifice; Christ *sits* at the right hand of God. Theirs is the position of a servant; His is the position of a monarch. Jesus is the King come home. His task is accomplished and His victory won. There is a *wholeness* about the life of Jesus that it may well be that we ought to think more about. His life is incomplete without His death; His death is incomplete without His resurrection; His resurrection is incomplete without His return to glory. It is the same Jesus who lived and died and rose again and who is at the right hand of God. He is not simply a saint who lived a lovely life; He is not simply a martyr who died an heroic death; He is not simply a risen and restored figure who returned to walk the earth and company with His friends. He is the Lord of glory. His life is like a panelled tapestry. To look at one panel is to see only a little bit of the story. The tapestry must be looked on as a whole before the full story is unfolded and the full greatness disclosed.

(iii) He stresses *the final triumph of Jesus*. He awaits the final subjugation of His enemies. Nothing can stop the destined end. In the end there must come a universe in which Jesus Christ is supreme. How that will come is not ours to know; but it may be that we are allowed to think that this final subjugation will not consist in the smashing and the breaking and the extinction of His enemies, but in their submission to His love. After all, it is not so much the power, but the love of God, which must conquer in the end.

Finally, as is his habit, the writer to the Hebrews clinches his argument with a quotation from scripture. He quotes Jeremiah 31: 33, 34 where Jeremiah speaks of the new covenant which will not be imposed on a man from outside but which will be written on his heart. That passage ends: " I will not remember any more their sins and their breaches of the law." In Jesus the new covenant, the new relationship between God and man, has come, and because of what Jesus was and did and is the barrier of sin is for ever taken away.

THE LETTER TO THE HEBREWS

THE MEANING OF CHRIST FOR US

Hebrews 10: 19-25

Since, then, brothers, in virtue of what the blood of
Jesus has done for us, we can confidently enter into
the Holy Place, by the new and living way which
Jesus inaugurated for us through the veil—that is,
through His flesh—and since we have a great High
Priest who is over the house of God, let us approach
the presence of God with a heart wherein the truth
dwells, and with the full conviction of faith, with our
hearts so sprinkled that they are cleansed from all
consciousness of evil, and with our bodies washed with
pure water. Let us hold fast to the undeviating hope
of our creed, for we can rely absolutely on Him who
made the promises; and let us put our minds to the
task of spurring each other on in love and fine deeds.
Let us not abandon our meeting together—as some
habitually do—but let us encourage one another, and
all the more so as we see the Day approaching.

THE writer to the Hebrews now comes to the practical
implication of all that he has been saying. From theology
he turns to practical exhortation. He is one of the deepest
theologians in the New Testament, but all his theology
is governed by the pastoral instinct. He does not think
merely for the pleasure of thinking, or for the thrill of
academic and intellectual satisfaction. He thinks only
that he may the more forcibly appeal to men to enter
into the presence of God.

He begins by saying three things about Jesus.

(i) *Jesus is the living way to the presence of God.* He says
that we enter into the presence of God by means of the
veil, that is, by the flesh of Jesus. That is a difficult thought,
but what he means is this. Before the Holy of Holies in
the Tabernacle the veil hung. That veil shut off and
screened off the presence of God. In order that men should
enter into the presence of God that veil would have to
be rent in twain so that the presence might be revealed.

Now Jesus' flesh is that which veiled His godhead. Charles Wesley in his great hymn appealed to men:

" Veiled in flesh the godhead see."

It was when the flesh of Christ was rent upon the Cross that men really saw God. All Jesus' life shows us God; but it is on the Cross that the love of God is really and finally revealed. As the rending of the Tabernacle veil opened the way to the presence of God, so the rending of the flesh of Christ revealed the full greatness of the love of God. In Jesus, then, we have one who opens up the way to God, by showing us the love of God, and by bringing to God the perfect sacrifice of perfect obedience.

(ii) *Jesus is the High Priest of God, over God's house, in the heavens.* As we have seen so often, the function of the priest was to build a bridge between man and God. So, to put it very simply, this means that Jesus not only shows us the way to God; but also when we get there He introduces us to the very presence of God. A man might be able to direct an enquirer how to get to Buckingham Palace, but he might be very far from having the right to take the enquirer into the presence of the Queen. Jesus does not only show us the way that leads to God; He takes us, as High Priest, into the presence of God. Because of what He did there is nothing to close the door or bar the way any more.

(iii) *Jesus is the one person who can really cleanse.* In the priestly ritual, as we have seen, the holy things were cleansed by being sprinkled with the blood of the sacrifices. Again and again the High Priest bathed and cleansed himself in the laver of clear water. But these things were in the end ineffective to remove the real pollution of sin. Only Jesus can really cleanse a man's heart and body until he is pure. His is no external purification; by His presence and His Spirit He cleanses the inmost thoughts of the heart and the inmost desires of a man's being until he is really clean.

From this the writer to the Hebrews goes on to urge us to do three things.

(i) *Let us approach the presence of God.* That is to say, Let us never forget the duty of worship. It is given to every man to live in two worlds. He lives in this world of space and time; and he lives in the world of the spirit and of eternal things. Our danger is that we become so involved in this world of earthly things that we forget the other world. In the morning as the day begins; in the evening as the day ends; ever and again in the midst of the day's activities, we must turn aside, if only for a moment or a second, and enter into the presence of God. Every man carries with him his own secret shrine; but so many men forget to enter it. As Matthew Arnold wrote:

> " But each day brings its petty dust
>   Our soon-choked souls to fill;
> And we forget because we must,
>   And not because we will."

(ii) *Let us hold fast to our creed.* That is to say, Let us never lose our grip of what we believe. The mocking and the cynical voices try to take our faith away; the materialist and his arguments try to make us forget God; the events of life can be such that they conspire to shake our faith. It was Stevenson who said that he believed in the ultimate decency of things, and if he woke up in hell he would still believe in it. We must have a grip on the faith that nothing can loosen.

(iii) *Let us put our minds to the task of taking thought for others.* That is to say, Let us remember that we are Christians, not only for our own sake, but also for the sake of others. No man ever saved his soul who devoted his whole time and energy to saving it. Many a man saved his soul by being so concerned for others that he forgot that he himself had a soul to save. It is easy to drift into a kind of selfish Christianity, but a selfish Christianity is a contradiction in terms.

But the writer to the Hebrews goes on to outline our duty to others in the most practical way. He sees that that duty extends in three directions.

(i) *We must spur and incite each other to noble living.* Best of all we can do that by setting the fine example. We can do it by reminding others of their traditions, their duties, their privileges, their responsibilities when they are likely to forget them. It has been said that a saint is someone in whom Christ stands revealed. We can seek ever to incite others to goodness by showing them Christ. We will remember how the dying soldier lad looked up at Florence Nightingale and murmured: " You're Christ to me."

(ii) *We must worship together.* There were some amongst those to whom the writer of the Hebrews was writing who had abandoned the habit of meeting together. It is still possible for a man to think that he is a Christian, and yet to abandon the habit of meeting with and worshipping with God's people in God's house on God's day. He can try to be what Moffatt called " a pious particle," a Christian in isolation. Moffatt distinguishes three reasons which may keep a man from worshipping with his fellow Christians. (*a*) He may not go to Church because of *fear*. He may be ashamed to show his loyalty by being seen going to Church. He may live or work among people who laugh at those who go to Church. He may have friends who have no use for that kind of thing, and he may fear their criticism and their contempt. He may try to be a secret disciple; but it has been well said that to be a secret disciple is impossible because either " the discipleship kills the secrecy, or the secrecy kills the discipleship." It would be well if we remembered that, apart from anything else, to go to Church is to demonstrate where our loyalty lies. Even if the sermon be poor and the worship tawdry, the Church still gives us the chance to show to men what side we are on. (*b*) He may not go because of *fastidiousness*.

He may dislike the common people; he may shrink from contact with people who are "not like himself." There are churches, even in this country, which are as much clubs as they are churches. They may be in neighbourhoods where the social status has come down; and the members who have remained faithful to them would be as much embarrassed as delighted if the poor people and the slum-dwellers in the area came flooding in. We must never forget that there is no such thing as a "common" man in the sight of God. It was for *all* men, not only for the respectable classes, that Christ died. (c) He may not go because of *conceit*. Frankly, he may believe and state that he does not need the Church; that he is intellectually beyond the standard of preaching there. Social snobbery may be bad; spiritual and intellectual snobbery is worse. The wisest man is a fool in the sight of God; and the strongest man is weak in the moment of temptation. There is no man who can live the Christian life and neglect the fellowship of the Church. If any man feels that he can do so let him remember that he comes to Church, not only *to get*, but *to give*. He ought to come not only to receive, but to make his own contribution to the life of the Church. If he feels that the Church has faults, it is his duty to come in and to help to mend them.

(iii) *We must encourage one another*. One of the highest of human duties is the duty of encouragement. There is a regulation of the Royal Navy which says: "No officer shall speak discouragingly to another officer in the discharge of his duties." Eliphaz unwillingly paid Job a great tribute. As Moffatt translates it: "Your words have kept men on their feet" (Job 4: 4). Barrie somewhere wrote to Cynthia Asquith: "Your first instinct is always to telegraph to Jones the nice thing Brown said about him to Robinson. You have sown a lot of happiness that way." It is easy to laugh at men's ideals; it is easy to pour cold water on their enthusiasm; it is easy to discourage others. The world is full of discouragers. We have a Christian duty to encourage one another. Many a time a word of praise or thanks or appreciation or cheer has kept a man on his feet. Blessed is the man who speaks such a word.

Finally, the writer to the Hebrews says that our Christian duty to each other is all the more pressing for the time is short. The Day is approaching. He is thinking of the Second Coming of Christ, when things as we know them will be ended. The early Church lived in that expectation. Whether or not we still do so, we must still realize that no man knows when the summons to rise and go will come to us also. In the time we have it is surely our duty to do all the good we can to all the people we can in all the ways we can.

THE THREAT AT THE HEART OF THINGS

Hebrews 10: 26-31

> For, if we deliberately sin after we have received full knowledge of the truth, no sacrifice for sin is left. All that we can expect is to wait in terror for judgment, and for that flaming wrath which will consume the adversaries of God. Anyone who regards the law of Moses as a dead letter dies without pity on the evidence of two or three witnesses. Of how much worse punishment, do you think, that man will be deemed worthy who has trampled underfoot the Son of God, who has failed to regard the blood of the new covenant, with which he was made fit for God's presence, as a sacred thing, and who has insulted the Spirit, through whom God's grace comes to us? For we know who it was who said: " Vengeance belongs to me; it is I who will repay," and again: " The Lord will judge His people." It is a terrifying thing to fall into the hands of the living God.

EVERY now and again the writer to the Hebrews speaks with a sternness that is almost without parallel in the New Testament. There are few writers who have such a sense of the sheer horror and terror of sin. In this passage his thoughts are going back to the grim instruction in

Deuteronomy 17: 2-6. It is there laid down that, if any person shall be proved to have gone after strange gods and to have worshipped them, " thou shalt bring forth that man or that woman, which have committed that wicked thing, unto thy gates, even that man or that woman, and shalt stone them with stones till they die. At the mouth of two witnesses or three witnesses shall he that is worthy of death be put to death; but at the mouth of one witness he shall not be put to death. And the hands of the witnesses shall be first upon him to put him to death, and afterwards the hands of all the people. So shalt thou put the evil away from among you."

The writer to the Hebrews has this horror of sin for two reasons. First, he lived in a day when the Church had been under attack and would be under attack again. The greatest peril the Church ran was from the possible evil living and apostasy of its members. A Church in such circumstances could not afford to carry members who were a bad advertisement for the Christian faith. Such people would be an insuperable handicap to the Church. A Church in such circumstances could not afford apostates. Its members must be loyal or nothing. The age in which this writer lived made loyalty an utter and absolute necessity if the Church was to survive. That is still true. Dick Sheppard spent much of his life preaching in the open air to people who were either hostile or indifferent to the Church. From their questions and from their arguments and from their criticisms he said that he had learned that " the greatest handicap the Church has is the unsatisfactory lives of professing Christians." The unsatisfactory Christian was and is the man who undermines the very foundations of the Church. Second, the writer to the Hebrews was sure that sin had become doubly serious because of the new knowledge of God and of God's will for men which Jesus had brought. One of the old divines wrote a kind of catechism. He ends by asking what happens if men disregard the truth and the appeal of the offer of Jesus Christ. His answer is that condemnation must necessarily follow, " and so much the more *because thou hast read this book.*" The greater the knowledge, the greater the sin. The conviction of the writer to the Hebrews was that, if under the old law, apostasy was a terrible thing, it had become a doubly terrible thing now that Christ had come.

He gives us three definitions of sin.

(i) *Sin is to trample Christ under foot.* Sin is to take love's offer and to trample that offer under foot. Sin is not any mere rebelliousness against law; sin is the wounding of love. A man can stand almost any attack on his body; the thing that beats him to his knees in defeat is a broken heart. It is told that in the days of the Hitler terror there was a man in Germany who was arrested, tried, tortured and put into a concentration camp. He faced it all with courage and gallantry and emerged erect and unbroken. Finally, with his body broken but with his head unbowed and his spirit unconquered, he emerged. And then by accident he discovered who it was in the first place who had informed and laid information against him. The informer to whom his arrest was due was his own son. The discovery broke him, and he died. The attack by an enemy he could bear; the attack of one whom he loved killed him. When Caesar was murdered he faced his assassins with complete and almost disdainful courage. But when he saw the hand of his friend Brutus raised to strike, he wrapped his head in his mantle and died. Once Christ had come the awfulness of sin lay not in its breaking of the law; it lay in the fact that sin is trampling the love of Christ under foot. Sin has become the most terrible crime in the world— the crime against love.

(ii) *Sin is the failure to see the sacredness of sacred things.* Nothing produces a shudder like sacrilege. During students' day collections for charity the students are very properly allowed a great deal of latitude. Stunts are the order of the day, and the authorities and the public regard them with tolerance and find a good deal of pleasure in them. But during a certain students' week a certain group of students carried out a strip-tease act on the base of the cenotaph of a great city. True, it was done in ignorance and the person mainly involved in it would never have done it had the facts been realized. But at that act there was a public gasp of horror. The sanctity of the cenotaph had been violated; a sacred thing had been used as if it had no sanctity. The writer to the Hebrews says in effect: " Look at what has been done for you; look at the shed blood and the broken body of Christ; look at what your new relationship to God cost; can you treat it as if it did not matter? Don't you see what a sacred thing this is? " Sin is the failure to realize the sacredness of that sacrifice upon the Cross.

(iii) *Sin is the insult to the Holy Spirit.* It is the Holy Spirit who speaks within us, who tells us what is right and wrong, who seeks to check us when we are on the way to sin, and to spur us on when we are drifting into an easy-going lethargy. To ignore and to disregard these voices and these warnings is to insult the Spirit. To refuse a good and wise man's advice, contemptuously to neglect his invitation, to abuse his hospitality is to insult him. Completely to ignore the pleadings, the invitations, the commands of the Spirit and to go one's own way is to insult the Spirit, and to grieve the heart of God.

All through this, one thing comes out. Sin is not disobedience to an impersonal law; it is the disturbance and the wrecking of a personal relationship. To sin is not to sin against the law; it is to defy and wound and violate the heart of the God whose name is Father.

And then the writer to the Hebrews finishes his appeal with a threat. He quotes Deuteronomy 32: 35, 36 where the sternness of God is clearly seen. At the heart of Christianity there remains for ever a threat. To remove that threat is to emasculate the faith. At the end of the day

141

it is not all one for the good and for the bad man alike, for no man can ever evade the fact that in the end judgment comes.

THE DANGER OF DRIFT

Hebrews 10: 32-39

> Remember the former days. Remember how, after you had been enlightened, you had to go through a hard struggle of suffering, partly because you yourselves were held up to insult and involved in affliction, and partly because you had become partners with people whose life was like that. For you gave your sympathy to those in prison; you accepted the pillaging of your goods with joy; for you knew that you yourselves hold a possession which is better and which lasts. Do not throw away your confidence, for it is a confidence that has a great reward. You need fortitude, so that, after you have done the will of God, you may receive the promise. For in a short time, a very short time, " He who is to come will come and He will not delay. And my just man shall live by faith; but if he shrinks back, my soul will not find pleasure in him." We are not men to shrink back from things and so to come to disaster, but we are men of a faith which will enable us to possess our souls.

THERE had been a time when those to whom this letter was written had been up against it. When first they had become Christians they had known persecution and plundering of their goods; and they had learned what it is to become involved with those who are under suspicion and who are unpopular. They had met that situation with gallantry and with honour; and now, when they are in danger of drifting away, the writer to the Hebrews reminds them of their former loyalty.

It is a truth of life that in many ways it is easier to stand adversity than it is to stand prosperity. Ease has ruined far more men than trouble ever did. The classic example of that is what happened to the armies of Hannibal.

Hannibal of Carthage was the one general who had routed the Roman legions. He alone had conquered the conquerors. But the Romans were a people who often lost a battle but who seldom lost a campaign. Winter came and the campaign had to be suspended. Hannibal wintered his troops in Capua which he had captured. Capua was a city of luxury. And one winter in Capua did what the Roman legions had not succeeded in doing. One winter there with its luxury so sapped the morale of the Carthaginian troops that when the spring came and the campaign was resumed they were unable to stand before the Romans. Ease had ruined them when struggle had only toughened them. That is often true of Christian life. Often a man can meet with honour the great hour of testing and of trial; it is the routine of the everyday which saps his strength and emasculates his faith.

The appeal of the writer to the Hebrews is an appeal that could be made to every man. In effect, he says: " Be what you once were at your best." If only we were always what we can be at our best, life would be very different. Christianity does not demand the impossible. If we were always as straight, as honest, as kind, as courageous, as courteous as we can be at our best, life would be a very different thing. Any man might well take as a motto, " Never to sink below my best."

To be such we need certain things.

(i) *We need to keep our hope before us.* The athlete will make his great effort because the tape and the goal beckon him on. He will submit to the discipline of any training because of the end in view. If life is only a day to day doing of the routine things, then we may well sink into a policy of drift; but if we are on the way to heaven and heaven's crown then life must always be at full tension and effort always at full pitch.

(ii) *We need fortitude.* Perseverance is one of the great unromantic virtues. Most people can start well; almost everyone can be fine in spasms. Most people have their good days. Most men have their great moments. To everyone it is sometimes given to mount up with wings as eagles; in the moment of the great effort everyone can run and not be weary; but the greatest gift of all is to walk and not to faint.

(iii) *We need the memory of the end.* The writer to the Hebrews makes a quotation from Habbakuk 2: 3. There the prophet tells his people that if they hold fast to their loyalty to God, God will see them through their present situation; but the victory comes only to the man who holds on. To the writer to the Hebrews life was a thing that was on its way to the presence of Christ. Life was therefore never something that could be allowed to drift; it was never something in which a man could be allowed to flinch and shrink from the demands of loyalty. It was the end of life which made the process of life all important, and only the man who endured to the end would be saved.

Here is a summons to us never to be less than our best; always to seek for the unromantic but essential virtue of perseverance; and always to remember that the end comes. If life is the road to Christ then none can afford to miss the road or to stop half-way.

THE CHRISTIAN HOPE

Hebrews 11: 1-3

> Faith means that we are certain of the things we hope for, convinced of the thing we do not see. It was because of faith that the men of old time had their record attested. It is by faith that we understand that the world was fashioned by the word of God, so that that which is seen came into being out of that which is unseen.

To the writer to the Hebrews faith is a hope that is absolutely certain that what it believes is true, and that what it expects will come. It is not the hope which looks forward

THE LETTER TO THE HEBREWS

with wistful longing; it is the hope which looks forward with utter certainty. It is not the hope which takes refuge in a perhaps; it is the hope which is founded on a conviction. In the early days of persecution they brought a humble Christian before the judges. He told them that nothing they could do could shake him because he believed that, if he was true to God, God would be true to him. " Do you really think," asked the judge, " that the like of you will go to God and His glory? " " I do not think," said the man, " I know." In the days of his uncertainty Bunyan was tortured by uncertainty. " Everyone doth think his own Religion rightest," he said, " both Jews and Moors and Pagans; and how if all our Faith and Christ and Scriptures should be but a ' Think so ' too? " But when the light broke he ran out crying out, " Now I know! I know!" The Christian hope is more than hope; it is a hope that has turned to certainty.

This Christian hope is such that it dictates all a man's conduct. It dominates his actions. He lives in this hope and he dies in this hope, and it is the possession of this hope which makes him act as he does.

As Silesius sang:

> " With Hope for pilgrim's staff I go,
>   And Patience is my travelling dress
> Wherewith through earthly weal and woe,
>   I fare to everlastingness."

Moffatt distinguishes three directions in which this hope operates.

(i) The Christian hope is *belief in God against the world.* If we follow the world's standards we may well have ease and comfort and prosperity; if we follow God's standards we may well have pain and loss and discomfort and unpopularity, and we may well have to give up the world's prizes. It is the conviction of the Christian hope that it is better to suffer with God than to prosper with the world. In the book of *Daniel,* Shadrach, Meshach and Abed-nego are confronted with the choice of obeying Nebuchadnezzar and worshipping the king's image or obeying God and entering the burning, fiery furnace. Without any hesitation they chose God (Daniel 3). When Bunyan was due for trial he said: "With God's comfort in my poor soul, before I went down to the justices, I begged of God that if I might do more good by being at liberty than in prison, that then I might be set at liberty. But if not, His will be done." The whole Christian attitude is that in terms of eternity a man cannot lose by being true to God. The Christian has no possible doubt that it is better to stake everything on God than to trust to the rewards of the world.

(ii) The Christian hope is *belief in the spirit against the senses*. The senses say to a man: "Take what you want. Take what you can touch and taste and handle and enjoy."

> " Gather ye rosebuds while ye may,
>   Old time is still a-flying;
> And this same flower that smiles to-day,
>   To-morrow will be dying."

The senses tell us to grasp the thing of the moment; the spirit tells us that there is something far beyond that. The Christian believes the spirit rather than the senses.

(iii) The Christian hope is *belief in the future against the present*. Long ago Epicurus said the chief end of life is pleasure. But he did not mean what so many people think he meant. He insisted that we must take the long view. The thing which is pleasant at the moment may bring pain in the long run, in which case it is not a good thing. The thing which hurts like fury at the moment may bring joy in the long run, in which case it is a good thing. The Christian is certain that in the long run no man can hang or exile the truth. He is certain that " great is truth, and in the end she will prevail." At the moment it looked as if his judges had eliminated Socrates and as if Pilate had crushed Christ; but the verdict of the future reversed the verdict of the moment. Fosdick somewhere says that Nero once condemned Paul, but the years pass on and the time comes when men call their sons

Paul, and their dogs Nero. It is easy to argue: " Why should I refuse the pleasure, the profit, the escape, the safety of the moment for an uncertain and a problematical future? " The Christian answer is that the future is *not* uncertain, because the future belongs to God. In every case the Christian hope believes that God's promises are true *and acts on that belief.* It is enough for the Christian that God has commanded a thing and that God has promised a thing. His conviction is that it is not a hope he has got but a certainty, because his hope is in God.

The writer to the Hebrews goes on to say that it was precisely because the great heroes of the faith lived on that principle that they were attested and approved by God. Every one of them refused the greatness of what the world calls a great career, refused the safety of what the world calls a safe decision, and staked everything on God—and history proved them right. The Christian hope is not an assumption; it is a certainty that is backed by all the evidence in the world.

The writer to the Hebrews goes further. He says that it is an act of faith to believe that God made this world. Then he goes on to say that the things which are seen emerged from the things which are not seen. Now when he said that he was aiming a blow at current belief. It was current belief that God created the world out of already existing matter, and not out of nothing. Further, it was current belief that this existing matter was flawed and that therefore from the beginning this is a flawed world because it is made from flawed material. The writer to the Hebrews insists that God did not work with existing material; God created the world from nothing. Now when he argued like this he was not interested in cosmological speculation. He was not interested in the scientific side of the matter. What he wanted to stress was the fact that *this is God's world.* If we can grip the fact that this is God's world, that God is responsible for it, then two things follow. First, we will use it as such. We will remember that everything in it is God's and we will try to use it as God would have us use it. Second, we will remember that, even when it does not look like it, somehow God is in control. If we believe that this is God's world then there comes the faith and the hope which enable us to do the most difficult thing in the world—to accept what we cannot understand. If we believe that this is God's world then into life there comes a new sense of responsibility and into life there comes a new power of acceptance, for everything belongs to God, and all is in the hands of God.

THE FAITH OF THE ACCEPTABLE OFFERING

Hebrews 11: 4

> It was by faith that Abel offered to God a fuller sacrifice than Cain, and so gained the verdict of being a just man, for God Himself witnessed to that fact on the grounds of the gifts he brought: and although he died because of his faith, he is still speaking to us.

THE writer to the Hebrews begins his honour roll of faith with the name of Abel. The Cain and Abel story is in Genesis 4: 1-15. As it stands it is a mysterious story. Cain tilled the ground and brought to God an offering of the fruits of the ground; Abel was a flock-master and brought to God an offering from his flocks. God preferred the gift of Abel to the gift of Cain, and Cain, moved to bitter jealousy, murdered his brother and became an outcast upon the earth. In the original story the meaning of the story is difficult. There is no indication why God preferred the gift of Abel to the gift of Cain. To us it seems quite arbitrary, and there seems little reason or justice in the strange story. The meaning of the story may well be that the only offering which a man can bring to God is the offering of the most precious thing that life supplies. Now the most precious thing that life supplies is *life itself*; and to the Hebrews blood always stood for life. The life was the blood, and the blood was the life. We can well understand that, because when the blood flows away, life ebbs away. If that principle be accepted, then the only true sacrifice to God, in those primitive days, was a sacrifice of blood, because blood is life, the most precious thing. Abel's sacrifice was a sacrifice of a living creature; Cain's was not; and therefore Abel's was the more acceptable.

But it may well be that the writer to the Hebrews is not thinking only of the story as it is in Genesis, but that he is also thinking of the legends and elaborations which gathered round about it in Jewish folk-lore. It is clear that the Jews themselves found the story puzzling and elaborated it, in order to find a reason for God's rejection of Cain and for Cain's murder of Abel. The earliest legend tells how every time Eve bore children she bore twins, a boy and a girl; and that the twins were given to each other as man and wife. In the case of Abel and Cain, Adam tried to change this, and he planned to give the twin sister of Cain to Abel. Cain was bitterly dissatisfied. To settle the matter, Adam said to them: " Go, my sons, sacrifice to the Lord; and he whose sacrifice is accepted shall have the young girl. Take each of you offerings in your hand, and go, sacrifice to the Lord, and He will decide." So Abel, who was a shepherd, took from his flock the fattest and the best lamb and took it to the place of sacrifice; but Cain, who was a tiller of the ground, took the poorest and the most meagre sheaf of corn that he could find and laid it on the altar. Whereupon fire descended from heaven and consumed the offering of Abel so that not even the cinders were left, but Cain's offering was left untouched. Adam them gave the girl to Abel and Cain was sorely vexed. One day Abel was asleep upon a mountain; and Cain came upon him and took a stone and crushed his head. Then he threw the dead body on his back and carried it about because he did not know what to do with it. He saw two crows fighting and one killed the other; the crow that had killed the other dug a hole in the ground with its beak and buried the other. Cain said: " I have not the sense of this bird. I too will lay my brother in the ground," and he did so.

The Jews had still another story to explain the first murder. Cain and Abel could not agree as to what they should possess. So Abel devised a scheme whereby they might divide everything and bring an end to contention. Cain took the earth and everything that is stationary; Abel took everything that is moveable. But in Cain's heart there was still bitter envy. One day he said to his brother: " Remove thy foot; thou standest on my property; the plain is mine." Abel ran to the hills, but Cain pursued him, saying: " The hills are mine." Abel took refuge on the mountains, but Cain still pursued him saying: " The mountains too are mine." And so, in his envy, he hunted his brother, until he killed him.

At the back of this story there lie two great truths. First, at the back of the whole matter there lies *envy*. Even the Greeks saw the horror of envy. Demosthenes said: " Envy is the sign of a nature that is altogether evil." Euripides said: " Envy is the greatest of all diseases among men." There was a Greek proverb which said: " Envy has no place in the choir of God." Envy leads to bitterness; bitterness leads to hatred; and hatred leads to murder. Envy is the drop of that poison which can poison all life, and kill all goodness in a man's soul. Second, there is a strange and eerie thought here. Cain was the man who discovered a new sin. One of the old Greek fathers said: " Up to this time no man had died so that Cain should know how to kill. The devil instructed him in this in a dream." Up to that time there had been no such thing as murder. Cain had introduced that sin into the world. There is condemnation for the sinner; but there is still greater condemnation for the man who teaches another to sin. No fate can be too hard for the man who teaches one of the little ones to stumble, the man who introduces some sin into a life that was innocent. Such a man, even as Cain was, is banished from the face of God.

So the writer to the Hebrews says: " Although he died for his faith, he is still speaking to us." Moffatt finely comments: " Death is never the last word in the life of a righteous man." When a man leaves this world, he leaves something in it. He may leave something which will grow and spread like a canker or like a virulent weed or like a poison seeping through life. He may leave something fine which blossoms and flourishes without end. He leaves an influence of good or ill; he leaves an example of goodness or of sin. Every one of us, when we die, still speaks. May God grant to us to leave behind, not the germ of evil, but the lovely thing in which the lives of those who come afterwards will find their blessing.

WALKING WITH GOD

Hebrews 11: 5, 6

It was by faith that Enoch was transferred from this to the other life so that he did not die, but passed from men's sight, because God took him from one life to the other. For, before this change came to him, it was testified that he pleased God. Apart from faith it is impossible to please God, for he who approaches God must believe that God is, and that He is the rewarder of those who spend their lives seeking Him.

IN the Old Testament the life of Enoch is summed up in one sentence: " And Enoch walked with God; and he was not, for God took him " (Genesis 5: 24). Many legends gathered around Enoch's name. He was said to have been the first man who was skilled in tailoring and in sewing, and that he instructed men how to cut out skins in the proper shape to make garments. He is said to have been the first to teach men to make shoes to protect their feet. He is said to have been the first to put pen to paper and to instruct men from books. Legend tells that with Enoch the Angel of Death made a compact of friendship. Enoch made three requests of the angel. First, that he might die and come back again so that he might know what death was like. Second, that he might see the abode of the wicked so that he might know what the punishment of the evil was like. Both these requests were granted to him, and his third request was that he might be permitted to see into Paradise that he might see what the blessed enjoyed. This also was granted, but Enoch, having been granted a glimpse of Paradise, never came back to earth again.

The simple statement in Genesis has a kind of mystical quality about it. In itself, if taken literally, it does not say how Enoch died. It simply says that in God's good time he passed peacefully and serenely from this earth. There were two specially famous interpretations of the death of Enoch. (i) *The Book of Wisdom* (4: 10ff) has the idea that God took Enoch to Himself when he was still young to save him from the infection of this world. " He was taken away while he lived amidst sinners. . . . He was snatched away lest evil should change his understanding or guile deceive his soul." This would be another way of putting the famous classical saying: " Whom the gods love die young." It would look on death as a reward. It would mean that God loved Enoch so much that He could not bear to see him tainted by the contagion of this world, and removed him before age and degeneration descended hand in hand upon him. (ii) Philo, the great Alexandrian Jewish interpreter, saw in Enoch the great type and pattern of *repentance*. Enoch was changed from one life to another. He was changed—so Philo saw it—by repentance from the life that is apart from God to the life that walks with God. But surely the meaning is much simpler than that. The writer to the Hebrews reads into the simple statement of the Old Testament passage the idea that Enoch did not die at all, but that in some mystic way God took him to Himself. But surely the idea behind it all is that in a wicked and corrupt generation Enoch walked with God, and so when the end came to him, there was no shock, no break, no interruption, and that death simply took him into God's nearer presence. Because he walked with God, when other men were walking away from God, he daily came nearer and nearer to God, and for him death was simply the last step that took him into the presence of that God with whom he had always walked.

We cannot think of Enoch without thinking of the different attitudes to death. The sheer serenity of the Old Testament statement, so simple and yet so moving, makes us think of how we ought to feel towards death.

(i) There are those who have thought of death as *mysterious and inexplicable*. William Morris wrote:

" Death have we hated, knowing not what it meant."

Bacon said: " Men fear death as children fear to go in the dark." To some, death has always been the terrifying unknown with what Hamlet called " that dread of something after death."

(ii) There are those who simply saw in death *the one inevitable thing in life*. Shakespeare makes Caesar say in *Julius Caesar*:

> " It seems to me most strange that men should fear;
> Seeing that death, a necessary end,
> Will come when it will come."

And in *Cymbeline* he writes with a strange fatalistic beauty:

> " Fear no more the heat o' the sun,
>   Nor the furious winter's rages;
> Thou thy worldly task hast done,
>   Home art gone and ta'en thy wages:
> Golden lads and girls all must,
> As chimney-sweepers, come to dust.

> " Fear no more the frown o' the great,
>   Thou art past the tyrant's stroke:
> Care no more to clothe and eat;
>   To thee the reed is as the oak:
> The sceptre, learning, physic must
> All follow this, and come to dust.

THE LETTER TO THE HEBREWS

> " Fear not more the lightning flash,
>   Nor the all-dreaded thunder-stone;
> Fear not slander, censure rash;
>   Thou hast finish'd joy and moan:
> All lovers young, all lovers must
> Consign to thee, and come to dust."

Death is inevitable, and there is nothing to be gained by struggling against the inevitable.

(iii) Some have seen in death *sheer extinction*. It was that loveliest of Roman poets, Catullus, who pled with Lesbia for her kisses for the night was coming:

> " Lesbia mine, let's live and love!
> Give no doit for tattle of
> Crabbed old censorious men;
> Suns may set and rise again,
> But when our short day takes flight
> Sleep we must one endless night."

To die was to go out to nothingness, to cease to be, to be lost in the eternal dreamless and unwaking sleep.

(iv) Some have seen in death *the supreme terror, the unmitigated evil*, the robber of all earthly loveliness. In *Measure for Measure* Shakespeare makes Claudio say:

> " Death is a fearful thing.
> Ay, but to die, and go we know not where;
> To lie in cold obstruction and to rot;
> This sensible warm motion to become
> A kneaded clod; and the delighted spirit
> To bathe in fiery floods, or to reside
> In thrilling region of thick-ribbed ice;
> To be imprisoned in the viewless winds,
> And blown with restless violence round about
> The pendent world. . . .
> The weariest and most loathed worldly life
> That age, ache, penury and imprisonment
> Can lay on nature is a paradise
> To what we fear of death."

To Claudio the worst and bitterest of life was to be preferred to death. W. S. Gilbert wrote in *The Yeomen of the Guard*:

> " Is life a boon?
> If so, it must befall
> That Death, whene'er he call,
> Must call too soon."

Robert Burns wrote of the early death of Highland Mary:

> " But oh! fell death's untimely frost
> That nipt my flower sae early! "

There are those who have seen only the grim terroriser and despoiler in death.

(v) There are many who have seen in death *release*. Weary of the world and of life, they have seen in death escape from life. It was Keats who said that he had been " half in love with easeful death." It was Shakespeare in one of the sonnets who cried:

> " Tir'd with all these, for restful death I cry."

Nicholas Rowe wrote: " Death is the privilege of human nature." The Stoics held that the gods had given men the gift of life, and the still greater gift of taking their own lives away. It was Swinburne who best of all caught this mood of world-weariness in *The Garden of Proserpine*:

> " From too much love of living,
> From hope and fear set free,
> We thank with brief thanksgiving
> Whatever gods may be
> That no man lives forever,
> That dead men rise up never;
> That even the weariest river
> Winds somewhere safe to sea.
>
> Then star nor sun shall waken,
> Nor any change of light;
> Nor sound of waters shaken,
> Nor any sound or sight;
> Nor wintry leaves nor vernal
> Nor days nor things diurnal;
> Only the sleep eternal
> In an eternal night."

There are those for whom death has been good only because it is the end of life.

(vi) There are some who have seen in death *transition*, not an end, but a stage in the way; not a closure, but a moving on; not a door closing, but a door opening. Longfellow wrote:

> " There is no Death! What seems so is transition;
>   This life of mortal breath
> Is but a suburb of the life elysian,
>   Whose portal we call death."

George Meredith wrote:

> " Death met I too,
> And saw the dawn glow through."

To such, death has always been a call to come up higher, a crossing from the dark to the dawn.

(vii) There are those to whom death has been an *adventure*. As Barrie made Peter Pan say: " To die will be an awfully big adventure." Charles Frohman, who had known Barrie so well, went down with the *Lusitania* in that disaster of 7th May, 1915. His last words were: " Why fear death? It is the most beautiful adventure in life." There was an old scholar who was dying, and who turned to his friends: " Do you realize," he said, " that in an hour or two I will know the answers for which we have been searching all our lives? " To such, death is the adventure of supreme discovery at last.

(viii) And, above all, there are those, like Enoch, to whom death is but an *entering into the nearer presence* of Him with whom they have lived so long. If we have lived with Christ, then we can also die with Him, certain that, in dying, we go to be for ever with our Lord.

But in this passage the writer to the Hebrews lays down in addition the two great foundation acts of faith of the Christian life.

(i) *We must believe in God.* It is clear that there can be no such thing as religion without God. Religion began when men became aware of God; religion ceases when men live a life in which for them God has ceased to exist.

(ii) *We must believe that God is interested.* As the writer to the Hebrews put it, we must believe that God is the rewarder of those who diligently seek Him. There were those in the ancient world who believed in the gods, but they believed that the gods lived out in the spaces between the worlds, entirely detached, entirely happy, entirely unaware of these strange animals called men. " God," said Epicurus as a first principle, " does nothing." There are many who believe in God, but who do not believe that God cares. It has been said that no astronomer can be an atheist; but it has also been said that an astronomer is bound to believe that God is a mathematician. But a God who is a mathematician need not care. Men have called God The First Principle, The First Cause, The Creative Energy, The Life Force. No doubt all these things are true; they are the statements of men who believe in God, but not in a God who cares. When Marcus Aurelius was asked why he believed in the gods, he said: " True, the gods are not discernible by human sight, but neither have I seen my soul and yet I honour it. So then I believe in the gods and I honour them, because again and again I have experienced their power." Not logic, but life convinced him of the gods. Seneca said: " The first essential of the worship of the gods is to believe that there are gods . . . and to know those gods who preside over the world, because they control the universe with their power, and work for the safety of the whole human race, while they still remember each individual person." Epictetus said: " You must know that the most important thing in reverence for the gods is to have right beliefs that they are and that they order all things righteously and well." We must believe, not only that God exists, but also that God cares, that God is involved in the human situation; and, for the Christian, that is easy, for God came to the world in Jesus Christ to tell us how much He cares.

THE LETTER TO THE HEBREWS

THE MAN WHO BELIEVED IN GOD'S MESSAGE

Hebrews 11: 7

> It was by faith that Noah, when he had been informed by God about things that were still unseen, reverently accepted the message and built an ark to preserve his household in safety. Through that faith he passed judgment on the world, and became an heir of the righteousness which is the result of faith.

THE Old Testament story of Noah is in Genesis chapters 6 to 8. The earth was so wicked that God decided that there remained nothing to do but to destroy it. He told Noah His purpose of judgment and instructed him to build an ark in which he and his family and the representatives of the animal creation might be saved. With reverence and obedience Noah took God at His word, and believed what God told him, and so in the destruction of the world he was preserved.

As is usually the case, legend adds many a detail to this story. The writer to the Hebrews must have known these legends and they must have helped to add vividness to the picture that was in his mind. One story tells how Noah was in doubt as to the shape he was to give the ark. God revealed to him that it was to be modelled on the plan of a bird's belly, and that it was to be constructed of teak wood. Noah planted a teak tree, and in twenty years it grew to such a size that out of it he was able to build the entire ark. Another story tells that, after he had been forewarned by God, Noah made a bell of plane wood, about five feet high, and that he sounded it every day, morning, noon and evening. When he was asked why he did so, he answered: " To warn you that God will send a deluge to destroy you all." Another story tells that, when Noah was building the ark, the people mocked him and laughed at him and counted him mad. But he said to them: " Though you rail at me now, the time will come when I shall rail at you; for you will learn to your cost who it is that punishes the wicked in this world, and

158

reserves for them a further punishment in the world to come."

Even more than Abel and Enoch, Noah stands out as the man of faith.

(i) *Noah took God at His word.* He believed the message which God sent him. The message might look foolishness at the moment; it might look as if it had little chance of coming true. But Noah accepted God's word and staked everything on it. Obviously if Noah was going to accept that word of God, he had to lay aside his normal activities and work and concentrate on doing what this message commanded. Noah's life was one continued and concentrated preparation for that which God had said would come. The choice comes to every man, either to listen to, or to disregard the message of God. He may live as if the message of God was of no importance, or he may live as if the message of God was the most important thing in the world. We may put it in another way—Noah was the man who heeded the warning of God. And it was because he heeded it that he was saved from disaster. God's warning comes to us in many ways. It may come from conscience; it may come from some direct word of God to our souls; it may come from the advice or the rebuke of some good and godly man; it may leap out at us from God's Book, or challenge us in some sermon. Wherever it comes from, we neglect the warning of God at our peril.

(ii) *Noah was the man who was not deterred by the mockery of others.* When the sun was shining, Noah's conduct must have looked like the conduct of a fool. Who ever in his senses built a great hulk of a ship on the dry land far from the sea and the water? It may often happen that the man who takes God's word looks like a fool. He may have to adopt a course of action which looks like madness. He may have to abandon many of the things on which the world sets a high value, because he has discovered a new scale of values. We have only to think of the early days of the Church. One man might meet a friend. He might

say to him: " I have decided to become a Christian."
The other man would certainly reply: " You know what
happens to the Christians? They are outlaws. They
are imprisoned, thrown to the lions, crucified, burned."
He would reply: " I know." And the first man would
say despairingly: " All I can say is, you must be mad."
It is one of the hardest challenges of Christianity that
we have sometimes to be prepared to be a fool for the sake
of Jesus Christ. After all we can never forget that there
was a day when Jesus' friends came and tried to get Him
to go home because they thought that He was mad. The
wisdom of God is so often foolishness with men.

(iii) *Noah's faith was a judgment on others.* That is
why, at least in one sense, it is dangerous to be a Christian.
It is not that the Christian is self-righteous; it is not
that the Christian is censorious; it is not that the Christian
goes about finding fault with other people; it is not that
the Christian says: " I told you so." It often happens
that the Christian simply by being himself is passing
judgment on other people. Alcibiades that brilliant, but
wild, young man of Athens used to say to Socrates:
" Socrates, I hate you, for every time I meet you, you
show me what I am." One of the finest men who ever
lived in Athens was Aristides, who was called " the just."
But they voted to banish and to ostracise him. One man,
being asked why he had so voted, answered: " Because
I am tired of hearing Aristides called ' the just.' " There
is a danger in goodness, for in the light of goodness evil
stands condemned.

(iv) *Noah was righteous through faith.* It so happens that
Noah is the first man in the Bible to be called *dikaios,
just* (Genesis 6: 9). His goodness consisted in the fact
that he had taken God at His word. When other men
broke God's commandments, Noah kept them; when
other men were deaf to God's warnings, Noah listened
to them; when other men laughed at God, Noah reverenced
Him. It has been said of Noah that " he threw the dark

scepticism of the world into relief against his own shining faith in God." In an age when men forgot and disregarded God, God for Noah was the supreme reality in the world. He was the one lonely man who stood for God in a day when all men were abandoning Him.

THE ADVENTURE AND THE PATIENCE OF FAITH

Hebrews 11: 8-10

> It was by faith that Abraham, when he was called, showed his obedience by going out to a place which he was going to receive as an inheritance, and he went out not knowing where he was to go. It was by faith that he sojourned in the land that had been promised to him, as though it had been a foreign land, living in tents, in the same way as did Isaac and Jacob, who were his coheirs in the promise of it. For he was waiting for the city which has foundations, whose architect and builder is God.

In the Old Testament the call of Abraham is told with dramatic simplicity in Genesis 12: 1. Jewish and eastern legends gathered largely round Abraham's name, and some of them must have been known to the writer to the Hebrews, and they add still more vividness to the story. The legends tell how Abraham was the son of Terah, who was the commander of the armies of Nimrod. When Abraham was born a very vivid star appeared in the sky, and seemed to obliterate the other stars. Nimrod sought to murder the infant Abraham but Abraham was concealed in a cave and his life was saved. The story tells how it was in that cave the first vision of God came to Abraham. When he was a youth he came out of the cave and stood looking across the face of the desert. The sun rose in all its glory and Abraham said: " Surely the sun is God, the Creator! " So he knelt down and worshipped the sun. But when evening came the sun sank in the west, and Abraham said: " No! the Author of creation cannot set! " So the moon arose in the east and the stars came out. Then Abraham said: " This moon must indeed be God, and the stars are His host! " So he knelt down and adored the moon. But after the night was passed the moon sank and the sun rose again. Then Abraham said: " Truly these heavenly bodies are no gods, for they obey law; I will worship Him who imposed the law upon them." The Arabs have a different legend. They tell how Abraham saw many flocks and herds and said to his mother: " Who is the lord of these? " She answered: " Your father, Terah." " And who is the lord of Terah? " the lad Abraham asked. " Nimrod," said his mother. " And who is the lord of Nimrod? " asked Abraham. And his mother bade him be quiet and not push questions too far; but already Abraham's thoughts were reaching out to the God who is the God of all. The legends go on to tell that Terah, Abraham's father, not only worshipped twelve idols, one for each of the months, but that he was also a manu-facturer of idols. One day Abraham was left in charge of the shop. People would come in to buy idols. Abraham would ask them how old they were, and they would answer perhaps fifty or sixty years of age. " Woe to a man of such an age," said Abraham, " who adores the work of one day! " A strong and hale man of seventy! came in to buy an idol. Abraham asked him his age, and then said: " You fool to adore a god who is younger than yourself! " A woman came in with a dish of meat for the gods. Abraham took a stick and smashed all the idols but one, in whose hands he set the stick he had used. Terah returned and was angry. Abraham said: " My father, a woman brought this dish of meat for your gods; they all wanted to have it and the strongest knocked the heads off the rest, lest they should eat it all." Terah said: " That is impossible for they are made of wood and stone." And Abraham answered: " Let thine own ear hear what thine own mouth has spoken! " All these legends give us a vivid picture of Abraham searching after God, and dissatisfied with the idolatry of his people. So when God's call came to

Abraham, he was ready to go out into the unknown to find God. Abraham is the supreme example of faith.

(i) Abraham's faith was *the faith that was ready for adventure*. God's summons meant that he had to leave home and family and career and business; yet he went. He had to go out into the unknown; and yet he went. In the best of us there is a certain timorousness. We wonder just what will happen to us if we take God at His word, and act on His commands and His promises. Bishop Newbigin tells of the negotiations which led to the formation of the United Church of South India. He had a share in these negotiations and in the long discussions which were necessary. Things were frequently held up by cautious and prudent people who wished to know just where each step was taking them, and what was going to happen if they did this or that, until in the end the chairman had to remind them that a Christian is a man who has no right to ask where he is going. It is true that in the faith of most of us there is a dull unadventurousness. We most of us live a cautious life on the principle of safety first. To live the Christian life there is necessary a certain reckless willingness to adventure. If faith does not involve risk, it is not faith. If faith can see every step of the way, it is not faith. It is sometimes necessary for the Christian to take the right way, the way to which the voice of God is calling him, without knowing what the consequences will be. Like Abraham he has to go out not knowing where he is going.

(ii) Abraham's faith was *the faith which had patience*. When Abraham reached the promised land, he was never allowed to possess it. He had to wander in it, a stranger and a tent-dweller, as the people were some day to wander in the wilderness. To Abraham God's promise never came fully true; and yet he never abandoned his faith. It is characteristic of the best of us that we are in a hurry. To wait is even harder than to adventure. The hardest time of all is the time in between. At the moment of decision there is the excitement and the thrill; at the moment of achievement there is the glow and glory of satisfaction; but in the in-between time there is necessary the ability to plod and to wait and to work and to watch when nothing seems to be happening. It is then that we are so liable to give up our hopes and lower our ideals and sink into an apathy whose dreams are dead. The man of faith is the man whose hope is flaming bright, whose effort is intensely strenuous even in the grey days when there is nothing to do but to wait.

(iii) Abraham's faith was *the faith which was looking beyond this world*. The later legends believed that at the moment of his call Abraham was given a vision and a glimpse of the new Jerusalem. In the *Apocalypse of Baruch* God says: " I showed it to my servant by night " (4: 4). In 4 *Ezra* the writer says: " It came to pass when they practised ungodliness before Thee, that Thou didst choose one from among them whose name was Abraham; him Thou didst love and to him only Thou didst reveal the end of the times, secretly, by night " (4: 13). No man in this world ever did anything great without a vision. The vision of the goal made him able to face the difficulties and discouragements of the way. To Abraham there was given the vision. It was not in earthly things to satisfy his longing; he would only find satisfaction when he reached the home of the soul; and, even when his body was wandering in Palestine, his soul was at home with God. God cannot give us the vision unless we give Him the chance to give it to us. If we wait upon God, even in earth's desert places, God will send us the vision, and with the vision the toil and trouble of the way become all worth while.

BELIEVING THE INCREDIBLE

Hebrews 11: 11, 12

It was by faith that Sarah too received power to conceive and to bear a son, although she was beyond the age for it, for she believed that He who gave the promise could be absolutely relied upon. So from one man, and he a man whose body had lost its vitality, there were born descendants, as many as the stars of the sky in multitude, as countless as the sand upon the seashore.

THE story of the promise of a son to Abraham and to Sarah is told in Genesis 17: 15-22; 18: 9-15; 21: 1-8. The wonder of the story is that both Abraham and Sarah were ninety years of age, and long past the age of begetting or bearing a child; and yet, according to the old story, that promise came to them and that promise came true.

When we read the Old Testament story, we see that the reaction of Abraham and Sarah to the promise of God followed a threefold course.

(i) It began with sheer *incredulousness*. When Abraham heard the promise he fell upon his face and laughed (Genesis 17: 17). When Sarah heard it she laughed within herself (Genesis 18: 12). When we first hear the promises and the offer and the invitation to God, the human reaction is bound to be that this is far too good to be true.

> " How Thou canst think so well of us,
> And be the God Thou art,
> Is darkness to my intellect,
> But sunshine to my heart."

There is no mystery in all creation like the love of God. That God should love men, and suffer for men, and die for men is something that staggers men into sheer incredulity. That is why the Christian message is the *gospel*, it is *good news*, news so good that it is almost impossible to believe that it is true.

(ii) It passed into *dawning realisation*. After the incredulity there came the dawning realisation that *this was God who was speaking*. And if God speaks, it is bound to be true. God cannot lie. The Jews used to lay it down as a primary law for a teacher that he must never promise his pupils that which he was unwilling or unable to perform, because if he did so he accustomed the pupils thus early to the broken word and the broken promise. But when we remember that the one who makes the promise is *God*, then there comes the realisation that however astonishing and incredible the promise may be, it must nonetheless be true.

(iii) It culminated in *the ability to believe in the impossible.* That Abraham and Sarah should have a child seemed, and indeed humanly speaking was, impossible. As Sarah said: " Who would have said that Sarah would have given children suck? " (Genesis 21: 7). But, by the grace and the power of God, the impossible became true. There is something here to challenge and uplift the heart of every man. Cavour said that the first essential of a statesman is " the sense of the possible." When we listen to men planning and arguing and thinking aloud, we get the impression of the vast number of things in this world which men know to be desirable but which they dismiss as impossible. So many magnificent visions and dreams and plans are knocked on the head with the verdict: " It can't be done." Men spend the greater part of their lives putting limitations on the power of God. Faith is the ability to lay hold on that strength which is made perfect in our weakness, that grace which is sufficient for all things, in such a way that the things which are humanly impossible become divinely possible. With God all things are possible, and, therefore, the word impossible is a word which should have no place in the vocabulary of the Christian and of the Christian Church.

SOJOURNERS AND STRANGERS

Hebrews 11: 13-16

All these died without obtaining possession of the promises. They only saw them from far away, and greeted them from afar, and they admitted that they were strangers and sojourners upon the earth. Now people who speak like that make it quite clear

THE LETTER TO THE HEBREWS

that they are searching for a fatherland. If they were thinking of the land from which they had come out, they would have had time to return. In point of fact they were reaching out after something better, I mean, the heavenly country. It was because of that that God was not ashamed to be called their God, for He had prepared a city for them.

NONE of the patriarchs entered into the full possession of the promises that God had made to Abraham. To the end of their days they were nomads, and they never lived a settled life in a settled land. They had to be for ever moving on. Certain great and permanent truths emerge from them.

(i) They lived for ever as strangers. The writer to the Hebrews uses three vivid Greek words about them. (a) In 11: 13 he calls them *xenoi*. *Xenos* is the Greek word for *a stranger and a foreigner*. In the ancient world the fate of the stranger was hard. He was regarded with hatred and suspicion and contempt. In Sparta *xenos* was the equivalent of *barbaros*; the stranger and the barbarian were one and the same thing. A man writes complaining that he was despised " because I am a *xenos*, a foreigner." Another man writes saying that, however poor a home is, it is better to live at home than *epi xenēs*, in a foreign country. When clubs had their common meal, those who sat down to it were divided into *members* and *xenoi*, *members* and *outsiders*. This word *xenos* can even mean a *refugee*. All their lives the patriarchs were foreigners in a land that never was their own. (b) In 11: 9 he uses the word *paroikein*, *to sojourn*, of Abraham. In any country a *paroikos* was *a resident alien*. The word is used of the Jews when they were captives in Babylon and in Egypt. The *paroikoi* were not very much above the slaves in the social scale. A *paroikos* had to pay an alien tax. He was a kind of licensed sojourner in a place. He was always an outsider and only on sufferance and on payment a member of the community. To put it in modern language, all their lives the patriarchs never had any human society,

167

other than their own clans, to which they belonged.
(c) In 11: 13 he uses the word *parepidēmos*. In any community a *parepidēmos* was a person who was staying there temporarily and who had his permanent home somewhere else. Sometimes his stay was strictly limited. A man is ordered to stay in a place, for instance, not more than twenty days. A *parepidēmos* is a man in lodgings, a man without a home in the place where life has sent him. All their lives the patriarchs were men who had no settled place that they could call home. It is to be noted that to dwell in a foreign land was a much more humiliating thing in the ancient days than it is now. To the foreigner in a foreign country a certain stigma attached. In the *Letter of Aristeas* the writer says: " It is a fine thing to live and to die in one's native land; a foreign land brings contempt to poor men and shame to rich men, for there is the lurking suspicion that they have been exiled for the evil they have done." In *Ecclesiasticus* (29: 22-28) there is a wistful passage:

" Better the life of the poor under a shelter of logs
    Than sumptuous fare in the house of strangers.
  With little or much be contented:
    So wilt thou not have to bear the reproach of thy
        wandering.

An evil life it is to go from house to house,
    And where thou art a stranger thou must not open
        thy mouth.
  A stranger thou art in that case and drinkest
        contempt;
    And besides this thou wilt have to hear bitter
        things:
' Come hither, sojourner, and furnish my table,
    And if thou hast aught feed me therewith ';
  Or, ' Get thee gone, sojourner, from the face of
        honour,
    My brother is come as my guest, I have need of
        my house.'
  These things are grievous to a man of understanding:
    Upbraiding concerning sojourning, and the
        reproach of a money-lender."

At any time it is an unhappy thing to be a stranger in a strange land, but in the ancient days to the natural unhappiness there was added the bitterness of humiliation. All their days the patriarchs were strangers in a strange land. That picture of the sojourner, the stranger, the pilgrim, the foreigner became a picture of the Christian life. Tertullian said of the Christian: " He knows that on earth he has a pilgrimage, but that his dignity is in heaven." Clement of Alexandria said: " We have no fatherland on earth." Augustine said: " We are sojourners exiled from our fatherland." It was not that the Christians were foolishly other-worldly; it was not that they detached themselves from the life and the work of this world; but they always remembered that they were on the way. There is an unwritten saying of Jesus: " The world is a bridge. The wise man will pass over it but will not build his house upon it." The Christian regards himself as the pilgrim of eternity.

(ii) In spite of everything these men never lost their vision and their hopes. However long that hope might be in coming true, the light of it shone in their eyes. However long the way might be, they never stopped tramping along it. Robert Louis Stevenson said: " It is better to travel hopefully than to arrive." They never gave up; they never drifted; they never wearily gave up the journey. They lived in hope and died in expectation.

(iii) In spite of everything they never wished to go back. Their descendants, the children of Israel, when they were in the desert, often wished to go back to the fleshpots of Egypt. But not the patriarchs. They had begun and it never struck them to turn back. In flying there is a point which is called *the point of no return*. When the aeroplane has reached that point *it cannot go back*. Its petrol supply has reached such a level that there is nothing left to do but to go on. One of the tragedies of life is the number of people who turn back just a little too soon. One further effort, a little more waiting, a little more hoping would make the dream come true. Immediately a Christian has set out on some enterprise sent to him by God, immediately he has set out on the Christian way, he should feel that he has already passed the point of no return.

(iv) These men were able to go on because they were haunted by the things beyond. The man with the wanderlust is lured on by the thought of the countries he has never seen. The great artist or composer is haunted and driven by the thought of the performance he has never yet given and the wonder he has never yet produced. Stevenson tells of an old byreman who spent all his days amidst the muck of the byre. Someone asked him if he never got tired of it all. He answered: " He that has something ayont (beyond) need never weary." These men had the something beyond—and so have we.

(v) Because these men were what they were, God was not ashamed to be called their God. Above all things, God is the God of the gallant adventurer. God loves the man who is ready to venture for His name. The prudent, cautious, comfort-loving man is the very opposite of God. The man who goes out into the unknown and who keeps going on will in the end arrive at God.

THE SUPREME SACRIFICE

Hebrews 11: 17-19

It was by faith that Abraham offered up Isaac, when he was put to the test. He was willing to offer up even his only son, although it had been said to him: " It is in Isaac that your descendants will be named." He was willing to do this for he reckoned that God was able to raise him even from the dead. Hence he did receive him back which is a parable of the resurrection.

THE Isaac story is told in Genesis 22: 1-18. There we read that most dramatic of stories of how Abraham met the supreme test of the demand for the life of his own son. To some extent this story has fallen into disrepute nowadays. It does not appear in syllabuses of religious education because it is held to teach a view of God that can no longer be accepted. Or, failing that, it is held to teach that the point of the story is that it was in this way that Abraham learned that God did not desire human sacrifice. There were days when men considered it a sacred duty to offer up their first-born sons to God, before they learned that God would never desire a sacrifice like that. No doubt that is true; but if we want to see this story at its greatest, and if we want to see it as the writer to the Hebrews saw it, we must take it at its face value. It was the response of a man who was asked to offer to God his own son.

(i) This story teaches us that we must be ready to sacrifice that which is dearest to us for the sake of loyalty to God. There have been many who have sacrificed their careers to what they took to be the will of God. J. P. Struthers was the minister of the Reformed Presbyterian Church in Greenock. He was the minister of a little congregation in a little Church, which it is neither false nor unkind to say, had a great past but no future. Had he been willing to forsake the Church of his fathers, any pulpit in the land was open to him. The most dazzling ecclesiastical prizes were his; but he sacrificed them all for the sake of what he considered to be loyalty to God's will for him. Sometimes a man may have to sacrifice personal relationships. A man may feel called to some task by God, called to a task in a sphere which is hard and difficult and in a place that is unattractive. He may be sure that that is God's will for him. It may be that the girl whom he was to marry will not face it with him, will not accept the rigours and the discomforts and the straiter circumstances and life and work in an area where life is

in the raw. The man must choose between the will of
God and the relationship which means so much to him.
When Bunyan was in gaol he was thinking of what must
happen to his family, if he was executed. Especially the
thought of his little blind daughter, who was so dear to
him, haunted him: " O," he said, " I saw in this condition
I was a man who was pulling down his house upon the
head of his wife and children; yet, thought I, I must do
it, I must do it."

> " The dearest idol I have known,
>   Whate'er that idol be,
> Help me to tear it from Thy throne,
>   And worship only Thee."

Abraham was the man who would sacrifice even the dearest
thing in life for God. Time and again in the early Church
it happened. In a home one partner became a Christian
and the other did not; the children became Christians
and the parents did not. The sword came down upon
that home; and unless there had been those who had
counted Christ dearer than all beside, there would be no
such thing as Christianity to-day. God must come first
in our lives, or He comes nowhere. There is a story of
two children who had been given a toy Noah's Ark as a
present. They had been listening to the Old Testament
stories and so they determined that they too would offer
a sacrifice. They examined the animals in their toy ark
with a view to picking one to be offered as a sacrifice,
and finally they decided on *a sheep with a broken leg*. The
only thing they would offer was a broken toy they could
well do without. That is the way in which so many people
would like to sacrifice to God; but only the dearest and
the best is good enough for Him.

(ii) Abraham is the pattern of the man who accepts
what he cannot understand. To Abraham there had come
this completely incomprehensible demand. It did not
make sense. The promise was that in Isaac his seed would
grow and grow until he became a mighty nation in which

all nations would be blessed. On the life of Isaac depended the promise; and now God seemed to demand that life to take it away. As Chrysostom put it: " The things of God seemed to fight against the things of God, and faith fought with faith, and the commandment fought with the promise." Into life for everyone at some time there comes something for which there seems to be no reason, something which passes comprehension and something which defies explanation. It is then that a man is faced with life's hardest battle—the battle to accept when he cannot understand. At such a time there is only one thing to do— to submit, to accept, to obey; and to do so without resentment and without rebellion, saying: " God, Thou art love! I build my faith on that."

(iii) Abraham is the pattern of the man who, with the test, found a way of escape. If we take God at His word, and if we stake everything on Him, even when there seems to be nothing but a blank wall in front of us, the way of escape will open up.

THE FAITH WHICH DEFEATS DEATH

Hebrews 11: 20-22

It was by faith that Isaac blessed Jacob and Esau in the things concerning the future. It was by faith that Jacob, when he was dying, blessed each of the sons of Joseph, and prayed leaning on the head of his staff. It was by faith that Joseph, as he came to the end, had in his mind the days when the children of Israel would leave Egypt, and gave instructions concerning his bones.

THERE is one thing that links these three examples of faith together. In each case the faith was the faith of a man to whom death was very near. The blessing which Isaac gave is in Genesis 27: 28, 29, 39, 40. It was given after Isaac had said: " Behold now, I am old, I know not the day of my death " (Genesis 27: 2). The blessing

was: " God give thee of the dew of heaven, and of the
fatness of the earth and plenty of corn and wine: let
people serve thee and nations bow down to thee." The
blessing of Jacob is given in Genesis 48: 9-22. The story
has just said that " the time drew nigh that Israel must
die " (Genesis 47: 29). The blessing was: " Let my name
be named upon them, and the name of my fathers Abraham
and Isaac; and let them grow into a multitude in the
midst of the earth " (Genesis 48: 15, 16). The incident
from the life of Joseph comes from Genesis 50: 22-26.
When Joseph was near to death he made the Israelites
take an oath that they would not leave his bones in Egypt,
but that they would take them with them when they
went out to possess the promised land, a promise which
in due time they kept (Exodus 13: 19; Joshua 24: 32).

The point which the writer to the Hebrews wishes to
make is that all these three men died without having
entered into the promise that God had made, the promise
of the Promised Land, and of greatness to the nation of
Israel. Isaac was still a nomad and a wanderer; Jacob
was an exile in the land of Egypt; Joseph had attained
to greatness, but still that greatness was the greatness of a
stranger in a strange land; and yet they never doubted
that the promise would come true. They died, not in
despair, but in hope. Their faith defeated death. Death
might come to them, but the promise of God could never die.

Now there is something of permanent greatness here.
The thought that was in the mind of all these men was
the same thought. If we could have seen into their minds
and if we could have heard their thoughts speaking, we
would have heard them say something like this: " God's
promise is true, for God never breaks a promise; I may
not live to see it; death may come to me before that
promise becomes a fact and that dream a reality; but
I am a link in the fulfilment of that promise; whether
or not that promise comes depends on me." Here is the
great function of life. Our dream may not come true;

our hopes may never be realised; but we must live in such a way that we shall hasten that hope, in such a way that it will be easier to enter into that dream. It may not be given to every man to enter into the fullness of the promises of God, but it is given to him to live with such fidelity and service that he will bring nearer the day when others will enter into it. To us is given the tremendous task of helping God to make His promises come true.

FAITH AND ITS SECRET

Hebrews 11: 23-29

> It was by faith that Moses, when he was born, was kept hidden for three months by his parents, because they saw that the child was beautiful: and they did not fear the edict of the king. It was by faith that Moses, when he grew to manhood, refused to be called the son of Pharaoh's daughter, and chose rather to suffer evil with the people of God than to enjoy the transient pleasures of sin, for he considered that a life of reproach for the sake of the Messiah was greater wealth than the treasures of Egypt, for he kept his eyes fixed upon his reward. It was by faith that he left Egypt, unmoved by the blazing anger of the king, for he could face all things, as one who sees Him who is invisible. It was by faith that he carried out the Passover and the sprinkling of blood, so that the destroying angel might not touch the children of his people. It was by faith that they crossed the Red Sea, as if they were going through dry land, and that the Egyptians, when they ventured to try to do so, were engulfed.

To the Hebrews Moses was the supreme figure in their history. He was the leader who had rescued them from slavery and who had received the Law of their lives from God. To the writer of the letter to the Hebrews Moses was pre-eminently the man of faith. In this story, as Moffatt points out, there are five different acts of faith. As with the other great characters whose names are included in this roll of honour of God's faithful ones, many legends and elaborations had gathered round the name of Moses and doubtless the writer of the letter to the Hebrews had them also in his mind.

(i) There was the faith of Moses' parents. The story of their action is told in Exodus 2: 1-10. Exodus 1: 15-22 tells how the king of Egypt in his hatred tried to wipe out the children of the Israelites by having them killed at birth. Legend tells how Amram and Jochebed, the parents of Moses (Numbers 6: 20), were troubled by the decree of Pharaoh. As a result Amram put away his wife, not because he did not love her, but because he would spare her the sorrow of seeing her children killed, if she should bear them. For three years she was put away, and then Miriam prophesied: "My parents shall have another son, who shall deliver Israel out of the hands of the Egyptians." She said to her father: "What hast thou done? Thou hast sent thy wife away, out of thine house, because thou couldst not trust the Lord God, that he would protect the child that might be born to thee." So Amram, shamed into trusting God, took back his wife; and in due time Moses was born. He was so lovely a child that his parents determined to hide him in their house. This they did for three months. Then, the legend tells, the Egyptians struck upon a cruel scheme. The king was determined that even hidden children should be sought out and killed. Now when a child hears another child cry, he will cry too. So the Egyptians sent Egyptian mothers into the homes of the Israelites with their babies. When they got into the Israelites houses the Egyptian mothers pricked their babies and the babies cried. This would make the hidden children of the Israelites cry too, and so the children were discovered and killed. In view of this, Amram and Jochebed decided to make a little ark and to entrust their child to it on the waters of the Nile. That Moses was born at all was an act of faith; that he was preserved was another act of faith. Moses began by being the child of faith. Without the faith of his parents he would never have been born and he would never have been preserved.

(ii) The second act of faith was Moses' loyalty to his own people. The story is told in Exodus 2: 11-14. Again the legends help to light up the picture. When Moses was entrusted to the waters of the Nile, he was found by the daughter of Pharaoh, whose name is given as Bithia, or more commonly Thermouthis. She was entranced by his beauty. Legend says that when she drew the ark out of the water, the archangel Gabriel boxed the ears of the little baby to make him cry, so that the heart of Thermouthis might be touched as she saw the little face puckered in sorrow and the baby's eyes full of tears. Thermouthis, much to her sorrow, was childless; so she took the baby Moses home, and trained and educated and cared for him as her own son. He grew to be so beautiful that people turned on the street, and even ceased their work, to look at him. He was so wise that he was far beyond all other children in learning and in knowledge. When he was still a child Thermouthis took him to Pharaoh and told him how she had found him. She placed him in Pharaoh's arms, and Pharaoh was so entranced by the child that he embraced him, and, at the request of Thermouthis, promised to make him his heir. By way of jest he took his crown and he placed it on the child's head; but the infant snatched the crown from his head and flung it on the ground and trampled it under foot; and Pharaoh's wise men were full of foreboding that this child would some day trample Pharaoh's royal power under foot. They say that the wise men wished to destroy the baby Moses there and then. But a test was proposed; they would set before the child a bowl of precious stones and a bowl of live coals. If the child put out his hand and touched the jewels, that would prove that he was so wise that he was a danger; if he put out his hands and touched the coals, that would prove that he was so witless that he was no danger. The infant Moses was about to touch the jewels, but Gabriel took his hand and put it on the coals. His finger was burnt; he put the burnt finger in his mouth and burnt his mouth; that, they say, was why Moses was not a good speaker (Exodus 4: 10) but stammered all his life. So Moses was spared. He was brought up in all luxury. He was heir to the kingdom. He became one of the greatest of all Egyptian generals; in particular he conquered the Ethiopians when they were threatening Egypt, and in the end was married to an Ethiopian princess. But all the time he had never forgotten his people and his fellow countrymen; and the day came when he decided to ally himself with the downtrodden Israelites and to say goodbye to the future of riches and ease and comfort and royalty that he might have had. Moses was the man who gave up all earthly glory for the sake of the people of God. Christ gave up His glory for men. He became despised and rejected; He abandoned the glory of heaven for the buffets and the scourging and the shame inflicted by men. Moses in his day and generation shared in the sufferings of Christ. Moses was the man who chose the loyalty that led to suffering rather than the ease which led to earthly glory. He would rather suffer for the right than enjoy luxury with the wrong. He knew that the prizes of earth were contemptible compared with the ultimate reward of God.

(iii) There came the day when Moses, because of his intervention on behalf of his people, had to withdraw from Egypt to Midian (Exodus 2: 14-22). Because of the order in which it comes that must be what verse 27 refers to. Some people have found difficulty here, because the Exodus narrative says that it was because Moses feared Pharaoh that he fled to Midian (Exodus 2: 14), while the writer to the Hebrews says that he went out not fearing the blazing wrath of the king. There is no real contradiction. It is simply that the writer of the letter to the Hebrews saw even more deeply into the story. For Moses to withdraw to Midian was not an act of fear; it was an act of courage. It showed the courage of the man who has learned to wait. The Stoics were wise; they held that a man should not throw his life away by needlessly provoking the wrath of a tyrant. Seneca wrote: " The wise man will never provoke the wrath of mighty men; nay, he will turn aside from it; in just the same way as sailors in sailing will not deliberately court the danger of the storm." At that moment Moses might have gone on; but his people were not ready; if he had gone on recklessly he would simply have thrown his life away and the deliverance from Egypt might never have happened. Moses was big enough and brave enough to know when to wait. He had the patience and the courage to wait until God said: " Now is the hour." Moffatt quotes a saying of A. S. Peake: " The courage to abandon work on which one's heart is set, and accept inaction cheerfully as the will of God, is of the rarest and highest kind, and can be created and sustained only by the clearest spiritual vision." When our fighting instincts say: " Go on," it takes a big and a brave man to wait. It is human to fear to miss the chance; it is great to wait for the time of God—even when it seems like throwing a chance away.

(iv) There came the day when Moses had to make all the arrangements in Egypt for the first Passover. The account is in Exodus 12: 12-48. The unleavened bread had to be made; the Passover lamb had to be slain; the door post had to be smeared with the blood of the lamb so that the Angel of Death would see the blood and pass over that house, and not slay the first-born in it; but the really amazing thing is that, according to the Exodus story, Moses not only made these regulations for the night on which the children of Israel were leaving Israel; he also laid it down that *they were to be observed annually for all time.* That is to say, Moses never doubted the success of the enterprise; Moses never doubted that the people would be delivered from Egypt; Moses never doubted that some day they would reach the promised land; even with the might of Pharaoh hot upon them, Moses never doubted the escape and the future triumph of the people. Here was a band of wretched Hebrew slaves about to set off on a journey across an unknown desert to an unknown promised land; here was the whole power of Egypt hot upon their heels; and yet Moses never doubted that God would bring His people safely through. Moses was preeminently the man who had faith to believe that if God gave His people an order He would also give them the strength to carry it out, that if God set His people an enterprise He would also give them the power to bring it to a triumphant conclusion. Moses knew well that God does not summon His servants to a great task, and then leave it at that. God goes with them every step of the way.

(v) Finally there was the great act of the crossing of the Red Sea. The story is told in Exodus 14. There we read the story of how the children of Israel were wondrously enabled to pass through the Red Sea, and of how the Egyptians were engulfed when they tried to do the same. It was at that moment that the faith of Moses communicated itself to the people, and drove them on when they might well have turned back. Here we have the faith of a leader and of a people who were prepared to attempt the impossible at the command of God, who realised that the greatest barrier in the world is no barrier if God be there to help us to overpass it. The book *As in Adam* has a sentence like this: " The business of life, the way to life, consists in getting over fences, not in lying down and moaning on the hither side." To Moses there belonged the faith to attempt what appeared to be the most insurmountable fences in the certainty that God would help the man who refused to turn back and who insists on going on.

Finally, this passage not only tells us of the faith of Moses; it also tells us of *the source of that faith*. Verse 27 tells us that Moses was able to face all things as one who

sees Him who is invisible. The great outstanding characteristic of Moses was the close intimacy of his relationship
with God. In Deuteronomy 33: 9-11 we read of how
Moses went into the Tabernacle; " and the Lord spake
unto Moses face to face, as a man speaketh unto his friend."
In Numbers 12: 7, 8 we read of God's verdict on Moses
when there were those who were ready to rebel against
him: " with him will I speak mouth to mouth." To put
it very simply and very humanly—the secret of the faith
of Moses was that Moses knew God personally. To every
task he came out from the presence of God. It is told
that, before a great battle, Napoleon would stand in his
tent alone; he would send for his commanders to come
to him, one by one; when they came in, he would say
no word to them, but he would look them in the eyes,
and shake them by the hand; and they would go out
prepared to battle and to die for the general whom they
loved. That is like Moses and God. Moses had the faith
he had because he knew God in the way he did. When
we come to any task straight from the presence of God,
no task can ever defeat us. Our failure and our fear is
so often due to the fact that we try to do things alone.
The secret of victorious living is to face God before we
face men.

THE FAITH WHICH DEFIED THE FACTS

Hebrews 11: 30, 31

> It was by faith that the walls of Jericho fell down,
> after they had been encircled for seven days. It
> was by faith that Rahab, the harlot, did not perish
> with the disobedient, because she had welcomed the
> scouts in peace.

UP to this point the writer to the Hebrews has been citing
as examples of faith the great figures of the time before
Israel entered into the Promised Land. Now he takes
two figures from the period of the struggle during which

the children of Israel were winning a place for themselves within Palestine.

(i) The first is the story of the fall of Jericho. That strange old story is told in Joshua 6: 1-20. Jericho was a strong city, barred and fortified. To take it seemed an impossible task. It was God's commandment that for six days, once each day, the people should march round it, led by seven priests, marching in front of the ark and bearing trumpets of rams' horn. For these six days the encircling march was to be carried out in silence. Then on the seventh day the priests were to blow upon the trumpets, after the city had been encircled seven times, and the people were to shout with all their might, " and the wall of the city shall fall down flat." As the old story tells it, so it was done and so it happened. That story left an indelible mark upon the memory of Israel. Centuries after this Judas Maccabaeus and his men were facing the city of Caspis, which was so secure in its strength that its defenders laughed in their safety. " Wherefore Judas with his company, calling upon the great Lord of the world, who without any rams or engines of war did cast down Jericho in the time of Joshua, gave a fierce assault against the walls, and took the city by the will of God " (2 Maccabees 12: 13-16). The people never forgot what great things God had done for them, and, when some great effort was called for, they nerved themselves for it by reminding themselves of what God had done.

Herein is the very point that the writer to the Hebrews wishes to make. The taking of Jericho was the result of an act of faith. It was taken by men who thought, not of what they could do, but of what God could do for them. They went to the task, not in their own might, but in the might of God. They were prepared to believe that God could make them able to achieve the impossible, that God could make their obvious weakness able for an incredible task. After the smashing of the Spanish Armada, there was erected on Plymouth Hoe a monument with

THE LETTER TO THE HEBREWS

the inscription: " God sent His wind and they were scattered." In other words, when the people of England saw how the storm and the gale had shattered the Spanish Armada, they said: " God did it." When we are faced with any great and demanding task, our thought should be, not what we can do, but what God can do with us and for us. When we are assessing our resources, God is the one ally whom we must never leave out of the reckoning. That which to us alone is impossible is always possible with God.

(ii) The second story that the writer to the Hebrews takes is the story of Rahab. It is told in Joshua 2: 1-21 and finds its sequel in Joshua 6: 25. When Joshua sent out spies to spy out the situation in Jericho, they found a lodging in the house of Rahab, who was a harlot. She protected them and enabled them to make their escape; and in return, when Jericho was taken, she and her family were saved from the general slaughter. It is an extraordinary thing how Rahab became imprinted on the memory of Israel. James (2: 25) quotes her as a great example of the good works which demonstrate faith. The Rabbis, who could do so, were proud to trace their descent to her. And, amazingly, she is one of the names which appear in the genealogy of Jesus Himself (Matthew 1: 25). Clement of Rome quotes her as an outstanding example of one who was saved " by faith and hospitality."

When the writer to the Hebrews cites her, what is the point that he desires to make? The point is this—Rahab in face of all the facts believed in the God of Israel. She said to the spies whom she welcomed and hid: " I know that the Lord hath given you the land. . . . For the Lord your God, He is God in heaven above, and in earth beneath " (Joshua 2: 9-11). At the moment at which she was speaking, there seemed not one chance in a million that the children of Israel could capture Jericho. These nomads from the desert had no artillery and no siege-engines. It must have seemed fantastically improbable that they could ever breach the walls of Jericho and storm the city. Yet Rahab believed—and staked her whole future on the belief— that God would make the impossible possible. She believed in God against the evidence of the facts. When common-sense pronounced the situation hopeless she had the uncommon sense to see beyond the situation. She had the adventurous courage to fling in her lot with God, when it seemed that to do so was to back the losing side. The real faith and the real courage are the faith and courage which can take God's side when that side seems doomed to defeat. As Faber had it:

> " Thrice blest is he to whom is given
> The instinct that can tell
> That God is on the field when He
> Is most invisible.

> For right is right, since God is God,
> And right the day must win;
> To doubt would be disloyalty,
> To falter would be sin."

The Christian believes in God against the facts; he believes that no man who takes the side of God can ever ultimately be on the losing side, for, even if he knows earth's defeats, there is a victory whose trophies are in heaven.

THE HEROES OF THE FAITH

Hebrews 11: 32-34

And what more shall I say? Time will fail me if I try to recount the story of Gideon, of Barak, of Samson, of Jephthah, of David, of Samuel and of the prophets, men who, through faith, mastered kingdoms, did righteousness, obtained promises, shut the mouths of lions, quenched the power of fire, escaped the edge of the sword, from weakness were made strong, showed themselves strong in warfare, routed the ranks of aliens.

THE LETTER TO THE HEBREWS

In this passage the writer of the letter to the Hebrews lets his mind's eye roam back over the history of his people; and out of it there springs to his memory name after name of those who were heroic souls. He does not take them in any particular order, but, as we shall see when we look at the outstanding characteristics of each one of them, there is a line of thought which binds them all together.

The story of Gideon is told in Judges 6 and 7. With only three hundred men Gideon won a victory over the Ammonites, in the days when they had terrorised Israel, a victory which went ringing down the centuries. The story of Barak is in Judges 4 and 5. Under the inspiration of the prophetess Deborah, Barak assembled his ten thousand young men, and faced the fearful odds of the Canaanites with their nine hundred chariots of iron, and won an almost incredible victory. It was as if a band of almost unarmed infantry routed a division of tanks. The story of Samson is in Judges 13 to 16. Always Samson was fighting alone. In the isolation of his splendid strength again and again he faced the most amazing odds and emerged triumphant. He, the one lonely figure, was the scourge of the Philistines. The story of Jephthah is in Judges 11 and 12. Jephthah was an illegitimate son; he was driven into a kind of exile and into the life of an outlaw; but when the Ammonites were putting Israel into fear, the forgotten outlaw was called back, and won his tremendous victory, although his vow to God cost him the life of his daughter. There was David, the king who had once been a shepherd lad, and who, to his own and everyone else's astonishment, was anointed king in preference to all his brothers (I Samuel 16: 1-13). There was Samuel, born to his mother so late in life (I Samuel I), and again and again moving alone as the only strong and faithful man of God amongst an easily frightened, a discontented and a rebellious people. There were the prophets, man after man of them bearing a faithful and an isolated witness to God.

The whole list is a list of men who faced incredible odds for God. It is a list of men who never believed that God was on the side of the big battalions, men who were willing to take tremendous and even terrifying risks for God. It is a list of men who cheerfully and courageously and confidently accepted God-given tasks which, on human terms, were impossible. They were all men who were never afraid to stand alone and to face apparently undefeatable hostile hordes for the sake of their loyalty to God. The honour roll of history is the roll of men who chose to be in God's minority rather than with earth's majority.

In the second part of the passage, when the writer to the Hebrews tells what these men, and men like these did, he does it in a series of machine-gun-like phrases. It may be that most of us lose a great deal of the impact of these phrases, for this reason—*phrase after phrase is a reminiscence.* As those who knew the scriptures well in their Greek version would know, phrase after phrase rings a bell in the mind. The word which is used for *mastering kingdoms* is the very word that Josephus, the Jewish historian, used of David. The phrase that is used for *wrought righteousness* is the very description of David from 2 Samuel 8: 15. The expression that is used for *stopping the mouths of lions* is the very expression that is used of Daniel in *Daniel* 6: 18, 23. The phrase about *quenching the violence of fire* goes straight back to the story of Shadrach, Meshach and Abed-nego in *Daniel* 3: 19-28. To speak about *escaping the edge of the sword* was to direct men's thoughts to the way in which Elijah escaped threatened assassination in I Kings 19: 1ff, and Elisha in 2 Kings 6: 31ff. The trumpet call about being *strong in warfare* and *routing the ranks of the aliens* would immediately make men think of the unforgettable glories of the Maccabaean days, which we will speak of in our next section. The phrase about *being made strong out of weakness* would conjure up many a picture. It might paint the mental picture of the extra-ordinary healing of Hezekiah, after he had turned his face to the wall to die (2 Kings 20: 1-7). Perhaps more likely, in the time in which the writer to the Hebrews wrote, it would remind his hearers of that epic but blood-thirsty incident which is told of in the *Book of Judith*, which is one of the apocryphal books. There was a time when Israel was threatened by the armies of Nebuchad-nezzar, led by his general Holofernes. The Jewish town of Bethulia had determined to surrender in five days' time for its supplies of food and water were at an end. In the town there was a widow called Judith. She was wealthy and she was beautiful, but she had lived in lonely mourning since her husband Manasses had died. She dressed in all her finery and persuaded her own people to let her out of the town; she went straight to the camp of the Assyrians. She gained an entry into the presence of Holofernes. She persuaded him that she was convinced of the defeat of her people as a punishment for their sins. She offered him a way into Jerusalem by stealth; and then, having gained his confidence, she slew him in his drunken sleep with his own dagger, cut off his head, and carried it back to her people. The traitors within the camp were silenced and looming defeat was turned into tumultuous victory. A woman's weakness had become strong to save her country.

The writer to the Hebrews is here seeking to inspire new courage and a new sense of responsibility by making his hearers remember their past. He does not do it blatantly; he does it with infinite artistry; he does not so much himself tell them what to remember; by his delicate hints he compels them to remember for themselves. When Oliver Cromwell was arranging for the education of his son Richard, he said: " I would have him learn a little history." When we are discouraged, let us look back and remember and take heart again. God's arm is not shortened; His power is not grown less. What God did once He can do again, for the God of history is the same God whom we worship to-day.

THE LETTER TO THE HEBREWS

THE DEFIANCE OF SUFFERING

Hebrews 11: 35-40

> Women received back their own folk as if they had
> been raised from the dead. Others were crucified
> because they refused to accept release, for they were
> eager to obtain a better resurrection. Others went
> through scoffing and scourging, yes, and chains and
> imprisonment. They were stoned; they were sawn
> asunder; they underwent every kind of trial; they
> died by the murder of the sword. They went about in
> sheepskins, in goatskins, they were in want, they were
> oppressed, they were maltreated—the world was
> not worthy of them—they wandered in desert places
> and on the mountains, they lived in caves and in
> holes of the earth. All these, though they were attested
> through their faith, did not receive the promise,
> because God had some better plan for us, that they,
> without us, should not find all His purposes fulfilled.

In this passage the writer to the Hebrews is intermingling
different periods of history. Sometimes he takes his
illustrations from the biblical period of history; but still
more he takes them from the Maccabaean period which
falls between the Old and the New Testament.

First let us take the things that can be explained against
the Old Testament background. In the life of Elijah
(I Kings 17: 17ff) and in the life of Elisha (2 Kings 4:
8ff) we read how, by the power and the faith of the prophets,
women did receive back again their children who had
died. Some were stoned to death. 2 Chronicles 24: 20-22
tells how the prophet Zechariah was stoned by his own
people because he told them the truth. Legend had it
that, down in Egypt, Jeremiah was stoned to death by
his own fellow-countrymen. Jewish legend tells that
Isaiah was sawn asunder. Hezekiah the good king died;
and Manasseh came to the throne. He worshipped idols
and he tried to compel Isaiah to take part in his idolatry
and to approve of it. Isaiah refused and he was condemned
to be sawn asunder with a wooden saw. While his enemies
tried to make him recant his faith he steadfastly defied

them, and prophesied their doom. " And whilst the saw
cut into his flesh, Isaiah uttered no complaint and shed
no tears; but he ceased not to commune with the Holy
Spirit till the saw had cloven him to the middle of his body."
The mind and memory of the writer to the Hebrews is
going back to the story of men who were enabled to do
mighty deeds for God and who were given strength to
withstand tortures and agonies for His name.

But even more the mind of the writer to the Hebrews
is going back over the history of the terrible days of the
Maccabaean struggle. That is a struggle of which every
Christian should know something, for if, in these terrible
killing days, the Jews had surrendered their faith and had
given up God, Jesus could not have come. It was because
they clung to their faith, and because they defied their
torturers, that God's purpose in Israel was able to be
worked out. The story is like this.

About the year 170 B.C. there was on the throne of
Syria a king called Antiochus Epiphanes. He was a good
governor, but he had an almost abnormal love for all
things Greek, and he saw himself as a missionary for the
Greek way of life and worship. He tried to introduce
this way of life into Palestine. He had some success;
there were those who were willing to accept Greek culture,
Greek drama, Greek athletics. Greek athletes trained naked,
and some of the Jewish priests even went so far as to seek
to obliterate the mark of circumcision from their bodies,
so that they might become completely hellenized. So far,
Antiochus had only succeeded in causing a division in
the nation; the greater part of the Jews were unshakably
true to their faith and could not be moved. So far force and
violence had not been used. Then about 168 B.C. there
came the day when the matter came as it were to boiling-
point. Antiochus had an interest in Egypt. He amassed
an army and invaded that country. To his deep humiliation
the Romans ordered him home. The way of his home-
going made the humiliation worse. The Romans did not

send an army to oppose him; such was the might of Rome that they did not need to. They sent a senator called Popilius Laena with a small and quite unarmed suite. Popilius and Antiochus met on the boundaries of Egypt. They talked; they both knew Rome and they had been friendly. Then, very gently, Popilius told Antiochus that Rome did not wish him to proceed with the campaign but wished him to go home. Antiochus said that he would consider it. Popilius took the staff which he was carrying and drew a circle in the sand round about Antiochus. Very quietly he said: " Consider it now; you will give me your decision before you leave that circle." Antiochus thought for a moment; he realized that to defy Rome was impossible. " I will go home," he said. That was a shattering humiliation for a king.

So Antiochus turned home, almost mad with rage; and as he went he turned aside to Jerusalem. He attacked the city and captured it almost without an effort. It was said that 80,000 Jews were killed and 10,000 sold into captivity. But there was worse to come. He sacked the Temple. The golden altars of the shewbread and of the incense, the golden candlestick, the golden vessels, even the curtains and the veils were taken. The treasury was sacked. Still worse was to come. On the altar of the burnt offering he offered sacrifices of swines' flesh to Zeus; and he turned the Temple chambers into brothels. There was no act of sacrilege that he omitted. But worse yet was to come. He completely forbade circumcision and he completely forbade the possession of the scriptures and of the law. He tried to compel the Jews to eat meats which were unclean and to sacrifice to the Greek gods. Inspectors went throughout the land to see that these commands were carried out. And if any were found to defy them, they " underwent great miseries and bitter torments; for they were whipped with rods and their bodies were torn to pieces; they were crucified while they were still alive and breathed; they also strangled those women and their sons whom they had circumcised, as the king had appointed, hanging their sons about their necks as if they were upon their crosses. And if there were any sacred book of the law found, it was destroyed; and those with whom they were found miserably perished also " (Josephus, *Antiquities of the Jews*, 12: 5, 4). Never in all history has there ever been such a sadistic and deliberate attempt to wipe out a people's religion.

It is easy to see how this passage can be read against the terrible happenings of these days. The Book of Fourth Maccabees has two famous stories which were undoubtedly in the mind of the writer to the Hebrews when he wrote the list of the things that the man of faith has had to suffer. The first is the story of Eleazar, the aged priest (4 Maccabees 5-7). He was brought before Antiochus and ordered to eat swine's flesh, and was threatened with the direst penalties if he refused. He did refuse. " We, Antiochus," he said, " who are convinced that we live under a divine law, consider no compulsion to be so forcible as obedience to our law." He would not comply with the king's order, " no, not if you pluck out my eyes and consume my bowels in the fire." They stripped him naked and scourged him with whips, while a herald stood by him, saying: " Obey the king's commands," His flesh was torn off by the whips, and he streamed down with blood, and his flanks were laid open by wounds. He collapsed and one of the soldiers kicked him violently in the stomach to make him rise. In the end even the guards were moved to wondering compassion. They suggested to him that they would bring him dressed meat which was not pork, and that he should eat it pretending that it was pork. He refused. " We should thus ourselves become an example of impiety to the young, if we became to them an excuse for eating the unclean." In the end they carried him to the fire; they threw him on it, " burning him with cruelly contrived instruments and pouring stinking liquids into his nostrils." So he died, declaring: " I am dying by fiery torments for the law's sake." That was one at least of the stories to which the writer to the Hebrews is referring when he speaks of the sufferings of those who died for their faith.

The second story is the story of the seven brothers (4 Maccabees 8-14). They too were given the same choice and confronted with the same threats. They were confronted with " the wheels and racks and hooks and catapults and caldrons and frying pans, and finger racks and iron hands and wedges and hot cinders." The first brother refused to eat the unclean things. They lashed him with whips; they tied him to the wheel, until he was dislocated and fractured in every limb. " They heaped up fuel, and, setting fire to it, strained him upon the wheel still more. And the wheel was besmeared all over with blood, and the heap of coals was extinguished with the droppings of gore, and pieces of flesh flew about the axles of the machine." But he withstood their tortures, and died faithful. The second brother they bound to the catapults. They donned spiked iron gloves. " These wild beasts, fierce as panthers, first dragged all the flesh off his sinews with their iron gauntlets to his chin, and tore off the skin of his head." So he too died still faithful. The third brother was brought forward. " The officers, impatient at the man's boldness, dislocated his hands and feet with racking engines, and wrenching them from their sockets, pulled his limbs asunder. And they fractured his fingers and his arms and his legs and his elbows." In the end they tore him apart on the catapult and flayed him alive. And he too died faithful. They cut out the tongue of the fourth brother before they submitted him to like tortures. The fifth brother they bound to the wheel, bending his body round the edge of it, and then fastened him with iron fetters to the catapult and tore him in pieces. The sixth they broke upon the wheel " while a fire roasted him from beneath. Then they heated sharp spits and applied them to his back; and piercing through his sides they burned

away his bowels." He too died in the faith. The seventh
brother they roasted alive in a gigantic frying pan. These
are the things of which the writer to the Hebrews is thinking; and these are things which we do well to remember.
It was due to the faith of these men that the Jewish faith
was not completely destroyed. And if that Jewish faith
had been destroyed, what would have happened to the
purposes of God? How could Jesus have been born into
the world if the Jewish faith had ceased to exist? It is
the simple fact of history that we owe our Christianity
to these martyrs of the killing times when Antiochus
made his deliberate attempt to wipe out the Jewish religion.

But there came a day when the whole situation ignited.
The agents of Antiochus had gone to a town called Modin,
and had erected an altar there to make the inhabitants
do sacrifice to the Greek gods. The emissaries of Antiochus
tried to persuade a certain Mattathias to set an example
by offering sacrifice, for he was a distinguished and an
influential man. He refused in anger. But another Jew,
seeking to curry favour and to save his own life, came
forward and was about to sacrifice. Mattathias, moved
to uncontrollable wrath, seized a sword and leapt forward
and slew his apostate countryman, and the king's com-
missioner with him. The standard of rebellion was raised.
Mattathias and his sons and those who were like-minded
with them took to the hills; and once again the phrases
that are used to describe their life there were in the mind
of the writer to the Hebrews and he has echoes of them
over and over again. " So Mattathias and his sons fled
into the mountains, and left all that they ever had in the
city " (I Maccabees 2: 28). " Judas Maccabaeus (and
his friends) withdrew himself into the wilderness and lived
in the mountains, after the manner of beasts " (2 Maccabees
5: 27). " Others, who had run together into caves near
by, to keep the Sabbath day secretly, being discovered . . .
were all burnt together " (2 Maccabees 6: II). " They
wandered in the mountains and in the dens like beasts "

THE LETTER TO THE HEBREWS

(2 Maccabees 10: 6). In the end under Judas Maccabaeus and his brothers the Jews regained their freedom and the Temple was cleansed and their faith flourished again.

In this passage, the writer to the Hebrews has done the same again. He does not actually mention these things. Far better that his hearers should be moved by this and that phrase to remember them for themselves. Let them look back and remember the terrible cost of the faith that had given them their own religion.

In the end he says a great thing. All these died before the final unfolding of God's promise, before the coming of God's Messiah into the world. It was as if God had so arranged things, that the full blaze of His glory and revelation should not be revealed until we and they can enjoy it together. The writer to the Hebrews is saying: " See! the glory of God has come. But see what it cost to enable it to come! That is the faith which gave you your faith. What can you do but be true to a heritage and a tradition like that? "

THE RACE AND THE GOAL

Hebrews 12: 1, 2

> Therefore, since we have so great a cloud of witnesses enveloping us, let us strip off every weight, and let us rid ourselves of the sin which so persistently surrounds us, and let us run with steadfast endurance the course that is marked out for us, and, as we do so, let us keep our gaze fixed on Jesus, who, in order to win the joy that was set before Him, steadfastly endured the Cross, thinking nothing of its shame, and has now taken His seat at the right hand of the throne of God.

THIS is one of the great, moving passages of the New Testament; and in it the writer to the Hebrews has given us a well-night perfect summary of the Christian life.

(i) In the Christian life we have *a goal*. The Christian life is a race along a course that is set out before us. The Christian is not an unconcerned stroller along the byways of life; he is a wayfarer on the high road. He is not a tourist, who returns each night to the place from which he started; he is a pilgrim who is for ever on the way. The goal is nothing less than Christ Himself, the presence of Christ, the likeness of Christ. The Christian life is going somewhere, and it would be well if, at each day's ending, we were to ask ourselves: " Am I any farther on? "

(ii) In the Christian life we have *an inspiration*. We have the thought of the unseen cloud of witnesses; and they are witnesses in a double sense, for they are those who have witnessed their confession to Christ and they are now those who are witnesses of our performance. The Christian is like a runner in some crowded stadium. As he presses on, the crowd looks down; and the crowd who look down upon him are those who have already won the crown. Longinus, in his great work *On The Sublime*, has a recipe for greatness in literary endeavour. " It is a good thing," he writes, " to form the question in our souls, ' How would Homer perhaps have said this? How would Plato or Demosthenes have lifted it up to sublimity? How would Thucydides have put it in his history? ' For when the faces of these people come before us in our emulation, they will, as it were, illumine our road and will lift us up to those standards of perfection which we have imagined in our minds. It would be still better if we were to suggest this to our minds, ' What would this that I have said sound like to Homer, if he were standing by, or to Demosthenes, or how would they have reacted to it? ' In truth it is a supreme test to imagine such a judgment court and theatre for our own private productions, and, in imagination, to submit an account of our writings to such heroes as judges." An actor would act with double intensity if he knew that some famous dramatic master was sitting in the stalls watching him. An athlete would strive with double effort if he knew that a stadium of famous Olympic athletes was watching him. It is of the very essence of life that life is lived in the gaze of the heroes of the faith who lived and suffered and died in their day and generation. How can a man avoid the struggle for greatness with an audience like that looking down upon him?

(iii) In the Christian life we have *a handicap*. If we are encircled by all the greatness of the past, we are also encircled by the handicap of our own sin. No man can reach to greatness when he is burdened down. No man would seek to climb Mount Everest with a pantechnicon of lumber weighing him down. If we would travel far, we must travel light. There is in life an essential duty of discarding things. There may be habits, there may be pleasures, there may be self-indulgences, there may be associations which hold us back and hold us down. They have to be shed as the athlete sheds his outer cloak as he goes to the starting-mark. Whatever holds us back must go; and often we will need the help of Christ to enable us to let it go.

(iv) In the Christian life we have *a means*. That means is *steadfast endurance*. The word is *hupomonē*. That word does not mean the patience which sits down and accepts things; it does not mean the weary patience which sits with bowed head and folded hands and mind resigned and lets the tide of things flow over it and past it. It means the patience which masters things. This means which we possess is no romantic thing; it is not something which lends us wings to fly over the difficulties and the hard places. It is that determination, unhasting and unresting, unhurrying and yet undelaying, which goes steadily on, and which refuses to be deflected. Obstacles will not daunt it; delays will not depress it; discouragements will not take its hope away. It will halt neither for discouragement from within nor for opposition from without.

It is the steadfast endurance which will carry on until
in the end it gets there.

(v) In the Christian life we have *an example*. That
example is Jesus Himself. For the goal that was set before
Him, He endured all things. To win that goal meant the
abandonment of heaven's glory; it meant the deliberate
refusal of earth's triumph; it meant the way of the Cross.
The writer to the Hebrews has a flash of insight—*despising
the shame*, he says. Jesus was sensitive; never had any
person so sensitive a heart. A cross was a humiliating
thing. It was the end for criminals, for those whom society
regarded as the dregs of humanity—and yet He accepted
it. St. Philip of Neri has a counsel; he bids us " to despise
the world, to despise ourselves, and to despise the fact
that we are despised " (*spernere mundum, spernere te
ipsum, spernere te sperni*). If Jesus could endure like that,
then so must we.

(vi) In the Christian life we have *a presence*. That
presence is the presence of Jesus Himself. He is at once
the goal of our journey, and the companion of our way.
He is at once the one whom we go to meet, and the one with
whom we travel. The wonder of the Christian life is that
we press on surrounded by the saints, oblivious to everything but the glory of the goal, and for ever in the company
of Him who has already made the journey and who reached
the goal, and who waits to welcome us when we reach
the end.

THE STANDARD OF COMPARISON

Hebrews 12: 3, 4

> Consider Him who steadfastly endured such opposition
> at the hands of sinners, and compare your lives with
> His, so that you may not faint and grow weary in
> your souls. You have not yet had to resist to the point
> of blood in your struggle against sin.

THE LETTER TO THE HEBREWS

THE writer to the Hebrews uses two very vivid words
when he speaks of *fainting* and *growing weary*. They are
the words which Aristotle uses of an athlete who flings
himself on the ground in panting relaxation and collapse
after he has surged past the winning post of the race. So
the writer to the Hebrews is in effect saying: " Don't
give up too soon; don't relax before the tape; don't
collapse until the winning post is passed; stay on your feet
until you get to the end."

To urge them to that he uses two arguments.

(i) For them the struggle of Christianity has not yet
become a mortal struggle. When he speaks of resisting
to the point of blood, he uses the very phrase which the
Maccabaean leaders used when they called on their troops
to go out and to fight to the death. When the writer to the
Hebrews says that his people have not yet resisted to the
point of blood, as Moffatt says, " he is not blaming them,
he is *shaming* them." When they think of what the heroes
of the past went through to make their faith possible,
surely they cannot drift into lethargy or flinch from conflict.

(ii) He pleads with them to compare what they have to
suffer with what Jesus suffered. Jesus gave up the glory
which was His; He came into all the narrowness of the
life of manhood and humanity; He faced the enmity
and the hostility of men; in the end He had to die upon
a cross. So the writer to the Hebrews in effect demands:
" How can you compare what you have to go through
with what He went through? He did all that for you—
what are you going to do for Him? "

These two verses stress the essential costliness of the
Christian faith. It cost the lives of all the saints and the
martyrs; it cost the life of Him who was the Son of God.
A thing which cost so much cannot be lightly discarded.
A tradition like that is not a tradition that a man can let
down. A heritage like that is not something that he can

hand down tarnished and decadent and belittled. These two verses make the demand that comes to every Christian: " Show yourself worthy of the sacrifice that men and God have made for you."

THE DISCIPLINE OF GOD

Hebrews 12: 5-11

Have you forgotten the appeal, an appeal which reasons with you as sons?

" My son, do not treat lightly the discipline which the Lord sends;
Never lose heart when you are put to the test by Him;
For the Lord disciplines the man whom He loves, and scourges every son whom He receives."

It is for the sake of discipline that you must endure. It is because He is treating us as sons that God sends these things upon us. What son is there whom his father does not discipline? If you are left without discipline—that discipline which everyone must share —then you are bastards and not sons. Surely it is true that we have human fathers who discipline us, and we pay heed to them. Surely we are still more bound to submit to the Father of the spirits of men, for that is the only way in which we can find real life. It was only for a short time that our human fathers disciplined us, and they did it as they thought best; but God disciplines us for our highest good, and He does so to make us fit to share His own holiness. No discipline seems to be a thing of joy when we are actually undergoing it, but afterwards it yields a fruit which is all to our highest welfare—the fruit of a righteous life—to those who are trained by it.

HERE the writer to the Hebrews sets out still another reason why men should cheerfully bear trouble and affliction when it comes to them. He has urged them to bear it because the great saints of the past have borne it. He has urged them to bear it because anything we have to bear is a little thing compared with that which Jesus Christ had to bear. Now, he says that we must bear hardship and affliction because they are sent to us as a discipline from God, and no life can have any value apart from discipline. A father always disciplines his child. It would not be a mark of a father's love to let a son do what he likes and have nothing but an easy way. If a father did that it would not show that he loved the son; it would show that he regarded the son as no better than an illegitimate child to whom he felt neither love nor responsibility. We submit to an earthly father's discipline; we have only to do so for a short time, until we reach years of maturity. At the best there is an element of arbitrariness in an earthly father's discipline; the earthly father is the father to whom we owe our bodily life. How much more should we submit to the discipline of God, to whom we owe our immortal spirits, who is altogether wisdom, and who, in His wisdom, seeks for nothing but our highest good which He alone can know. There is a curious and an interesting passage in Xenophon's *Cyropaedia*. There is an argument about whether the man who makes men laugh or makes men weep is of most use in the world. Aglaitidas says: " He that makes his friends laugh seems to me to do them much less service than he who makes them weep; and if you will look at it rightly, you, too, will find that I speak the truth. At any rate, fathers develop self-control in their sons by making them weep, and teachers impress good lessons on their pupils in the same way, and laws, too, turn the citizens to justice by making them weep. But could you say that those who make us laugh either do good to our bodies or make our minds any more fitted for the management of our private business or the affairs of state? " It was the view of Aglaitidas that it was the man who exerted discipline who really cared for and who really did good to his fellow men.

There is no doubt that this passage would come to those who heard it for the first time with a double impact, for all the world knew of that amazing thing the *patria potestas*, the father's power. A Roman father had by law absolute power over his family. If his son should marry, the father continued to have absolute power both over him and any grandchildren there might be. It began at the very beginning. A Roman father could keep or discard his newborn child as he liked. He could bind or scourge his son; he could sell him into slavery; and he even had the right to execute his own son. True, when a father was about to take serious steps against a member of his family, he usually called a council of all the adult male members of the family, but he did not need to, and he did not need to take their advice. True, in later days public opinion would not permit the execution of a son by a father, but it happened as late as the days of Augustus. Sallust, the Roman historian, tells us of an incident during the Catiline conspiracy. Catiline rebelled against Rome; there were those who went out to support him and to join his forces. Amongst them there was Aulus Fulvius, the son of a Roman senator. He was arrested and brought back, and his own father tried him and judged him and ordered him to be put to death. In regard to the *patria potestas* a Roman son never came of age. He might have engaged on a state career; he might be holding the highest magistracies; he might be held in honour by the whole country; all that did not matter; he was still directly and completely under his father's power, so long as his father survived. If ever a people knew what parental discipline was the Romans did ; and when the writer to the Hebrews talked about the way in which an earthly father disciplined his son, his hearers well knew what he was talking about.

So, then, the writer to the Hebrews insists that we must look on all the hardships of life as the discipline of God; and we must look on them as sent to work, not for our injury or for our harm, but for our ultimate and highest good. To prove his point he makes a quotation from Proverbs 3: 11, 12. There are many ways in which a man may look at the disciplines which God sends him.

(i) He may resignedly *accept* discipline. That is what the Stoics did ; they held that nothing in this world happens outside the will of God. Therefore, they argued, there is nothing to do but to accept it. To do anything else is simply to batter one's head against the walls of the universe, and to attempt to refuse to accept the inevitable. That is certainly acceptance; it may possibly be the acceptance of supreme wisdom; but nonetheless it remains the acceptance, not of a father's love, but of a father's power. It is not a willing but a defeated acceptance.

(ii) A man may accept discipline in life *with the grim sense of getting it over as soon as possible.* A certain famous Roman said: " I will let nothing interrupt my life." If a man accepts discipline like that he accepts it with grim determination, but he regards it as an infliction and an affliction which is to be struggled through with defiance, and certainly not with gratitude.

(iii) A man may accept discipline *with the self-pity which leads in the end to collapse.* There are some people who, when they are caught up in some difficult situation, give the impression that they feel that they are the only people in the world whom life ever hurt and to whom life ever brought sorrow. They are lost in self-pity. Even if it be a case of a loss of a loved one through death, it is *themselves* for whom they are sorry all the time.

(iv) A man may accept discipline *as a punishment which he resents.* It is strange that at this time the Romans saw in national and personal disasters nothing but the vengeance of the gods. Lucan wrote: " Happy were Rome indeed, and blessed citizens would she have, if the gods were as much concerned with caring for men as they are with exacting vengeance from them." Tacitus held that the disasters of the nation were the proof that not men's safety but men's punishment was the interest of the gods.

There are still people who regard God as a vindictive God. When something happens to them or to those whom they love their question is: " What did I do to deserve this? " And the question is asked in such a spirit and in such a tone as to make it clear that they regard the whole matter as an unjust and unmerited punishment from God. It never dawns upon them to ask: " What is God trying to teach me, what is God trying to make me, what is God trying to do with me through this experience which has come to me? "

(v) So we come to the last attitude. There are those who see in the hard things of life *the discipline of a loving father*. Jerome said a paradoxical but true thing: " The greatest anger of all is when God is no longer angry with us when we sin." He meant that the supreme punishment is when God lets us alone as unteachable, incurable, and unenlightenably blind. The true Christian knows that whatever comes to him comes from a God who is a Father, and that " a father's hand will never cause his child a needless tear." He knows that everything that comes means something, is meant for some purpose, is designed to make him a wiser and a better man. As Robert Browning wrote in Rabbi ben Ezra:

> " Then welcome each rebuff
>   That turns earth's smoothness rough,
> Each sting that bids nor sit nor stand but go!
>   Be our joy three-parts pain!
>   Strive and hold cheap the strain;
> Learn, nor account the pang; dare, never grudge the
>   throe!
>
>   For thence—a paradox
>   Which comforts while it mocks—
> Shall life succeed in that it seems to fail;
>   What I aspired to be,
>   And was not, comforts me.
> A brute I might have been, but would not sink i' the
>   scale."

We shall cease from self-pity, from resentment and from rebellious complaint if we remember that there is no discipline of God which does not take its source in love, and which is not aimed at good.

DUTIES, AIMS AND DANGERS

Hebrews 12: 12-17

So, then, lift up the slack hands. Strengthen the weak knees. And make straight the paths of your feet, so that the bones of the lame may not be completely dislocated, but rather may be cured. Make peace your aim—and do it all together—and aim at that holiness without which no one can see the Lord. Watch that no one misses the grace of God. Watch that no pernicious influence grows up to involve you in troubles. And watch that the main body of your people are not soiled by any such thing. Watch that no one falls into sexual impurity, or turns to an unhallowed life, as Esau did, Esau who, for a single meal, gave away his birthright. For you are well aware of how when he afterwards wanted to claim the blessing he ought to have inherited, he was rejected—for he had no opportunity to change his mind—although he sought that blessing with tears.

WITH this passage the writer to the Hebrews comes to the problems of everyday Christian life and living. He knew that sometimes it is given to a man to mount up with wings as an eagle; he knew that sometimes a man is enabled to run and not be weary in the pursuit of some great moment of endeavour; but he also knew that of all things it is hardest to walk every day and not to faint. In this passage he is thinking of the daily life and struggle of the Christian way.

(i) He begins by reminding them of their *duties*. In every congregation, and in every Christian society, there are those who are weaker and who are more likely to go astray and to be led astray and to abandon the struggle.

THE LETTER TO THE HEBREWS

It is the duty of those who are stronger to put more life and vigour into those who are almost giving up the battle. They must put fresh vigour into the listless hands and fresh strength into failing feet. The phrase that is used for *slack hands* is the same phrase as is used to describe the children of Israel in the days when they wished to abandon the rigours of the journey across the wilderness and to return to the ease and the fleshpots of Egypt. *The Odes of Solomon* (6: 14ff) have a description of the work of those who are true servants and ministers:

> " They have assuaged the dry lips,
> And the will that fainted they have raised up . . .
> And limbs that had fallen
> They have straightened and set up."

One of life's greatest glories is to be an encourager of the man who is near to despair and a strengthener of the man whose strength is failing. To help these people we have to make their ways straight. A Christian man has a double duty; he has a duty to God and a duty to his fellow men. *The Testimony of Simeon* (5: 2, 3) has an illuminating description of the duty of the good man. " Make your heart good in the sight of the Lord; and make your ways straight in the sight of men; so you will find favour in the sight of the Lord and of men." To God a man must present a clean heart; to men a man must present an upright life. To show a man the right way wherein to walk, by personal example to keep him on the right road, to remove from the path of life something that would make a man stumble, and to make the journey easier for faltering and lagging feet, is a Christian duty. A man must offer his heart to God, and his service and example to his fellow men.

(ii) Second, the writer to the Hebrews turns to the *aims* which must ever be before the Christian man. (*a*) He must aim at *peace*. In Hebrew thought and language peace was no negative thing; it was intensely positive. It was not simply freedom from trouble. It was two things. First, it was everything which makes for a man's highest good; it meant the highest welfare that a man could enjoy; it meant that in which manhood finds its highest peak. As the Hebrews saw it, that supreme welfare and that highest good were to be found in obedience to God. The writer of the *Proverbs* says: " My son, forget not my law; but let thine heart keep my commandments: for length of days and long life and *peace* shall they add unto thee." The Christian man must aim at that complete obedience to God in which life finds its highest happiness, its greatest good, its perfect consummation, its *peace*. Second, *peace* means right relationships between man and man. It means a state when hatred is banished, and when each man seeks nothing but his neighbour's good; it means the bond of love, forgiveness and service which ought to bind men together. The writer to the Hebrews says: " Seek to live together as Christian men ought to live, in the real unity which comes from living in Christ." The peace which is to be sought is the peace which comes from obedience to God's will, which raises a man's life to its highest realisation, and which enables him to live in and to produce right relationships between his fellow men.

One thing remains to be noted—that kind of peace is to be our *aim*; it is to be *pursued*. That kind of peace requires an effort. It is not something which just happens. It is the product of effort and discipline and mental and spiritual toil and sweat. Rudyard Kipling wrote:

" Our England is a garden, and such gardens are not made
By singing:—' Oh, how beautiful!' and sitting in the shade,
While better men than we go out and start their working-lives
At grubbing weeds from gravel-paths with broken dinner-knives."

The gifts of God are given, but they are not given away;

they have to be *won*, for God's gifts can only be received on God's conditions—and the supreme condition is obedience to Himself.

(*b*) He must aim at *holiness* (*hagiasmos*). *Hagiasmos* has in it the same root as the adjective *hagios*, which is usually translated *holy*. The root meaning of this word is always *difference* and *separation*. Although he lives in the world, the man who is *hagios* must always in one sense be different from the world and separate from the world. His standards are not the world's standards, nor is his conduct the world's conduct. His ideal is different; his reward is different; his aim is different. His aim is, not to stand well with men, but to stand well with God. *Hagiasmos*, *holiness*, as Westcott finely put it, is " the preparation for the presence of God." The life of the Christian man is dominated and directed by the constant memory that its greatest aim is to enter into the presence of God.

(iii) The writer to the Hebrews now goes on to point the *dangers* which threaten the Christian life.

(*a*) There is the danger of *missing the grace of God*. The word he uses might be paraphrased *failing to keep up with the grace of God*. The early Greek commentator Theophylact interprets this in terms of a journey of a band of travellers. Every now and again they have to check up and ask: " Has anyone fallen out? Has anyone lingered by the wayside? Has anyone been left behind while the others have pressed on? " In *Micah* there is a vivid text (4: 6). The Authorised Version translates the prophet's word from God: " I will assemble her that halteth." Moffatt translates it: " I will collect the stragglers." It is easy to straggle away, to linger behind, to drift instead of to march, and so to miss the grace of God. There is no opportunity in this life which cannot be missed. The grace of God brings to us the opportunity to make ourselves and to make life what they were meant to be. A man may, in his lethargy, his thoughtlessness, his unawareness, his procrastination, miss the chances which grace brings to him. Against that we must ever be upon the watch.

(b) We must beware of what the Authorised Version calls " a root of bitterness." The phrase comes from *Deuteronomy* 29: 18; and there it describes the man or woman who goes after strange gods, and encourages others to do so, and who thereby becomes a pernicious and poisonous influence on the life of the community. The writer to the Hebrews is warning against those who are a corrupting influence. There are always those who think the Christian standards unnecessarily strict and unnecessarily punctilious; there are always those who do not see why they should not become involved in the things the world calls success and pleasure; there are always those who would be well content to accept the world's standards of life and conduct. This was specially so in the early Church. The Church was a little island of Christianity surrounded by a sea of paganism; those who were members of it were only, at the most, one generation away from heathenism. It was fatally easy to relapse into the old standards. This is a warning against any influence which would make the Christian think more of the world and less of God. It is a warning against the infection of the world, sometimes deliberately, sometimes unconsciously, spread within the Christian society.

(c) The Christian has to beware lest any *fall into immorality or relapse into an unhallowed life*. The word that is used for *unhallowed* is the Greek word *bebēlos*. It has an illuminating background. It was used for ground that was *profane* in contradistinction to ground that was *consecrated*. The ancient world had its religions into which only the initiated could come. *Bebēlos* is used for the person who is *uninitiated* and *uninterested* in contradistinction to the man who is *devout*. It was applied to such men as

Antiochus Epiphanes, who was pledged to wipe out all true religion; it was applied to Jews who had become renegades and apostates and who had forsaken God. Westcott sums up this word; he says that it describes the man whose mind recognizes nothing as higher than earth; for whom there is nothing sacred; who has no divine reverence for the unseen. An *unhallowed* life is a life without any awareness of or interest in God. In its thoughts, its aims, its pleasures, its standards, it is completely earthbound. We have to have a care lest we drift into a frame of mind and heart which has no horizon beyond this world, for that way inevitably lie the failure of chastity and the loss of honour.

To sum it all up, the writer to the Hebrews cites the example of Esau. He really puts two stories together— the story in *Genesis* 25: 28-34 and the story in *Genesis* 27: 1-39. In the first of these stories Esau comes in from the field ravenously hungry and sells his birthright to Jacob for a share of the food which Jacob is preparing. The second of these two stories tells how Jacob subtly robbed Esau of his birthright by impersonating him when Isaac was old and blind, and so gained the blessing and the birthright which belonged to Esau as the elder of the two sons. It was when Esau sought the blessing that Jacob had shrewdly obtained and when he could not get it, that he lifted up his voice and wept (*Genesis* 27: 38). But there is more to this than lies upon the surface. In Hebrew legend and in rabbinic elaboration Esau had come to be looked upon as the entirely sensual man, the man who put the needs of his body first, the man who put the immediate pleasures and the passions of the hour first, the man who sold his birthright to fill his belly. Hebrew legend says that before Jacob and Esau were born—they were twins—while they were still in their mother's womb, Jacob said to Esau: " My brother, there are two worlds before us, this world and the world to come. In this world men eat and drink and traffic and marry and bring up sons and daughters; but all this does not take place in the world to come. If you like, take this world and I will take the other." And Esau was well content to take this world, because he did not believe that there was any other. On that very day when Jacob s subterfuge had gained him Isaac's blessing, legend said that Esau already had committed five sins—" he had worshipped with strange worship, he had shed innocent blood, he had pursued a betrothed damsel, he had denied the life of the world to come, and he had despised his birthright." Hebrew interpretation saw Esau as the man of the body, the sensual man, the man who saw no pleasures beyond the crude pleasures of this world. Any man like that sells his birthright. Any man throws away his inheritance when he throws away eternity. The writer to the Hebrews says, according to the Authorised Version, that Esau *found no place for repentance*. The word is *metanoia*, which literally means *a change of mind*. It is better to say that it was now impossible for Esau to change his mind. It is not that he was barred for ever from the forgiveness of God. It is something much simpler than that. It is just the grim fact that there are certain choices which cannot be unmade, and certain consequences which not even God can take away. To take a very simple example— if a young man loses his purity or a girl her virginity, nothing can ever bring it back. The choice was made and the choice stands. God can and will forgive, but God Himself cannot turn back the clock and unmake the choice or undo the consequences. We do well to remember that there is a certain finality in life. If, like Esau, we take the way of this world, if we make sensual, bodily things our final good, if we choose the pleasures of time in preference to the joys of eternity, God can and will still forgive, but something has happened that can never be undone. There are certain things in which a man cannot change his mind; his desire to do so has come too late; he must abide for ever by the choice that he has made.

THE LETTER TO THE HEBREWS

THE TERROR OF THE OLD AND THE GLORY OF THE NEW

Hebrews 12: 18-24

It is not to something that can be touched that you have come, to a flaming fire, to mist and gloom and stormblast, and to the blare of a trumpet, and to a voice which spoke such words that those who heard it begged that not another word should be further spoken unto them, for they could not bear the command: " If even a beast touches the mountain, it shall be stoned." So terrifying was the apparition that Moses said: " I am in utter fear and trembling." But you have come to Mount Sion, and to the city of the living God, the heavenly Jerusalem, to ten thousands of angels gathered in glad assembly, to the assembly of the honoured ones whose names are in the registers of heaven, to that God who is judge of all, to the spirits of just men who have come to that goal for which they were created, and to Jesus, the mediator of the new covenant, to the sprinkled blood which has a message greater than the blood of Abel.

THIS passage is a contrast between the old and the new. It is a contrast between the giving of the law on Mount Sinai and the new covenant of which Jesus is the mediator. Down to verse 21 it has echo after echo from the story of the giving of the law on Mount Sinai. Deuteronomy 4: 11 describes what that first law-giving was like: " And ye came near and stood under the mountain; and the mountain burned with fire unto the midst of heaven, with darkness, clouds and thick darkness. And the Lord spake unto you out of the midst of the fire." Exodus 19: 12, 13 tells of the unapproachability of that awful mountain: " And thou shalt set bounds unto the people round about, saying, Take heed to yourselves, that ye go not up into the mountain, or touch the border of it: whosoever toucheth the mountain shall be surely put to death: there shall not an hand touch it, but he shall surely be stoned, or shot through; whether it be beast or man, it shall not live: when the trumpet soundeth long, they shall come up to the mount." Deuteronomy 5: 23-27 tells how the people were so afraid to hear the voice of God for themselves that they besought Moses to go and to bring God's message to them. " If we hear the voice of the Lord our God any more, then we shall die." Deuteronomy 9: 19 tells of the fear and the terror of Moses, but the writer to the Hebrews has transferred these words to the giving of the law, when, in the original story, they were spoken by Moses when he came down from the mountain and found the people worshipping the golden calf. The whole passage down to verse 21 is a pattern of phrases and reminiscences from the story of the giving of the law at Mount Sinai. All the terrible and terrifying things have been gathered together to stress the shattering awfulness of that scene.

In the giving of the law at Mount Sinai three things are stressed. (i) There is stressed *the sheer majesty of God*. The whole story stresses the shattering might of God, and in it there is no love at all. (ii) There is stressed *the absolute unapproachability of God*. So far from the way being opened to God, it is barred; and he who tried to approach God met death. (iii) There is stressed *the sheer terror of God*. Here there is nothing but the awe-stricken fear which is afraid to look and even afraid to listen.

Then at verse 22 there comes the difference. The first section deals with all that man can expect under the old covenant and the old law; in it there is nothing in God but lonely majesty, complete separation from man, and prostrating fear. But to the Christian there has come the new covenant; there has come the new relationship with God.

In this passage the writer to the Hebrews makes a kind of list of the new glories that await the Christian and that are open to him.

(i) The new Jerusalem, the heavenly Jerusalem, awaits him. There awaits him a new creation. This world with all its impermanence, with all its fears, with all its mysteries, with all its separations is gone; life for the Christian is recreated and made new.

(ii) The angels await him in joyful assembly. The word that the writer to the Hebrews uses for *joyful assembly* is *panēguris*. This is the word for a joyful national assembly in honour of the gods. To the Greek it described a joyful holy day when all men celebrated and all men rejoiced. For the Christian, the joy of heaven is such that it makes even the angels break into rejoicing.

(iii) There await the Christian God's elected people. The writer to the Hebrews uses two words to describe them. He says literally that they are *the first-born*; now the characteristic of the *first-born* son is that the inheritance and the honour are his. He says that they are those whose names are written in the registers of God. In ancient days kings kept a register of their faithful citizens. The man whose name was in such a register was an accepted and an acknowledged citizen of the king. So there await the Christian all those whom God has honoured and all those whom God has reckoned amongst his faithful citizens.

(iv) There awaits the Christian God the Judge. Even amidst the joy there remains the awe. The writer to the Hebrews never forgot that, at the end, the Christian must stand the scrutiny of God. The glory is there; but the awe and the fear of God still remain. The New Testament is never in the faintest danger of sentimentalising the idea of God.

(v) There await the Christian the spirits of all good men who have achieved their goal. Once they encircled him in the unseen cloud; now he will be one of them. He himself goes to join those whose names are on the honour roll of God, those whose faith has been approved and attested by God.

(vi) Finally the writer to the Hebrews says that it was Jesus who initiated this new covenant; it was Jesus who made this new relationship with God possible; it was Jesus who took away the terror of Mount Sinai and gave to men the glory of the new relationship with God; it was Jesus, the perfect priest and the perfect sacrifice, who made the unapproachable approachable, and who took away the terror of God. And He did this at the cost of His blood; that is to say He had to die before this was possible. So the writer to the Hebrew ends the section with a curious contrast between the blood of Abel and the blood of Jesus. When Abel was slain his blood upon the ground called for vengeance (Genesis 4: 10). His death was something which called for revenge. But when Jesus was slain, His blood, His death did not call for vengeance; it opened up the way of reconciliation. His life, His death, His sacrifice made it possible for man to be friends with God.

Once men were under all the terror of the law; the relationship between them and God was a relationship of unbridgeable distance and shuddering fear, but after Jesus came and lived and died, the God who was far distant is brought near, and a way is opened to the God whose presence was once barried to man.

THE GREATER OBLIGATION

Hebrews 12: 25-29

> See that you do not refuse to listen to His voice; for if they who refused to listen to the one who brought the oracles of God upon earth did not escape, how much more shall we not escape if we turn away from Him who speaks from Heaven? Then His voice shook the earth, but now the voice of the promise is: " Still once more I will shake, not only the earth, but heaven also." That phrase " still once more " signifies the removal of the things that are shaken, because they are merely created things, in order that the things which cannot be shaken may remain. Therefore let us give thanks because we are receiving a kingdom that cannot be shaken, a kingdom in which we must worship God acceptably, with reverence and with fear, for our God, too, is a consuming fire.

HERE the writer to the Hebrews begins with a contrast

which is also a warning. Moses brought to earth the oracles of God. Now the word that he uses of Moses (*chrēmatizein*) implies that Moses was only the *transmitter* of these oracles. He was only the mouthpiece through which God spoke. And yet the man who broke the commandments which Moses transmitted did not escape punishment and condemnation. On the other hand there is Jesus. The word that is used of Him (*lalein*) implies the direct speech of God; He was not merely the transmitter of the voice of God; He *was* the voice of God; He did not speak with an earthly accent and an earthly message; heaven itself spoke in Him. If that be so, how much more will the man who refuses to obey Him find punishment and condemnation? If a man merits condemnation for neglecting the imperfect message of the law, how much more does he merit condemnation if he neglects the perfect message of the gospel? Just because the gospel is the full revelation of God, just because in it God spoke as He never spoke before and never will need to speak again, there is laid on the man who hears it a double and a terrible responsibility. Those who heard only the old law never had a chance to hear the whole truth; those who have heard the new gospel have heard the full revelation of God's truth; and a man's condemnation must be all the more if he neglects that perfect revelation of God.

Then the writer to the Hebrews goes on to draw out another thought. When the law was given the earth was shaken. " And Mount Sinai was altogether on a smoke, because the Lord descended upon it in fire; and the smoke thereof ascended as the smoke of a furnace, and the whole mount quaked greatly " (Exodus 19: 18). " Tremble thou earth at the presence of the Lord " (Psalm 114: 7). " The earth shook, the heavens also dropped at the presence of God " (Psalm 68: 8). " The voice of Thy thunder was in the heaven; the lightnings lightened the world; the earth trembled and shook " (Psalm 77: 18). That was what happened when first the law was given. Now the writer to the Hebrews finds another reference to the shaking of the earth in Haggai 2: 6. There the Greek version of the Old Testament says: " Still once more (the Hebrew says, " very soon ") I will shake, not only the earth, but heaven also." The writer to the Hebrews takes this to be an announcement of the day when this earth shall pass away and the new age will begin. In that day everything that can be shaken will be uprooted and destroyed; the only things that will remain are the things which can never be shaken; and chief among them is our relationship with God. All things may pass away; the world as we know it may be uprooted; life as we experience it may come to an end; but one thing cannot change or end or be shaken—the relationship of the Christian to God. Even if everything else is shattered into eternal destruction that relationship stands eternally sure.

If that be so there is a great obligation laid upon us. We must worship God with reverence; we must serve Him with fear; for nothing must be allowed to disturb that relationship which will be our salvation when the world passes away. So the writer to the Hebrews finishes with one of these threatening quotations which he so often flings like a thunderbolt at his hearers. It is a quotation from Deuteronomy 4: 24. There Moses is telling the people that they must never break their agreement with God; they must never relapse into idolatry and the worship of graven images; for God is a jealous God; they must worship Him and Him alone or they will find Him a consuming fire. It is as if the writer to the Hebrews said: " There is a choice before you. Remain unshakably true to God, and in the day when the universe is shaken into destruction, your relationship with God will still stand safe and secure. Be false to God, and that very God who might have been your salvation, will be to you a consuming fire of destruction." It is a grim thought; but in it there is the eternal truth, which there is no altering, that, if a man is true to God, he gains everything; and if he is untrue to God, he loses everything. In time and in eternity nothing matters save only loyalty to God.

THE MARKS OF THE CHRISTIAN LIFE

Hebrews 13: 1-6

Let brotherly love be always with you.

Do not forget the duty of hospitality, for, in remembering this duty, there are some who have entertained angels without knowing that they were doing so.

Remember those who are in prison, for you yourselves know what it is like to be a prisoner; remember those who are suffering ill-treatment, for the same thing can happen to you so long as you are in the body.

Let marriage be held in honour among you all, and never let the marriage bed be defiled. God judges those who are adulterers and immoral in their conduct.

Let your way of life be free from the love of money. Be content with what you have, for He has said: " I will never fail you and I will never forsake you "; so that we can say with confidence: " The Lord is my helper: I will not be afraid. What can man do to me? "

As he comes to the close of the letter, the writer to the Hebrews turns to practical things. Here he outlines five essential qualities of the Christian life.

(i) There is *brotherly love.* The very circumstances of the early Church sometimes threatened brotherly love. The very fact that they took their religion as seriously as they did was in one sense a danger. In a Church which is threatened from the outside and desperately earnest in the inside, there are always two dangers. First, there is the danger of heresy-hunting. The very desire to preserve the faith clean and pure tends to make men eager to track down and to eliminate the heretic and the man whose faith has gone astray. Second, there is the danger of stern and unsympathetic treatment of the man whose nerve

THE LETTER TO THE HEBREWS

and whose faith have failed. The very necessity of **unswerv-ing** loyalty in the midst of a heathen and a hostile world tends to add sternness and rigorousness to the treatment of the man who, in some crisis, had not the courage to stand for his faith. It is a great thing to keep the faith clean; but when the desire to do so makes us censorious, critical, fault-finding, condemning, harsh and unsympath-etic, brotherly love is destroyed, and we are left with a situation which is worse than the situation which we tried to avoid. Somehow or other we have to combine two things —a desperate earnestness in the faith and a kindness to the man who has strayed from it.

(ii) There is *hospitality*. The ancient world loved and honoured hospitality. The Jews had a saying: " There are six things, the fruit of which a man eats in this world and by which his horn is raised in the world to come." And the list begins: " Hospitality to the stranger and visiting the sick." The Greeks gave Zeus, as one of his favourite titles, the title *Zeus Xenios*, which means Zeus, the god of strangers. The wayfaring man and the stranger were under the protection of the king of the gods. Hospi-tality, as Moffatt says, was an article of ancient religion. In the ancient world inns were filthy, ruinously expensive, and of low repute. The Greek had always a shrinking from hospitality given for money. Inn-keeping seemed to him an unnatural affair. In *The Frogs* of Aristophanes, Dionysus asks Heracles, when they are discussing finding a lodging, if he knows where there are fewest fleas. Plato in *The Laws* speaks of the inn-keeper holding travellers to ransom. It is not without significance that Josephus says that Rahab, the harlot, who harboured Joshua's scouts in Jericho, kept an inn. When Theophrastus wrote his character sketch of the reckless man, he said that he was fit to keep an inn or run a brothel. He put both occu-pations on the same level. In the ancient world there was a rather wonderful system of what were called " guest friendships." Throughout the years families, even when

they had lost active touch with each other, had an arrange-
ment that at any time needful they would make accommo-
dation available for each other. This hospitality was even
more necessary in the circle of the Christians. Slaves
had no home of their own to which to go. Wandering
preachers and prophets were always on the roads. On
the ordinary business of life, Christians had journeys
to make. Both their price and their moral atmosphere
made the public inns impossible. There must in these
days have been many isolated Christians fighting a lonely
battle. Christianity was, and still should be, the religion
of the open door. The writer to the Hebrews says that
those who have given hospitality to strangers have sometimes, all unaware, entertained the angels of God. He
is thinking of the time when the angel came to Abraham
and Sarah to tell them of the coming of a son (Genesis
18: 1ff), and of the day when the angel came to Manoah
to tell him that he would have a son (Judges 13: 3ff).

(iii) There was *sympathy for those in trouble*. It is here
we see the Christian Church in its early days at its loveliest.
It often happened that the Christian landed in prison and
worse. It might be for his faith; it might be for debt,
for the Christians were poor; it might be that they were
captured by pirates or brigands. It was then that the
Christian Church went into action. Tertullian in *The
Apology* writes: " If there happen to be any in the mines,
or banished to the islands, or shut up in prisons for nothing
but their fidelity to the cause of God's Church, they become
the nurslings of their confession." Aristides the heathen
orator said of the Christians: " If they hear that any one
of their number is imprisoned or in distress for the sake
of their Christ's name, they all render aid in his necessity,
and, if he can be redeemed, they set him free." When
Origen was young it was said of him: " Not only was he
at the side of the holy martyrs in their imprisonment and
until their final condemnation, but, when they were led

to death, he boldly accompanied them into danger." Sometimes Christians were condemned to the mines, which was almost like being sent to Siberia or to Devil's Island. *The Apostolic Constitutions* lay it down: " If any Christian is condemned for Christ's sake to the mines by the ungodly, do not overlook him, but from the proceeds of your toil and sweat send him something to support himself and to reward the soldier of Christ." The Christians sought out their fellow Christians even in the wilds. There was actually a little Christian Church in the mines at Phaeno. Sometimes Christians had to be ransomed from robbers and brigands. *The Apostolic Constitutions* lay it down: " All monies accruing from honest labour do ye appoint and apportion to the redeeming of the saints ransoming thereby slaves and captives and prisoners, people who are sore abused or condemned by tyrants." When the Numidian robbers carried off their Christian friends, the Church at Carthage raised the equivalent of £1,000 to ransom them and promised more. There were actually cases when Christians sold themselves as slaves to find money to ransom their friends. The Christians were even prepared to bribe their way into gaol. The Christians became so notorious for their help to those in gaol, that, at the beginning of the fourth century, the Emperor Licinius passed new legislation that " no one was to show kindness to sufferers in prison by supplying them with food, and that no one was to show mercy to those starving in prison." It was added that those who were discovered so doing would be compelled to suffer the same sentence and fate as those they tried to help. These instances are taken from Harnack's *Expansion of Christianity*, and many others could be added. In the early days no Christian who was in trouble for his faith was ever neglected or forgotten by his fellow Christians.

(iv) There was *purity*. First, the marriage bond was to be universally respected. This may mean either of two almost opposite things. (*a*) There were ascetics who despised

marriage. Some even went the length of castrating themselves to secure what they thought was purity. Origen,
for instance, took that course. Even a heathen like Galen,
the physician, noted of the Christians that " they include
men and women who refrain from cohabiting all their
lives." The writer to the Hebrews insists against these
ascetics that the marriage bond is to be honoured and not
despised. (b) There were those who were ever liable to
relapse into morality. The writer to the Hebrews uses
two words. The one denoted adulterous living; the other
denotes all kinds of impurity, such as unnatural vice.
Into the world the Christians brought a new ideal of purity.
Even the heathen admitted that. Galen, the Greek doctor,
in the passage we have already quoted, goes on: " And
they also number individuals who in ruling and controlling
themselves, and in their keen pursuit of virtue, have
attained a pitch not inferior to that of real philosophers."
When Pliny, the governor of Bithynia, examined the
Christians and reported back to Trajan, the Emperor,
he had to admit, even although he was looking for a charge
on which to condemn them, that at their Lord's Day
meeting: " They bound themselves by an oath, not for
any criminal end, but to avoid theft or robbery or adultery,
never to break their word, or repudiate a deposit when
called upon to refund it." In the early days the Christians
presented such a purity to the world that not even their
critics and their enemies could find a fault in it.

(v) There is *contentment*. The Christian must be free
from the love of money. He must be content with what
he has, and why should he not be, for he possesses the
continual presence of God? The writer to the Hebrews
quotes two great Old Testament passages—Joshua I: 5
and Psalm 118: 6—to show that the man of God needs
nothing more because he has with him always the presence
and the help of God. Nothing that man can give him, no
gift that earthly ambition can wring from life, can improve
on that.

THE LETTER TO THE HEBREWS

THE LEADERS AND THE LEADER

Hebrews 13: 7, 8

> Remember your leaders, the men who spoke the word of God to you. Look back on how they made their exit from this life, and imitate their faith. Jesus Christ is the same yesterday and to-day and for ever.

IMPLICIT in this passage there is a description of the real leader of men.

(i) The real leader of the Church preaches Christ, and thereby brings men to Christ. It is not to himself that he draws attention, but to the person of Jesus Christ. Leslie Weatherhead somewhere tells a story of a public schoolboy who decided to enter the ministry. He was asked when he had come to that decision. He said that he had come to it after hearing a sermon in his school chapel. He was asked the name of the preacher. His answer was that he had no memory of the preacher's name; all he knew was that that preacher had shown him Jesus. The duty of the real preacher is to obliterate himself and to show men nothing but Jesus Christ.

(ii) The real leader of the Church lives in the faith, and thereby he brings Christ to men. A saint has been defined as " a man in whom Christ lives again." The duty of the real preacher is not so much to talk to men about Christ as to show men Christ in his own life and work and being. Men listen not so much to what the man is saying as to what the man is. His life is not an argument in words but a demonstration in living.

(iii) The real leader, if need be, dies in loyalty. He shows men how to live, and in the end he shows men how to die. He demonstrates a loyalty to which there is no limit. Jesus, having loved His own, loved them to the end. And the real leader, having loved Jesus, loves Him to the end. His loyalty never stops halfway.

(iv) Thereby the real leader leaves to those who come

after two things—he leaves an example and an inspiration. Quintilian, the Roman master of oratory, said: " It is a good thing to know, and always to keep turning over in the mind, the things which were illustriously done of old." Epicurus advised his disciples continuously to remember those of old time who lived with virtue.

If there is one thing more than another that the world and the Church need in every generation, it is leadership like that.

But then the writer to the Hebrews moves on to another great thought. It is in the nature of things that all earthly leaders must come and go. They have their day and they lead their generation, and then they must pass from the scene. They have their part in the drama of life, and then the curtain comes down. But Jesus Christ is the same yesterday and to-day and for ever. His pre-eminence is permanent; His leadership is for ever. And therein there lies the secret of earthly leadership. The real leader is the man who is led himself by Jesus Christ. The men who have made the Churches, the men who have led others on the upward way, are the men who in every age and every generation have themselves been led by the eternal and the unchanging Christ. He who walked the ways of Galilee is still as powerful as ever to smite evil and to love the sinner; and, even as then He chose twelve to be with Him, and then sent them out to do His work, so now He is still seeking those who will bring men to Him, and Him to men.

THE WRONG AND THE RIGHT SACRIFICE

Hebrews 13: 9-16

> Do not let yourselves be carried away by subtle and strange teachings, for it is a fine thing to have your heart made strong by grace, not by the eating of different kinds of food, for they never did any good to those who took that line of conduct. We have an altar from which those who serve in the tabernacle

have no right to eat. For the bodies of the animals, whose blood is taken by the High Priest into the Holy Place, as an offering for sin, are burned outside the camp. That was why Jesus suffered outside the gate, so that He might make men fit for the presence of God by His own blood. So then let us go to Him outside the camp, bearing the same reproach as He did, for here we have no abiding city, but we are searching for the city which is to come. Through Him, therefore, let us continually bring to God a sacrifice of praise, I mean, the fruit of lips which continually acknowledge their faith in His name. Do not forget to do good and to share everything, for God is well pleased with a sacrifice like that.

It may be that no one will ever discover the precise meaning which is behind this passage. Clearly there was some false teaching going on in the Church to which this letter was written. The writer to the Hebrews did not need to describe it to the people to whom he wrote; they knew all about it, because some of them had succumbed to it, and all were in danger of it. As to what it was, we have only indications and we can only deduce and guess.

We may start with one basic fact. The writer to the Hebrews is convinced that real strength only comes to a man's heart from the grace of God, and that what people eat and drink has nothing to do with their spiritual strength. So then in the Church to which he was writing there were some people who placed too much importance on laws about food. Here there are certain possibilities.

(i) The Jews had their rigid food laws. They are laid down at length in Leviticus 12. All the world knows that no Jew will eat pork. The Jew believed that he could serve and please God by eating and not eating certain foods. Possibly there were Christians in this Church who were ready to abandon their Christian freedom and liberty and once again to put themselves under the yoke of Jewish rules and regulations about food, thinking that by so doing they were going to add strength to their spiritual life and to their souls.

(ii) There were certain Greeks who had very definite ideas about food. Long ago Pythagoras had been like that. He believed in reincarnation; he believed that a man's soul passed from body to body until finally it had merited release. That release could be hastened by prayer and meditation and discipline and asceticism; and so the Pythagoreans were vegetarians and ate no meat. There were people called Gnostics who were much the same. They believed that matter was altogether bad, and that a man must concentrate on spirit which is altogether good. They therefore believed that the body was altogether bad and that a man ought to discipline his body and treat it with the greatest rigorousness and austerity. They would cut down food to the bare, irreducible minimum and they too abstained from meat. There were any number of Greeks who thought that by what they ate or refused to eat they were strengthening their spiritual life and releasing their soul.

(iii) But neither of these things seems quite to fit. This eating and drinking has something to do with the body of Jesus. The writer to the Hebrews goes back to the regulations for the Day of Atonement. Now according to these regulations, the body of the bullock, which was an offering for the sins of the High Priest, and the body of the goat which was an offering for the sins of the people, must be totally consumed with fire in a place outside the camp (Leviticus 16: 27). They were sin offerings and the point is that even if the worshippers had wished to eat their flesh they could not do so. The writer to the Hebrews sees Jesus as the perfect sacrifice. The parallel for him is complete, because Jesus too was sacrificed outside the gate, for Calvary was outside the city wall of Jerusalem. Crucifixions were always carried out outside a town. Jesus too, then, was the sin-offering for men; and it follows that, just as none could eat of the flesh of the sin-offering on the Day of Atonement, no one can eat of His flesh. It may be that here we have the clue. There may have been a little group in this Church who, either at the sacrament, or at some common meal where they consecrated their food to Jesus, claimed that they were in truth and in fact eating the body of Christ. They may have persuaded themselves that because they had consecrated their food to Christ, His body had entered into it. That was indeed what the religious Greeks believed about their own gods. When a Greek sacrificed he was given back part of the meat. Often he made a feast for himself and his friends within the temple where the sacrifice had been made; and he believed that when he ate the meat of the sacrifice, the god to whom that meat had been sacrificed was in the meat, and entered into him. With the meat the life of the god entered into his body and his heart. It may well be that certain Greeks had brought their own ideas into Christianity with them; and talked about eating the body of Christ. The writer to the Hebrews believed with all the intensity of his being that no food can bring Christ into a man, that Christ can enter into a man only by grace. It is quite likely that we have got here a reaction against an overstressing of the sacraments. It is a notable fact that the writer to the Hebrews never mentions the sacraments; they do not seem to come into his scheme at all. It is likely that, even thus early, there were those who took a mechanical view of the sacraments, and forgot that no sacrament in the world avails anything by itself; its only use is that in it the grace of God meets the faith of man. It is not the meat, but the faith and the grace which matter.

But this queer argument has set the writer to the Hebrews thinking. Christ was crucified outside the gate. He was exiled and banished from men. The reproach of a criminal was on Him. He was numbered with the transgressors. Therein the writer to the Hebrews sees a picture. We too have to sever ourselves from the life of the world. We too have to submit to going out of the world's gate. We too may have to bear the same reproach as Christ bore. The separation, the isolation, the humiliation may come to the Christian as they came to Christ. The Christian must be prepared to undergo the same treatment from the world as his Master underwent.

But the writer to the Hebrews goes further. If in the sacrament the Christian cannot again offer the sacrifice of Christ, what sacrifice can he offer? The writer to the Hebrews says he can offer certain things.

(i) He can offer his continual praise and thanks to God. The ancient peoples sometimes argued that a thank-offering was more acceptable to God than a sin-offering, for when a man offered a sin-offering he was trying to get something out of God, forgiveness for his sins, while a thank-offering was the unconditional offering of the grateful heart. The sacrifice of gratitude is a sacrifice that all can and are bound to bring.

(ii) He can offer his public and glad confession of his faith in the name of Christ. That is the offering of loyalty. The Christian can always offer to God a life that is never ashamed to show whose it is and whom it serves. Never to be ashamed of the gospel of Jesus Christ is also an offering.

(iii) The Christian can offer as a sacrifice to God deeds of kindness to and of sharing with his fellow men. In point of fact, that was something which a Jew knew well. After A.D. 70 the sacrifices of the Temple were at an end. They were no longer possible, for in that year the Temple was destroyed. What was left? The Rabbis taught that in these later days, when the Temple ritual was gone, theology, prayer, penitence, the study of the law, charity were sacrifices still equivalent to the ancient ritual. Rabbi Jochanan ben Zakkai comforted himself in those sorrowful days by believing that " in the practice of charity he still possessed a valid sacrifice for sin." An ancient Christian writer says: " I expected that thy heart would bear fruit, and that thou wouldst worship God, the Creator of all, and unto Him continually offer thy prayers by means of compassion; for compassion shown to men by men is a bloodless sacrifice and holy unto God." After all, Jesus Himself said: "Inasmuch as ye have done it unto one of the least of these my brethren ye have done it unto me" (Matthew 25: 40). And the best of all sacrifices to bring to God is the gift of help to one of His children who is in need.

OBEDIENCE AND PRAYER

Hebrews 13: 17-20

> Obey your leaders and submit to them, for they sleeplessly watch over your souls, conscious that they will have to give account of their trust. This do that they may carry out this task with joy and not with grief, for, if you grieve them, there would be no profit to you either in that. Keep on praying for us, for we believe that we have a clear conscience, for we wish in all things to live in such a way that our conduct will be fair. I urge you to do this all the more that I may the more quickly be enabled to return to you.

HERE the writer to the Hebrews lays down the duty of the congregation to its present leaders and its absent leader.

To the present leaders the duty of the congregation is obedience. A Church is a democracy, but not a democracy run mad; it must give obedience to the leaders whom it has chosen as its guides. That obedience is not to be given in order to gratify the leaders' sense of power, or to increase their prestige. It is to be given so that at the end of the day the leaders may be seen to have lost none of the souls which are committed to their care and to their charge. The greatest joy of the leader of any Christian fellowship is to see those whom he leads established in the Christian way. As John wrote: "I have no greater joy than to hear that my children walk in the truth" (3 John 4). The greatest sorrow of the leader of any Christian fellowship is to see those whom he leads getting further away from God.

THE LETTER TO THE HEBREWS

To the absent leader the duty of the congregation is the duty of prayer. It is a Christian duty always to bear our absent loved ones to the throne of God's grace. It is a Christian duty daily to remember before the throne of God's grace all those who bear the responsibility of leadership and of authority. When Mr. Baldwin, as he then was, became Prime Minister of Great Britain, his friends thronged round him to congratulate him. His answer to their congratulations was: " It is not your congratulations I need; it is your prayers."

We must give our respect and our obedience to those who are set in authority over us when they are present with us, and when they are absent we must ever remember them in our prayers.

A PRAYER, A GREETING AND A BLESSING

Hebrews 13: 20-24

> May the God of peace, who brought up from among the dead the great shepherd of the sheep, with the blood of the eternal covenant, it is our Lord Jesus I mean, equip you with every good thing that you may do His will, and may He create in you through Jesus Christ that which is well-pleasing in His sight. To Him be glory for ever and ever. Amen.
> Brothers, I appeal to you to bear with this appeal of mine, for indeed it is but a short letter that I have sent to you.
> I would have you know that our brother Timothy is at liberty again. If he comes soon I will see you along with him.
> Greet all your leaders and all God's dedicated people. The folk from Italy send you their greetings. Grace be with you all. Amen.

THE great prayer of the first two verses of this passage draws a perfect picture of God and of Jesus.

(i) God is the God of peace. Even in the most troublous and distressing situation, God can bring peace to men's souls. In any fellowship where there is division it is because men have forgotten God and only the memory of God's presence can bring back the lost peace. When a man's mind and heart are distracted, when he is torn in two between the two sides of his own nature, it is only by giving his life into the control of God that he can know peace. It is only God who can put a man into a right relationship with himself, with his fellow men and with eternity. It is only the God of peace who can make us at peace with ourselves, at peace with each other, and at peace with Himself.

(ii) God is the God of life. It was God who brought Jesus again from the dead. The love of God and the power of God are the only things which can bring a man peace in life and triumph in death. It was to obey the will of God that Jesus died, and that same will of God brought Him again from the dead. For the man who obeys the will of God there is no such thing as final disaster, and even death itself is conquered.

(iii) God is the God who both shows us His will and equips us to do it. God never gives us a task without also giving us the power to do it. With the vision He also sends the power. We are never asked to go to any task with only that which we can bring to it; if that were so we might well be daunted at the height of the demand of the Christian life. When God sends us out, He sends us out armed and equipped with everything we need.

Here, too, is the great threefold picture of Jesus.

(i) Jesus is the great shepherd of His sheep. The picture of Jesus as the good shepherd is something which is very precious to us, but, strangely enough, it is a picture that Paul never uses, and that the writer to the Hebrews uses only here. There is a lovely legend of Moses. It tells of a thing that Moses did when he had fled from Egypt and when he was keeping the flocks of Jethro in the desert. A sheep of the flock wandered far away. Moses patiently followed it, and when he found it, it was drinking at a mountain stream. Moses came up to it and put it upon his shoulder. "So it was because you were thirsty that you wandered away," said Moses gently, and, without anger at the toil the sheep had caused him, he carried it home. And when God saw it, He said: "If this man Moses is so compassionate to a straying sheep, he is the very man I want to be the leader of my people." A shepherd is one who is ready to give his life for his sheep. He is one who bears with the foolishness of the sheep and who never stops loving them. That is what Jesus does for us.

(ii) Jesus is the one who established the new covenant. That is to say, Jesus is the one who made possible the new relationship between God and man. It was Jesus who showed us what God is like, and who opened the door. He look away the terror and showed us the love of God.

(iii) Jesus is the one who died. To establish that new relationship, to show men what God was like, to open the way to God, cost the life of Jesus. Our new relationship to God cost the blood of Jesus. He died to bring us to God and to life.

So the letter finishes with some personal greetings. The writer to the Hebrews half apologises for the length of his letter. If he had dealt with these vast topics the letter would never have ended at all. It is short—Moffatt points out that you can read it aloud in less than an hour—in comparison with the greatness of the eternal and infinite truths with which it deals.

What the reference to Timothy means no one knows, but it sounds as if Timothy too had been in prison for the sake of Jesus Christ.

And so the letter comes to an end with a blessing. All through it has been telling of the grace of Christ which opens the way to God, and so we come to an end with a prayer that that wondrous grace may rest upon us.